PENGUIN BOOKS

SWEETNESS AND POWER

Sidney W. Mintz is professor of anthropology at Johns Hopkins University, whose faculty he joined after teaching for two decades at Yale. He is the author of *Worker in the Cane*, *Caribbean Transformations*, and *Tasting Food, Tasting Freedom: Excursions into Eating, Culture, and the Past*, co-author of *The People of Puerto Rico*, and editor of *Slavery, Colonialism and Racism*.

I do not know if coffee and sugar are essential to the happiness of Europe, but I know well that these two products have accounted for the unhappiness of two great regions of the world: America has been depopulated so as to have land on which to plant them; Africa has been depopulated so as to have the people to cultivate them.

—from Volume 1 of J. H. Bernardin de Saint Pierre's
Voyage to Isle de France, Isle de Bourbon,
The Cape of Good Hope...With New Observations on Nature
and Mankind by an Officer of the King (1773)

This engraving by William Blake, *Europe Supported by Africa and America*, was commissioned by J. G. Stedman for the *finis* page of his book *Narrative of a five years' expedition, against the Revolted Negroes of Surinam* (London: J. Johnson & J. Edwards, 1795). (Photo courtesy of Richard and Sally Price)

SIDNEY W. MINTZ

SWEETNESS AND POWER

THE PLACE OF SUGAR IN MODERN HISTORY

PENGUIN BOOKS

PENGUIN BOOKS
Published by the Penguin Group
Penguin Group (USA) Inc., 375 Hudson Street, New York, New York 10014, U.S.A.
Penguin Group (Canada), 90 Eglinton Avenue East, Suite 700, Toronto,
Ontario, Canada M4P 2Y3 (a division of Pearson Penguin Canada Inc.)
Penguin Books Ltd, 80 Strand, London WC2R 0RL, England
Penguin Ireland, 25 St Stephen's Green, Dublin 2, Ireland (a division of Penguin Books Ltd)
Penguin Group (Australia), 250 Camberwell Road, Camberwell,
Victoria 3124, Australia (a division of Pearson Australia Group Pty Ltd)
Penguin Books India Pvt Ltd, 11 Community Centre, Panchsheel Park,
New Delhi – 110 017, India
Penguin Group (NZ), 67 Apollo Drive, Rosedale, North Shore 0632, New Zealand
(a division of Pearson New Zealand Ltd)
Penguin Books (South Africa) (Pty) Ltd, 24 Sturdee Avenue, Rosebank,
Johannesburg 2196, South Africa

Penguin Books Ltd, Registered Offices: 80 Strand, London WC2R 0RL, England

First published in the United States of America by Viking Penguin Inc. 1985
Published in Penguin Books 1986

50

A portion of this book appeared originally in *Boston Review*.

LIBRARY OF CONGRESS CATALOGING IN PUBLICATION DATA
Mintz, Sidney Wilfred, 1922–
Sweetness and power.
Bibliography: p.
Includes index.
1. Sugar—Social aspects—History.
2. Sugar trade—Social aspects—History.   I. Title.
GT2869.M56   1986   394.1'2   86–781
ISBN 978-0-14-009233-2

Printed in the United States of America
Set in Sabon

For Jackie
with love and gratitude

Acknowledgments

T his book has a lengthy past. I began collecting data for it many years ago, without even knowing it; then writing it took time, too. I began to draft it in 1978, while enjoying a National Endowment for the Humanities fellowship. I thank the Department of Anthropology of the University of Pennsylvania, which bestowed on me a visiting title during the year I spent in Philadelphia; and Professor William H. Davenport, who generously afforded me, in addition to his company, half of his precious office space to use as my own.

During the spring of 1978, thanks to the hospitality of the Department of Anthropology of Princeton University, the Christian Gauss Lecture Committee, and their respective chairmen, Professor James Fernandez and Professor Joseph Frank, I was able to try out some of my ideas on thoughtful audiences. Insightful critics, including Professors Natalie Z. Davis, Stanley Stein, and Victor Brombert, did what they could to help me with their queries.

The summers of 1980 and 1981 were spent at that mecca of scholarship, the British Library. The Wenner-Gren Foundation and its director of research, Lita Osmundsen, made it possible for me to go to England during one of those summers. A research grant, provided through the good offices of a great Hopkins dean, the late Dr. George Owen, financed the other.

Of special importance were the people who helped me to find materials, copied and kept in order citations, documents, and references, and typed manuscript revisions. I am particularly grateful to Elise LeCompte, who surely worked as hard on the book as I did, before emigrating to graduate school. Marge Collignon typed the final draft with skill and celerity. Dr. Susan Rosales Nelson worked swiftly and efficiently in preparing the index.

To the librarians who showed me unfailing kindness at the Van Pelt Library (University of Pennsylvania), the British Library, the Wellcome Institute of Medicine Library, the Firestone Library (Princeton University), the Enoch Pratt Free Public Library of Baltimore, and, above all, the Milton S. Eisenhower Library (The Johns Hopkins University), I owe more than I can say. A special salute to the staff of the Interlibrary Loan Department of the Eisenhower Library, whose industry, dedication, and efficiency are unmatched.

Many good friends read and criticized portions of the manuscript at different points in its preparation. Among them I must mention my colleague Professor Ashraf Ghani, as well as Dr. Sidney Cantor, Professor Frederick Damon, Professor Stanley Engerman, Dr. Scott Guggenheim, Dr. Hans Medick, and Professor Richard Price. Rich and detailed critical commentary on the entire manuscript came from Mr. Gerald Hagelberg, Professor Carol Heim, Mr. Keith McClelland, Professor Rebecca J. Scott, Professor Kenneth Sharpe, and Dr. William C. Sturtevant. I have not been able to deal adequately with all of their criticisms and suggestions, but their help improved the text more than they will probably recognize. Special enlightenment was volunteered by a veteran member of the sugar tramp fraternity, Mr. George Greenwood, for which I am most grateful. I also want to thank the members of my department— faculty, staff, and students. Their encouragement and support during our first decade together have given new meaning to the word *collegiality*. My editor, Elisabeth Sifton, awed me with her skill and fired me with her enthusiasm; I thank her warmly.

If anyone suffered more with this book than I, it was my spouse, Jacqueline, to whom it is dedicated with all of my love and gratitude—a late present for our twentieth anniversary.

—*Sidney W. Mintz*

Contents

List of Illustrations

Introduction

This book has an odd history. Though it was completed only after a recent and sustained period of writing, much of it grew from skimmings and impressions collected over many years of reading and research. Because of its subject matter, it is a figurative sort of homecoming. For nearly the whole of my professional life, I have been studying the history of the Caribbean region and of those tropical products, mainly agricultural, that were associated with its "development" since the European conquest. Not all such products originated in the New World; and of course none of them, even those that were indigenous, became important in world trade until the late fifteenth century. Because they were produced thereafter for Europeans and North Americans, I became interested in how those Europeans and North Americans became consumers. Following production to where and when it became consumption is what I mean by coming home.

Most people in the Caribbean region, descendants of the aboriginal Amerind population and of settlers who came from Europe, Africa, and Asia, have been rural and agricultural. Working among them usually means working in the countryside; getting interested in them means getting interested in what they produce by their labor. Because I worked among these people—learning what they were like, what their lives were made into by the conditions they lived under—I inevitably wanted to know more about sugar and rum and coffee and chocolate. Caribbean people have always been entangled with a wider world, for the region has, since 1492, been caught up in skeins of imperial control, spun in Amsterdam, London, Paris, Madrid, and other European and North American centers of world power. Someone working inside the rural sectors of those little island societies would inevitably be inclined, I think, to view such networks of control and dependence from the Caribbean vantage point: to look up and out from local life, so to speak, rather than down and into it. But this insider's view has some of the same disadvantages as the firmly European perspective of an earlier generation of observers for whom the greater part of the dependent, outer, non-European world was in most ways a remote, poorly known, and imperfect extension of Europe itself. A view that excludes the linkage between metropolis and colony by choosing one perspective and ignoring the other is necessarily incomplete.

Working in Caribbean societies at the ground level, one is led to ask in just what ways beyond the obvious ones the outer world and the European world became interconnected, interlocked even; what forces beyond the nakedly military and economic ones maintained this intimate interdependence; and how benefits flowed, relative to the ways power was exercised. Asking such questions takes on a specific meaning when one also wants to know in particular about the histories of the products that colonies supply to metropolises. In the Caribbean case, such products have long been, and largely still are, tropical foods: spices (such as ginger, allspice, nutmeg, and mace); beverage bases (coffee and chocolate); and, above all, sugar and rum. At one time, dyes (such as indigo and annatto and fustic) were important; various starches, starch foods, and bases (such as cassava, from which tapioca is made, arrowroot, sago, and various species of *Zamia*) have also figured in the export trade; and a few industrial staples (like sisal) and essential oils (like vetiver) have mattered; bauxite, asphalt, and oil still do. Even some fruits, such as bananas, pineapples, and coconuts, have counted in the world market from time to time.

But for the Caribbean region as a whole, the steady demand overall and for most epochs has been for sugar, and even if it is now threatened by yet other sweeteners, it seems likely to continue to hold its own. Though the story of European sugar consumption has not been tied solely to the Caribbean, and consumption has risen steadily worldwide, without regard to where the sugar comes from, the Caribbean has figured importantly in the picture for centuries.

Once one begins to wonder where the tropical products go, who uses them, for what, and how much they are prepared to pay for them—what they will forgo, and at what price, in order to have them—one is asking questions about the market. But then one is also asking questions about the metropolitan homeland, the center of power, not about the dependent colony, the object and target of power. And once one attempts to put consumption together with production, to fit colony to metropolis, there is a tendency for one or the other—the "hub" or the "outer rim"—to slip out of focus. As one looks at Europe the better to understand the colonies as producers and Europe as consumer, or vice versa, the other side of the relationship seems less clear. While the relationships between colonies and metropolis are in the most immediate sense entirely obvious, in another sense they are mystifying.

My own field experiences, I believe, influenced my perceptions of the center-periphery relationship. In January 1948, when I went to Puerto Rico to start my anthropological fieldwork, I chose a south-coast municipality given over almost entirely to the cultivation of sugar cane for the manufacture of sugar for the North American market. Most of the land in that municipality was owned or leased by a single North American corporation and its landholding affiliate. After a stay in the town, I moved to a rural district (*barrio*); there, for slightly more than a year, I lived in a small shack with a young cane worker.

Surely one of the most remarkable things about Barrio Jauca—and, indeed, about the entire municipality of Santa Isabel at the time—was its dedication to sugar cane. In Barrio Jauca, one stands on a vast alluvial plain, created by the scouring action of once-great rivers—a fertile, fanlike surface extending from the hills down to the Caribbean beaches that form Puerto Rico's south coast. Northward, away from the sea and toward the mountains, the land rises in low foothills, but the coastal land is quite flat. A superhighway from northeast to southwest now passes nearby, but in 1948 there was only a single tarred road, running due east-west along the coast, linking the roadside villages and the towns—Arroyo, Guayama, Salinas, Santa Isabel—of what was then an immense, much-developed sugar-cane-producing region, a place where, I learned, North Americans had penetrated most deeply into the vitals of pre-1898 Puerto Rican life. The houses outside the town were mostly shacks built on the shoulders of roads—sometimes clustered together in little villages with a tiny store or two, a bar, and not much else. Occasionally, an unarable field could be found, its saline soil inhibiting cultivation, on which a few woebegone goats might graze. But the road, the villages stretched along it, and such occasional barren fields were the only interruptions to the eye between mountains and sea; all else was sugar cane. It grew to the very edge of the road and right up to the stoops of the houses. When fully grown, it can tower fifteen feet above the ground. At its mature glory, it turned the plain into a special kind of hot, impenetrable jungle, broken only by special pathways (*callejones*) and irrigation ditches (*zanjas de riego*).

All the time I was in Barrio Jauca, I felt as if we were on an island, floating in a sea of cane. My work there took me into the fields regularly, especially but not only during the harvest (*zafra*). At that time most of the work was still done by human effort alone, without machines; cutting "seed," seeding, planting, cultivating, spreading fertilizer, ditching, irrigating, cutting, and loading cane—it had to be loaded and unloaded twice before being ground—were all manual tasks. I would sometimes stand by the line of cutters, who were working in intense heat and under great pressure, while the foreman stood (and the *mayordomo* rode) at their backs. If one had read about the history of Puerto Rico and of sugar, then the lowing of the animals, the shouts of the *mayordomo*, the grunting of the men as they swung their machetes, the sweat and dust and din easily conjured up an earlier island era. Only the sound of the whip was missing.

Of course, the sugar was not being produced for the Puerto Ricans themselves: they consumed only a fraction of the finished product. Puerto Rico had been producing sugar cane (and sugar in some form) for four centuries, always mainly for consumers elsewhere, whether in Seville, in Boston, or in some other place. Had there been no ready consumers for it elsewhere, such huge quantities of land, labor, and capital would never have been funneled into this one curious crop, first domesticated in New Guinea, first processed in India, and first carried to the New World by Columbus.

Yet I also saw sugar being consumed all around me. People chewed the cane, and were experts not only on which varieties were best to chew, but also on how to chew them—not so easy as one might expect. To be chewed properly, cane must be peeled and the pith cut into chewable portions. Out of it oozes a sticky, sweet, slightly grayish liquid. (When ground by machine and in large quantities, this liquid becomes green, because of the innumerable tiny particles of cane in suspension within it.) The company went to what seemed like extreme lengths to keep people from taking and eating sugar cane—there was, after all, so much of it!—but people always managed to lay hands on some and to chew it soon after it was cut, when it is best. This provided almost daily nourishment for the children, for whom snagging a stalk—usually fallen from an oxcart or a truck—was a great treat. Most people also took the granular, refined kind of sugar, either white or brown, in their coffee, the daily beverage of the Puerto Rican people. (Coffee drunk without sugar is called *café puya*—"ox-goad coffee.")

Though both the juice of the cane and the granular sugars were sweet, they seemed otherwise quite unrelated. Nothing but sweetness brought together the green-gray cane juice (*guarapo*) sucked from the fibers and the granular sugars of the kitchen, used to sweeten coffee and to make the guava, papaya, and bitter-orange preserves, the sesame and tamarind drinks then to be found in Puerto Rican working-class kitchens. No one thought about how one got from those giant fibrous reeds, flourishing upon thousands of acres, to the delicate, fine, pure white granular food and flavoring we call sugar. It was possible, of course, to see with one's own eye how it was done (or, at least, up to the last and most profitable step, which was the conversion from brown to white, mostly carried out in refineries on the mainland). In any one of the big south-coast mills (*centrales*), Guánica or Cortada or Aguirre or Mercedita, one could observe modern techniques of comminution for freeing sucrose in a liquid medium from the plant fibers, the cleansing and condensation, the heating that produced evaporation and, on cooling, further crystallization, and the centrifugal brown sugar that was then

shipped northward for further refining. But I cannot remember ever
hearing anyone talk about making sugar, or wonder out loud about
who were the consumers of so much sugar. What local people were
keenly aware of was the *market* for sugar; though half or more of
them were illiterate, they had an understandably lively interest in
world sugar prices. Those old enough to remember the famous
1919–20 Dance of the Millions—when the world market price of
sugar rose to dizzying heights, then dropped almost to zero, in a
classical demonstration of oversupply and speculation within a
scarcity-based capitalist world market—were especially aware of
the extent to which their fates lay in the hands of powerful, even
mysterious, foreign others.

By the time I returned to Puerto Rico a couple of years later, I
had read a fair amount of Caribbean history, including the history
of plantation crops. I learned that although sugar cane was flanked
by other harvests—coffee, cacao (chocolate), indigo, tobacco, and
so on—it surpassed them all in importance and outlasted them.
Indeed, the world production of sugar has never fallen for more
than an occasional decade at a time during five centuries; perhaps
the worst drop of all came with the Haitian Revolution of 1791–
1803 and the disappearance of the world's biggest colonial producer; and even that sudden and serious imbalance was very soon
redressed. But how remote this all seemed from the talk of gold and
souls—the more familiar refrains of historians (particularly historians of the Hispanic achievement) recounting the saga of European
expansion to the New World! Even the religious education of the
enslaved Africans and indentured Europeans who came to the Caribbean with sugar cane and the other plantation crops (a far cry
from Christianity and uplift for the Indians, the theme of Spanish
imperial policy with which the conventional accounts were then
filled) was of no interest to anyone.

I gave no serious thought to why the demand for sugar should
have risen so rapidly and so continuously for so many centuries, or
even to why sweetness might be a desirable taste. I suppose I thought
the answers to such questions were self-evident—who doesn't like
sweetness? Now it seems to me than my lack of curiosity was obtuse;
I was taking demand for granted. And not just "demand" in the

abstract; world sugar production shows the most remarkable upward production curve of any major food on the world market over the course of several centuries, and it is continuing upward still. Only when I began to learn more Caribbean history and more about particular relationships between planters in the colonies and bankers, entrepreneurs, and different groups of consumers in the metropolises, did I begin to puzzle over what "demand" really was, to what extent it could be regarded as "natural," what is meant by words like "taste" and "preference" and even "good."

Soon after my fieldwork in Puerto Rico, I had a chance for a summer of study in Jamaica, where I lived in a small highland village that, having been established by the Baptist Missionary Society on the eve of emancipation as a home for newly freed church members, was still occupied—almost 125 years later—by the descendants of those freedmen. Though the agriculture in the highlands was mostly carried out on small landholdings and did not consist of plantation crops, we could look down from the lofty village heights on the verdant north coast and the brilliant green checkerboards of the cane plantations there. These, like the plantations on Puerto Rico's south coast, produced great quantities of cane for the eventual manufacture of granulated white sugar; here, too, the final refining was done elsewhere—in the metropolis, and not in the colony.

When I began to observe small-scale retailing in the busy market place of a nearby town, however, I saw for the first time a coarse, less refined sugar that harked back to earlier centuries, when haciendas along Puerto Rico's south coast, swallowed up after the invasion by giant North American corporations, had also once produced it. In the Brown's Town Market of St. Ann Parish, Jamaica, one or two mule-drawn wagons would arrive each market day carrying loads of hard brown sugar in "loaves," or "heads," produced in traditional fashion by sugar makers using ancient grinding and boiling equipment. Such sugar, which contained considerable quantities of molasses (and some impurities), was hardened in ceramic molds or cones from which the more liquid molasses was drained, leaving behind the dark-brown, crystalline loaf. It was consumed solely by poor, mostly rural Jamaicans. It is of course common to find that the poorest people in less developed societies are in many regards the most "traditional." A product that the poor eat, both because they are accustomed to it and because they have no choice, will be praised by the rich, who will hardly ever eat it.

I encountered such sugar once more in Haiti, a few years later. Again, it was produced on small holdings, ground and processed by ancient machinery, and consumed by the poor. In Haiti, where nearly everyone is poor, nearly everyone ate this sort of sugar. The loaves in Haiti were shaped differently: rather like small logs, wrapped in banana leaf, and called in Creole *rapadou* (in Spanish, *raspadura*). Since that time, I have learned that such sugars exist throughout much of the rest of the world, including India, where they were probably first produced, perhaps as much as two thousand years ago.

There are great differences between families using ancient wooden machinery and iron cauldrons to boil up a quantity of sugar to sell to their neighbors in picturesque loaves, and the massed men and machinery employed in producing thousands of tons of sugar cane (and, eventually, of sugar) on modern plantations for export elsewhere. Such contrasts are an integral feature of Caribbean history. They occur not only between islands or between historical periods, but even within single societies (as in the case of Jamaica or Haiti) at the same time. The production of brown sugar in small quantities, remnant of an earlier technical and social era, though it is of declining economic importance will no doubt continue indefinitely, since it has cultural and sentimental meaning, probably for producers as well as consumers.[1] Caribbean sugar industries have changed with the times, and they represent, in their evolution from antecedent forms, interesting stages in the world history of modern society.

I have explained that my first fieldwork in Puerto Rico was in a village of cane workers. This was nearly my first experience outside the continental United States, and though I had been raised in the country, it was my first lengthy encounter with a community where nearly everyone made a living from the soil. These people were not farmers, for whom the production of agricultural commodities was a business; nor were they peasants, tillers of soil they owned or could treat as their own, as part of a distinctive way of life. They were agricultural laborers who owned neither land nor any productive property, and who had to sell their labor to eat. They were wage earners who lived like factory workers, who worked in factories in the field, and just about everything they needed and used they bought from stores. Nearly all of it came from somewhere else: cloth and clothing, shoes, writing pads, rice, olive oil, building materials, medicine. Almost without exception, what they consumed someone else had produced.

The chemical and mechanical transformations by which substances are bent to human use and become unrecognizable to those who know them in nature have marked our relationship to nature for almost as long as we have been human. Indeed, some would say that it is those very transformations that define our humanity. But the division of labor by which such transformations are realized can impart additional mystery to the technical processes. When the locus of manufacture and that of use are separated in time and space, when the makers and the users are as little known to each other as are the processes of manufacture and use themselves, the mystery will deepen. An anecdote may make the point.

My beloved companion and teacher in the field, the late Charles Rosario, received his preparatory education in the United States. When his fellow students learned that he came from Puerto Rico, they immediately assumed that his father (who was a sociologist at the University of Puerto Rico) was a *hacendado*—that is, a wealthy owner of endless acres of tropical land. They asked Charlie to bring them some distinctive souvenir of plantation life when he returned from the island at the summer's end; what they would relish most, they said, was a machete. Eager to please his new friends, Charlie told me, he examined countless machetes in the island stores. But he was dismayed to discover that they were all manufactured in Connecticut—indeed, at a factory only a few hours' drive from the New England school he and his friends were attending.

As I became more and more interested in the history of the Caribbean region and its products, I began to learn about the plantations that were its most distinctive and characteristic economic form. Such plantations were first created in the New World during the early years of the sixteenth century and were staffed for the most part with enslaved Africans. Much changed, they were still there when I first went to Puerto Rico, thirty years ago; so were the descendants of those slaves and, as I later learned and saw elsewhere, the descendants of Portuguese, Javanese, Chinese, and Indian contract laborers, and many other varieties of human being whose ancestors has been brought to the region to grow, cut, and grind sugar cane.

I began to join this information to my modest knowledge of Europe itself. Why Europe? Because these island plantations had been the invention of Europe, overseas experiments of Europe, many of them successful (as far as the Europeans were concerned); and the history of European societies had in certain ways paralleled that of the plantation. One could look around and see sugar-cane plantations and coffee, cacao, and tobacco haciendas, and so, too, one could imagine those Europeans who had thought it promising to create them, to invest in their creation, and to import vast numbers of people in chains from elsewhere to work them. These last would be, if not slaves, then men who sold their labor because they had nothing else to sell; who would probably produce things of which they were not the principal consumers; who would consume things they had not produced, and in the process earn profit for others elsewhere.

It seemed to me that the mysteriousness that accompanied my seeing, at one and the same time, cane growing in the fields and white sugar in my cup, should also accompany the sight of molten metal or, better, raw iron ore, on the one hand, and a perfectly wrought pair of manacles or leg irons, on the other. The mystery was not simply one of technical transformation, impressive as that is, but also the mystery of people unknown to one another being linked through space and time—and not just by politics and economics, but along a particular chain of connection maintained by their production.

The tropical substances whose production I observed in Puerto Rico were foods of a curious kind. Most are stimulants; some are intoxicating; tobacco tends to suppress hunger, whereas sugar provides calories in unusually digestible form but not much else. Of all of these substances, sugar has always been the most important. It is the epitome of a historical process at least as old as Europe's thrustings outside itself in search of new worlds. I hope to explain what sugar reveals about a wider world, entailing as it does a lengthy history of changing relationships among peoples, societies, and substances.

The study of sugar goes back very far in history, even in European history.[2] Yet much about it remains obscure, even enigmatic. How and why sugar has risen to such prevailing importance among European peoples to whom it had at one time been hardly known is still not altogether clear. A single source of satisfaction—sucrose extracted from the sugar cane—for what appears to be a widespread, perhaps even universal, human liking for sweetness became established in European taste preferences at a time when European power, military might, and economic initiative were transforming the world. That source linked Europe and many colonial areas from the fifteenth century onward, the passage of centuries only underlining its importance even while politics changed. And, conversely, what the metropolises produced the colonies consumed. The desire for sweet substances spread and increased steadily; many different products were employed to satisfy it, and cane sugar's importance therefore varied from time to time.

Since sugar seems to satisfy a particular desire (it also seems, in so doing, to awaken that desire yet anew), one needs to understand just what makes demand work: how and why it increases under what conditions. One cannot simply assume that everyone has an infinite desire for sweetness, any more than one can assume the same about a desire for comfort or wealth or power. In order to examine these questions in a specific historical context, I will look at the history of sugar consumption in Great Britain especially between 1650, when sugar began to be fairly common, and 1900, by which time it had entered firmly into the diet of every working family. But this will require some prior examination of the production of the sugar that ended up on English tables in the tea, the jam, the biscuits and cakes and sweets. Because we do not know precisely how sugar was introduced to large segments of Britain's national population—at what rates, by what means, or under exactly what conditions—some speculation is unavoidable. But it is nevertheless possible to show how some people and groups unfamiliar with sugar (and other newly imported ingestibles) gradually became users of it—even, quite rapidly, daily users. Indeed, there is much evidence that many consumers, over time, would have gladly eaten more sugar had they been able to get it, while those who were already consuming it regularly were prepared only reluctantly to reduce or forgo its use. Because anthropology is concerned with how people stubbornly maintain past practices, even when under strong negative pressures, but repudiate other behaviors quite readily in order to act differently, these materials throw light upon the historical circumstances from a perspective rather different from the historian's. Though I cannot answer many questions that historians might bring to these data, I shall suggest that anthropologists ask (and try to answer) certain other questions.

Cultural or social anthropology has built its reputation as a discipline upon the study of non-Western peoples; of peoples who form numerically small societies; of peoples who do not practice any of the so-called great religions; of peoples whose technical repertories are modest—in short, upon the study of what are labeled "primitive" societies. Now, the fact that most of us anthropologists have *not* made such studies has not weakened the general belief that anthropology's strength as a discipline comes from knowing about societies the behaviors of whose members are sufficiently different from our own, yet are based on sufficiently similar principles, to allow us to document the marvelous variability of human custom while vouchsafing the unshakable, essential oneness of the species. This belief has a great deal to recommend it. It is, anyway, my own view. Yet it has unfortunately led anthropologists in the past to bypass willfully any society that appeared in one regard or another not to qualify as "primitive"—or even, occasionally, to ignore information that made it clear that the society being studied was not quite so primitive (or isolated) as the anthropologist would like. The latter is not an outright suppression of data so much as an incapacity or unwillingness to take such data into account theoretically. It is easy to be critical of one's predecessors. But how can one refrain from counterposing Malinowski's studied instructions about learning the natives' point of view by avoiding other Europeans in the field,[3] with his rather casual observation that the same natives had learned to play cricket in the mission schools years before he began his fieldwork? True, Malinowski never *denied* the presence of other Europeans, or of European influence—indeed, he eventually reproached himself for too studiedly ignoring the European presence, and called this his most serious deficiency. But in much of his work, the West in all its guises was played down or even ignored, leaving behind an allegedly pristine primitivity, coolly observed by the anthropologist-as-hero. This curious contrast—unspoiled aborigines on the one hand, hymn-singing mission children on the other—is not an isolated one. By some strange sleight of hand, one anthropological monograph after another whisks out of view any signs of the present and how it came to be. This vanishing act imposes burdens on those who feel the need to perform it; those of us who do not ought to have been thinking much more soberly about what anthropologists should study.

Many of anthropology's most distinguished contemporary practitioners have turned their attention to so-called modern or western societies, but they and the rest of us seem to want to maintain the illusion of what one of my colleagues has aptly dubbed "the uncontaminated McCoy." Even those of us who have studied non-primitive societies seem eager to perpetuate the idea that the profession's strength flows from our mastery of the primitive, more than from the study of change, or of becoming "modern." Accordingly, the movement toward an anthropology of modern life has been somewhat halting, and it has tried to justify itself by concentrating on marginal or unusual enclaves in modern societies: ethnic clusters, exotic occupations, criminal elements, the "underlife," etc. This surely has its positive side. Yet the uncomfortable inference is that such groups most closely approximate the anthropological notion of the primitive.

In the present instance, the prosaic quality of the subject matter is inescapable; what could be less "anthropological" than the historical examination of a food that graces every modern table? And yet the anthropology of just such homely, everyday substances may help us to clarify both how the world changes from what it was to what it may become, and how it manages at the same time to stay in certain regards very much the same.

Let us suppose that there is some value in trying to shape an anthropology of the present, and that to do so we must study societies that lack the features conventionally associated with the so-called primitive. We must still take into account the institutions anthropologists cherish—kinship, family, marriage, *rites de pas-*

sage—and puzzle out the basic divisions by which people are assorted and grouped. We would still try to find out more about fewer people than less about more people. We would still, I believe, put credence in fieldwork, and would value what informants say, as well as what they aspire to and what they do. This would, of course, have to be a different anthropology. As the archaeologist Robert Adams has suggested, anthropologists will no longer be able to invoke scientific "objectivity" to protect themselves from the political implications of their findings, if their subjects turn out simply to be fellow citizens who are poorer or less influential than they.[4] And this new anthropology does not yet wholly exist. The present book, mainly historical in nature, aspires to take a step in its direction. My contention is that the social history of the use of new foods in a western nation can contribute to an anthropology of modern life. It would, of course, be immensely satisfying to be able to declare that my brooding about sugar for thirty years has resulted in some clear-cut alignment, the solution to a puzzle, the resolution of some contradiction, perhaps even a discovery. But I remain uncertain. This book has tended to write itself; I have watched the process, hoping it would reveal something I did not already know.

The organization of the volume is simple. In chapter 1, I attempt to open the subject of the anthropology of food and eating, as part of an anthropology of modern life. This leads me to a discussion of sweetness, as opposed to sweet substances. Sweetness is a taste— what Hobbes called a "Quality"—and the sugars, sucrose (which is won principally from the cane and the sugar beet) among them, are substances that excite the sensation of sweetness. Since any normal human being can apparently experience sweetness, and since all the societies we know of recognize it, something about sweetness must be linked to our character as a species. Yet the liking for sweet things is of highly variable intensity. Hence, an explanation of why some peoples eat lots of sweet things and others hardly any cannot rely on the idea of the species-wide characteristic. How, then, does a particular people become firmly habituated to a large, regular, and dependable supply of sweetness?

Whereas fruit and honey were major sources of sweetness for the English people before about 1650, they do not seem to have figured significantly in the English diet. Sugar made from the juice of the cane had reached England in small quantities by about 1100 A.D.; during the next five centuries, the amounts of cane sugar available doubtless increased, slowly and irregularly. In chapter 2, I look at the production of sugar as the West began to consume more and more of it. From 1650 onward, sugar began to change from a luxury and a rarity into a commonplace and a necessity in many nations, England among them; with a few significant exceptions, this increased consumption after 1650 accompanied the "development" of the West. It was, I believe, the second (or possibly the first, if one discounts tobacco) so-called luxury transformed in this fashion, epitomizing the productive thrust and emerging intent of world capitalism, which centered at first upon the Netherlands and England. I therefore also focus on the possessions that supplied the United Kingdom with sugar, molasses, and rum: on their system of plantation production, and the forms of labor exaction by which such products were made available. I hope to show the special significance of a colonial product like sugar in the growth of world capitalism.

Thereafter, in chapter 3, I discuss the consumption of sugar. My aim is, first, to show how production and consumption were so closely bound together that each may be said partly to have determined the other, and, second, to show that consumption must be explained in terms of what people did and thought: sugar penetrated social behavior and, in being put to new uses and taking on new meanings, was transformed from curiosity and luxury into commonplace and necessity. The relationship between production and consumption may even be paralleled by the relationship between use and meaning. I don't think meanings inhere in substances naturally or inevitably. Rather, I believe that meaning arises out of use, as people use substances in social relationships.

Outside forces often determine what is available to be endowed with meaning. If the users themselves do not so much determine what is available to be used as add meanings to what is available, what does that say about meaning? At what point does the prerogative to bestow meaning move from the consumers to the sellers? Or could it be that the power to bestow meaning always accompanies the power to determine availabilities? What do such questions—and their answers—mean for our understanding of the operation of modern society, and for our understanding of freedom and individualism?

In chapter 4, I try to say something about why things happened as they did, and I attempt some treatment of circumstance, conjuncture, and cause. Finally, in chapter 5, I offer a few suggestions about where sugar, and the study of sugar in modern society, may be going. I have suggested that anthropology is showing some uncertainty about its own future. An anthropology of modern life and of food and eating, for example, cannot ignore fieldwork or do without it. My hope is that I have identified problems of significance concerning which fieldwork might eventually yield results useful for both theory and policy.

My bias in a historical direction will be apparent. Though I do not accept uncritically the dictum that anthropology must become history or be nothing at all, I believe that without history its explanatory power is seriously compromised. Social phenomena are by their nature historical, which is to say that the relationships among events in one "moment" can never be abstracted from their past and future setting. Arguments about immanent human nature, about the human being's inbuilt capacity to endow the world with its characteristic structures, are not necessarily wrong; but when these arguments replace or obviate history, they are inadequate and misleading. Human beings do create social structures, and do endow events with meaning; but these structures and meanings have historical origins that shape, limit, and help to explain such creativity.

SWEETNESS AND POWER

1 · Food, Sociality, and Sugar

Our awareness that food and eating are foci of habit, taste, and deep feeling must be as old as those occasions in the history of our species when human beings first saw other humans eating unfamiliar foods. Like languages and all other socially acquired group habits, food systems dramatically demonstrate the infraspecific variability of humankind. It is almost too obvious to dwell on: humans make food out of just about everything; different groups eat different foods and in different ways; all feel strongly about what they do eat and don't eat, and about the ways they do so. Of course, food choices are related in some ways to availability, but human beings never eat every edible and available food in their environment. Moreover, their food preferences are close to the center of their self-definition: people who eat strikingly different foods or similar foods in different ways are thought to be strikingly different, sometimes even less human.

The need for nourishment is expressed in the course of all human interaction. Food choices and eating habits reveal distinctions of age, sex, status, culture, and even occupation. These distinctions are immensely important adornments on an inescapable necessity. "Nutrition as a biological process," wrote Audrey Richards, one of anthropology's best students of food and ingestion, "is more fundamental than sex. In the life of the individual organism it is the more primary and recurrent want, while in the wider sphere of human society it determines, more largely than any other physiological function, the nature of social groupings, and the form their activities take."[1]

Nothing the newborn infant does establishes so swiftly its social connection with the world as the expression and satisfaction of its hunger. Hunger epitomizes the relation between its dependence and the social universe of which it must become a part. Eating and nurturance are closely linked in infancy and childhood, no matter how their connection may be altered later. Food preferences that emerge early in life do so within the bounds laid down by those who do the nurturing, and therefore within the rules of their society and culture. Ingestion and tastes hence carry an enormous affective load. What we like, what we eat, how we eat it, and how we feel about it are phenomenologically interrelated matters; together, they speak eloquently to the question of how we perceive ourselves in relation to others.

From the beginning, anthropology has concerned itself with food and ingestion. Robertson Smith, a founding father of anthropology, who examined eating together as a special social act (he was interested in the sacrificial meal, in connection with which he used the term "commensals" to describe the relation between gods and human beings), saw the breaking of bread by gods with men as "a symbol and a confirmation of fellowship and mutual social obligations." "Those who sit at meat together are united for all social effects; those who do not eat together are aliens to one another, without fellowship in religion and without reciprocal social duties."[2] But Robertson Smith also argued that "the essence of the thing lies in the physical act of eating together"[3]—a bond, created simply by partaking of food, linking human beings with one another.

In an early article, Lorna Marshall provided a glowing description of how sharing food serves to reduce individual and intragroup tension. The !Kung Bushmen, she reported, always consumed fresh meat immediately after it became available: "The fear of hunger is mitigated; the person one shares with will share in turn when he gets meat and people are sustained by a web of mutual obligation. If there is hunger, it is commonly shared. There are no distinct haves and have-nots. One is not alone.... The idea of eating alone and not sharing is shocking to the !Kung. It makes them shriek with an uneasy laughter. Lions could do that, they say, not men."⁴ Marshall described in detail how four hunters who killed an eland, following ten days of hunting and three days of tracking the wounded animal, bestowed the meat upon others—other hunters, the wife of the owner of the arrow that first wounded the prey, the relatives of the arrow's owner, etc. She recorded sixty-three gifts of raw meat and thought there had been many more. Small quantities of meat were rapidly diffused, passed on in ever-diminishing portions. This swift movement was not random or quixotic; it actually illuminated the interior organization of the !Kung band, the distribution of kinfolk, divisions of sex, age, and role. Each occasion to eat meat was hence a natural occasion to discover who one was, how one was related to others, and what that entailed.

The connections between food and kinship, or food and social groups, take radically different forms in modern life. Yet surely food and eating have not lost their affective significance, though as a means for validating existing social relations their importance and their form are now almost unrecognizably different. So an anthropological study of contemporary western food and eating may try to answer some of the same questions as are asked by our anthropological predecessors, such as Richards, Robertson Smith, and Marshall—but both the data and the methods will differ substantially. In this study, I have tried to place a single food, or category of foods, in the evolution of a modern western nation's diet. It involved no fieldwork *per se*—though I stumbled across issues that might be better understood if fieldwork were directed to their exposition. Moreover, though I touch on the social aspects of ingestion, I am concerned less with meals and more with mealtimes—how meals were adapted to modern, industrial society, or how that society affected the sociality of ingestion, how foods and the ways to eat them were added to a diet or eliminated from it.

Specifically, I am concerned with a single substance called sucrose, a kind of sugar extracted primarily from the sugar cane, and with what became of it. The story can be summed up in a few sentences. In 1000 A.D., few Europeans knew of the existence of sucrose, or cane sugar. But soon afterward they learned about it; by 1650, in

England the nobility and the wealthy had become inveterate sugar eaters, and sugar figured in their medicine, literary imagery, and displays of rank. By no later than 1800, sugar had become a necessity—albeit a costly and rare one—in the diet of every English person; by 1900, it was supplying nearly one-fifth of the calories in the English diet.

How and why did this happen? What turned an exotic, foreign, and costly substance into the daily fare of even the poorest and humblest people? How could it have become so important so swiftly? What did sugar mean to the rulers of the United Kingdom; what did it come to mean to the ordinary folk who became its mass consumers? The answers may seem self-evident; sugar is sweet, and human beings like sweetness. But when unfamiliar substances are taken up by new users, they enter into pre-existing social and psychological contexts and acquire—or are given—contextual meanings by those who use them. How that happens is by no means obvious. That human beings like the taste of sweetness does not explain why some eat immense quantities of sweet foods and others hardly any. These are not just individual differences, but differences among groups, as well.

Uses imply meanings; to learn the anthropology of sugar, we need to explore the meanings of its uses, to discover the early and more limited uses of sugar, and to learn where and for what original purposes sugar was produced. This means examining the sources of supply, the chronology of uses, and the combination of sugar with other foods—including honey, which is also sweet, and tea, coffee, and chocolate, which are bitter—in the making of new dietary patterns. The sources of sugar involve those tropical and subtropical regions that were transformed into British colonies, and so we must examine the relationships between such colonies and the motherland, also the areas that produced no sugar but the tea with which it was drunk, and the people who were enslaved in order to produce it.

Such an inquiry inevitably brings many more questions in its wake. Did the English come to eat more sugar just because they liked it; did they like it because they had too little of other foods to eat; or did other factors affect their disposition toward this costly food? We need to reflect on those social reformers, such as Jonas Hanway, who inveighed against the wastefulness and prodigality of the laboring classes because they came to want tea and sugar; and on their opponents, the sugar brokers and refiners and shippers, such as George Porter, who won out over the reformers because they envisioned sugar's benefactions for all Englishmen—and struggled to change the nature of the market. This also means seeing how, over time, the exigencies of work changed where, how, and when ordinary people ate, and how new foods were created, with new virtues. Perhaps most important of all, we must understand how, in the creation of an entirely new economic system, strange and foreign luxuries, unknown even to European nobility a few short centuries earlier, could so swiftly become part of the crucial social center of British daily life, the universal substances of social relationship for the farthest-flung empire in world history. And then we shall have returned—though on a different level of explanation—to our fellow humans the !Kung, dividing and redividing their eland meat as they validate the social worth of the links that bind them to one another.

Studying the varying use of a single ingestible like sugar is rather like using a litmus test on particular environments. Any such traceable feature can highlight, by its intensity, scale, and perhaps spread, its association with other features with which it has a regular but not invariant relation, and in some cases can serve as an index of them. Such associations can be broad and important—as between rats and disease, or drought and famine, or nutrition and fertility— or they may seem trivial, as between sugar and spices. The affinity between such phenomena may be intrinsic and explicable, as with, say, rats and disease. But of course the association may also be quite arbitrary, neither "causal" nor "functional," as in the case of sugar and spices—substances foreign to Europe, carried thence from distant lands, gradually entering into the diet of people trying them out for the first time; linked together mostly by the accident of usage and, to some extent, by origin, but overlapping and diverging as their uses overlapped and diverged and as the demand for them rose and fell. Sugar has been associated during its history with slavery, in the colonies; with meat, in flavoring or concealing taste;

with fruit, in preserving; with honey, as a substitute and rival. And sugar was associated with tea, coffee, and chocolate; much of its history in the late seventeenth and eighteenth centuries springs from that particular association. Sugar was also first associated with the rich and the noble classes, and it remained out of the reach of the less privileged for centuries.

In staying with sugar, the aim is not to de-emphasize other foods, but to make clear the changing uses and meanings of sugar itself over time. As uses change or are added on, as use both deepens and broadens, meanings also change. There is nothing "natural" or inevitable about these processes; they have no inbuilt dynamic of their own. The relationship between the production of sugar and its consumption changed over time and, as it did, the uses to which sugar was put and the meanings to which it gave rise also changed. By keeping sugar itself as the focus, we can actually see more clearly how its relationship to other foods, those with which it was combined and those which it eventually supplanted, was altered.

Nutritionists can construct diets for the species based on the best scientific information available, but there is no infallible guide to what is naturally the best food for human beings. We appear to be capable of eating (and liking) just about anything that is not immediately toxic. Cross-cultural studies of dietary preferences reveal eloquently that the universes that human groups treat matter-of-factly as their "natural environments" are clearly social, symbolically constructed universes. What constitutes "good food," like what constitutes good weather, a good spouse, or a fulfilling life, is a social, not a biological, matter. Good food, as Lévi-Strauss suggested long ago, must be good to think about before it becomes good to eat.

If we look at the whole sweep of human cultural evolution and concentrate on that last "minute" of geological time when the domestication of plants and animals occurs, we can see that almost all human beings who have ever lived were members of societies in which some one particular vegetable food was "good." Because plant domestication and purposeful cultivation greatly increased the stability of the food supply and, in consequence, the human population itself, most of us and our ancestors during these past ten or twelve thousand years have subsisted primarily on some one sort of vegetable food.[5]

Most great (and many minor) sedentary civilizations have been built on the cultivation of a particular complex carbohydrate, such as maize or potatoes or rice or millet or wheat. In these starch-based societies, usually but not always horticultural or agricultural, people are nourished by their bodily conversion of the complex carbohydrates, either grains or tubers, into body sugars. Other plant foods, oils, flesh, fish, fowl, fruits, nuts, and seasonings—many of the ingredients of which are nutritively essential—will also be consumed, but the users themselves usually view them as secondary, even if necessary, additions to the major starch. This fitting together of core complex carbohydrate and flavor-fringe supplement is a fundamental feature of the human diet—not of *all* human diets, but certainly of enough of them in our history to serve as the basis for important generalizations.

In her monographs on the Southern Bantu people called the Bemba, Audrey Richards has described luminously how a preferred starch can be the nutritive anchor of an entire culture:

> For us it requires a real effort of imagination to visualize a state of society in which food matters so much and from so many points of view, but this effort is necessary if we are to understand the emotional background of Bemba ideas as to diet.
>
> To the Bemba each meal, to be satisfactory, must be composed of two constituents: a thick porridge (*ubwali*) made of millet and the relish (*umunani*) of vegetables, meat or fish, which is eaten with it.... *Ubwali* is commonly translated by "porridge" but this is misleading. The hot water and meal are mixed in proportion of 3 to 2 to make *ubwali* and this produces a solid mass of the consistency of plasticine and quite unlike what we know as porridge. *Ubwali* is eaten in hunks torn off in the hand, rolled into balls, dipped in relish, and bolted whole.
>
> Millet has already been described as the main constituent of Bemba diet, but it is difficult for the European, accustomed as he is to a large variety of foodstuffs, to realize fully what a "staple crop" can mean to a primitive people. To the Bemba, millet porridge is not only necessary, but it is the only constituent of his diet which actually ranks as food.... I have watched natives

eating the roasted grain off four or five maize cobs under my very eyes, only to hear them shouting to their fellows later, "Alas, we are dying of hunger. We have not had a bite to eat all day...."

The importance of millet porridge in native eyes is constantly reflected in traditional utterance and ritual. In proverb and folktale the *ubwali* stands for food itself. When discussing his kinship obligations, a native will say, "How can a man refuse to help his mother's brother who has given him *ubwali* all these years?" or, "Is he not her son? How should she refuse to make him *ubwali*?"...

But the native, while he declares he cannot live without *ubwali*, is equally emphatic that he cannot eat porridge without a relish (*umunani*), usually in the form of a liquid stew....

The term *umunani* is applied to stews—meat, fish, caterpillars, locusts, ants, vegetables (wild and cultivated), mushrooms, etc.— prepared to eat with porridge. The functions of the relish are two: first to make the *ubwali* easier to swallow, and second to give it taste. A lump of porridge is glutinous and also gritty— the latter not only owing to the flour of which it is made, but to the extraneous matter mixed in with it on the grindstone. It needs a coating of something slippery to make it slide down the throat. Dipping the porridge in a liquid stew makes it easier to swallow. Thus the use of *umunani*, which to European eyes adds valuable constituents to the diet, is defended by the native on the ground that it overcomes the purely mechanical difficulty of getting the food down the throat.... The Bemba himself explains that the sauce is not food....

It prevents the food "coming back." Meat and vegetable stews are cooked with salt whenever possible, and there is no doubt that an additional function of the relish in native eyes is to give the porridge taste and to lessen the monotony of the diet. Groundnut sauce is also praised as bringing out the taste of a number of different relishes such as mushrooms, caterpillars, etc.

In general, only one relish is eaten at a meal. The Bemba do not like to mix their foods, and despise the European habit of eating a meal composed of two or three kinds of dishes. He calls this habit *ukusobelekanya* and one said, "It is like a bird first to pick at this and then at that, or like a child who nibbles here and there through the day."[6]

The picture Richards paints for us is in its more general features surprisingly common worldwide. People subsist on some principal complex carbohydrate, usually a grain or root crop, around which their lives are built. Its calendar of growth fits with their calendar of the year; its needs are, in some curious ways, their needs. It provides the raw materials out of which much of the meaning in life is given voice. Its character, names, distinctive tastes and textures, the difficulties associated with its cultivation, its history, mythical or not, are projected on the human affairs of a people who consider what they eat to be the basic food, to be *the* definition of food.

But some one such single food can be boring, too. People brought up in starch-centered cultures may feel they have not really eaten unless they have had *ubwali* (tortillas, rice, potatoes, bread, taro, yams, manioc cakes—whatever), but they will also feel that *ubwali* is not enough unless it is accompanied by *umunani*. Why this should be so is not entirely clear, but over and over again the centricity of the complex carbohydrates is accompanied by its contrastive periphery. Elisabeth and Paul Rozin call one aspect of this common structural pattern a "flavor principle" and they have drawn up lists of distinctive regional flavors, like the *nuoc mam* of Southeast Asia, the chili peppers (*Capsicum* species) of Mexico, West Africa, and parts of India and China, the *sofrito* of the Hispanic Americans, and so on.[7] But whether it be the sauce the Bemba eat to provide taste and to make the starch easier to swallow; the chili peppers that enliven a diet of maize-based *atole* and *tortillas*; or the fish and bean pastes and soys of the Far East which accompany rice or millet—these supplementary tastes gain their importance because they make basic starches ingestively more interesting. They also may supply important, often essential, dietary elements, but this never seems to be the reason people give for eating them.

Even in diets where a wider range of food possibilities appears to be available, a general relationship between "center" and "edge" is usually discernible. The Irish joke about "potatoes and point"— before eating one's potato, one would point it at a piece of salt pork hung above the table—is clear enough. The habits of bread-eating peoples, who use fats and salt to flavor the large quantities of bread they regularly eat, are also well known. (A common East European combination used to be black bread, chicken fat, raw garlic, and salt. There are scores of local variants.) Pasta is eaten with a sauce;

for even the most modest the sauce changes a monotonous meal into a banquet. Cornmeal, couscous, bulgur, millet, yams—it hardly matters which (though of course to those whose diet is built around such an item, it matters enormously): supplementary tastes round the diet out, punctuate it, and give it variable character.

These supplements are not ordinarily consumed in large quantities—hardly ever in quantities equal to those of the starches—and people who eat them regularly might find the idea of doing so nauseating. Their tastes and textures usually contrast noticeably with the smoothness, lumpiness, grittiness, chewiness, blandness, or dryness of the cooked starch, but they are usually blendable substances that can be eaten when the starch itself is eaten: they "go" with it. Commonly, they are liquid or semiliquid, soluble or meltable, often oily. Small quantities of such supplements will change the character of substantial quantities of liquid, especially if they have a strong or contrastive taste and are served hot—as sauces to be ladled over starches or into which a starch is dipped.

Often the supplemental food contains ingredients that are sun-dried, fermented, cured, smoked, salted, semiputrefied, or otherwise altered from a natural state. In these ways they contrast "processually" with the principal starch as well. Many of the main starches need only to be cleaned and cooked in order to be eaten.

The fringe additions need not be fish, flesh, fowl, or insect in origin; often they are grasses such as watercress, chives, mint, or seaweed (bitter, sour, pungent, chewy, slimy); lichens, mushrooms, or other fungi (moldy-bitter, crisp, "cold"); dried spices (tart, bitter, "hot," aromatic); or certain fruits, either fresh or preserved (sour, sweet, juicy, fibrous, tough). Because they may sting, burn, intensify thirst, stimulate salivation, cause tearing or irritate mucous membranes, be bitter, sour, salty, or sweet, they usually taste (and probably smell) very different from the starch itself. And there is no doubt that they increase the consumption of the core food.

In the last two or three centuries, whole societies—as opposed to what were once tiny, privileged, uppermost segments of older, more hierarchical societies—have apparently begun to stand such patterns on end. In these rare new cases—the United States would be one—complex carbohydrates decline as the central part of the diet, which is instead composed for the most part of flesh (including fish and fowl), fats of all kinds, and sugars (simple carbohydrates). These late-appearing adaptations, which typically require immense caloric input for every calorie delivered,[8] contrast with the archaic hunter/fisher/gleaner societies. In their own way, the United States, Argentina, and Australia–New Zealand are as nutritionally extraordinary as the Eskimos, the Tlingit, or the Masai.[9]

It should be superfluous to point out that the older dietary complexes carried important symbolic loads. What people eat expresses who and what they are, to themselves and to others. The congruence of dietary patterns and their societies reveals the way cultural forms are maintained by the ongoing activity of those who "carry" such forms, whose behavior actualizes and incarnates them. Given the remarkable capacity of human beings to change, and of societies to be transformed, one must nonetheless imagine what would be involved in turning the Mexican people into eaters of black bread, the Russian people into eaters of maize, or the Chinese into eaters of cassava. And it is important to note that the radical dietary changes of the last three hundred years have largely been achieved by revolutionary pressures in food processing and consumption and by adding on new foods, rather than simply cutting back on older ones. In any event, transformations of diet entail quite profound alterations in people's images of themselves, their notions of the contrasting virtues of tradition and change, the fabric of their daily social life.

The character of the English diet at the time when sugar became known to Englishmen—known and then desired—is relevant to our history. For during the period when sugar was first becoming widely known, most people in England and elsewhere were struggling to stabilize their diets around adequate quantities of starch (in the form of wheat or other grains), not to move beyond such consumption. What turns out to be most interesting about the British picture is how little it differed from eating habits and nutrition elsewhere in the world. As recently as a century ago, the combination diet of a single starch supplemented by a variety of other foods, and the constant possibility of widespread hunger—sometimes famine—would have characterized something like 85 percent of the world's population. Today, this picture still applies in much of Asia, Africa, and Latin America; and the pattern of one-starch "centricity" still typifies perhaps three-quarters of the world's population.

In 1650, the people of what was to become the United Kingdom also lived on a starch-centered diet. Within a single century, they began to move toward a pattern that has since been adopted by many other societies. This transformation exemplifies one sort of modernization. But it was not simply the consequence of other, more important changes; indeed, in a sense it may have been the other way around: this and like dietary transformations actively facilitated more fundamental changes in British society. In other words, the question becomes not only how the English people became sugar eaters, but also what this meant for the subsequent transformation of their society.

Similarly, if we ask what sugar meant to the people of the United Kingdom when it became a fixed and (in their view) essential part of their diet, the answer partly depends on the function of sugar itself, its significance, for them. "Meaning" in this case is not simply to be "read" or "deciphered," but arises from the cultural applications to which sugar lent itself, the uses to which it was put. Meaning, in short, is the consequence of activity. This does not mean that culture is only (or is reducible to only) behavior. But not to ask how meaning is put into behavior, to read the product without the production, is to ignore history once again. Culture must be understood "not simply as a product but also as production, not simply as socially constituted but also as socially constituting."[10] One decodes the process of codification, and not merely the code itself.

Researchers working with infants in the United States have concluded that there is a built-in human liking for sweet tastes, which appears "very early in development and is relatively independent of experience."[11] Though there are inadequate cross-cultural data to sustain that position, sweetness seems to be so widely favored that it is hard to avoid the inference of some inborn predisposition. The nutrition scholar Norge Jerome has collected information to show how sucrose-rich foods form part of the early acculturational experiences of non-western peoples in many world areas, and there seems to be little or no resistance to such items. It is perhaps noteworthy that sugar and sugary foods are commonly diffused with stimulants, particularly beverages. There may be some synergy involved in the ingestive learning of new users: to date, there have been no reports on any group with a nonsugar tradition rejecting the introduction of sugar, sweetened condensed milk, sweetened beverages, sweetmeats, pastries, confectionery, or other sweet dietary items into the culture. In fact, a recent study on sucrose intolerance in northern Alaskan Eskimos revealed that sucrose-intolerant individuals continued to consume sucrose despite the discomforts associated with the offending items.[12]

Many scholars have promoted the thesis that mammalian responsiveness to sweetness arose because for millions of years a sweet taste served to indicate edibility to the tasting organism.[13] Hominid evolution from arboreal, fruit-eating primate ancestors makes this thesis particularly persuasive, and has encouraged some students of the problem to go to logical extremes:

> ... the least natural environments may sometimes provide the best evidence about human nature.... Western peoples consume enormous per capita quantities of refined sugar because, to most people, very sweet foods taste very good. The existence of the human sweet tooth can be explained, ultimately, as an adaptation of ancestral populations to favor the ripest—and hence the sweetest—fruit. In other words, the selective pressures of times past are most strikingly revealed by the artificial, supernormal stimulus of refined sugar, despite the evidence that eating refined sugar is maladaptive.[14]

In fact, it can be argued equally well (and more convincingly, it seems to me) that the widely variant sugar-eating habits of contemporary populations show that no ancestral predisposition within the species can adequately explain what are in fact culturally conventionalized norms, not biological imperatives. That there are links between fruit eating, the sensation of sweetness, and the evolution of the primates is persuasive. That they "explain" the heavy consumption of refined sugar by some peoples in the modern world is not.

Indeed, all (or at least nearly all) mammals like sweetness.[15] That milk, including human milk, is sweet is hardly irrelevant. One scholar, seeking to push the link between human preferences and sweetness just a little further back, has even argued that the fetus experiences sweetness when nourished *in utero*.[16] The newborn infant usually lives exclusively on milk at first. Jerome notes that the use of sweetened liquids as a substitute for milk for infant feeding occurs across the world. The first nonmilk "food" that a baby is likely to receive in North American hospitals is a 5-percent glucose-and-water solution, used to evaluate its postpartum functioning because "the newborn tolerates glucose better than water."[17] On the one hand, that the human liking for sweetness is not just an acquired disposition is supported by many different kinds of evidence; on the other, the circumstances under which that predisposition is intensified by cultural practice are highly relevant to how strong the "sweet tooth" is.

Sweetness would have been known to our primate ancestors and to early human beings in berries, fruit, and honey—honey being the most intensely sweet, by far. Honey, of course, is an animal product, at least in the sense that its raw material is gathered from flowering plants by bees. "Sugar," particularly sucrose, is a vegetable product extracted by human ingenuity and technical achievement. And whereas honey was known to human beings at all levels of technical achievement the world over from a very early point in the historical record, sugar (sucrose) made from the sugar cane is a late product that spread slowly during the first millennium or so of its existence, and became widespread only during the past five hundred years. Since the nineteenth century, the sugar beet, a temperate crop, has become an almost equally important source of sucrose, and the mastery of sucrose extraction from it has altered the character of the world's sugar industries.[18] In the present century, other caloric sweeteners, particularly those from maize (*Zea mays*), have begun to challenge the primacy of sucrose, and noncaloric sweeteners have also begun to win a place in the human diet.

Sensations of sweetness must be carefully distinguished from the substances that give rise to them; and processed sugars, such as sucrose, dextrose, and fructose, which are manufactured and refined technochemically, must be distinguished from sugars as they occur in nature. For chemists, "sugar" is a generic term for a large, varied class of organic compounds of which sucrose is but one.

I concentrate in this book on sucrose, though there will be occasion to refer to other sugars, and this focus is dictated by the history of sucrose's consumption in recent centuries, which completely outstripped honey (its principal European competitor before the seventeenth century), and made largely irrelevant such other products as maple sugar and palm sugar. The very idea of sweetness came to be associated with sugar in European thought and language, though honey continued to play a privileged minor role, particularly in literary imagery. The lack of clarity or specificity in European conceptions of sweetness as a sensation is noticeable.

I have already remarked that, though there may be certain absolute species-wide features in the human taste apparatus, different peoples eat widely variant substances and have radically different ideas about what tastes good, especially relative to other edible substances. Not only do individuals differ in preferences and the degree of intensity of a particular taste that suits them, but also there is no adequate methodology to bracket or bound the range of tastes typical of persons in any group. To add to the difficulties, the lexicons of taste sensation, even if fully recorded, are immensely difficult to translate for comparative purposes.

Still, there is probably no people on earth that lacks the lexical means to describe that category of tastes we call "sweet." Though the taste of sweetness is not uniformly liked, either by whole cultures or by all of the members of any one culture, no society rejects sweetness as unpleasant—even though particular sweet things are tabooed or eschewed for various reasons. Sweet tastes have a privileged position in contrast to the more variable attitudes toward sour, salty, and bitter tastes; this, of course, does not rule out the common predilections for certain sour, salty, or bitter substances.

But to say that everyone everywhere likes sweet things says nothing about where such tastes fit into the spectrum of taste possibilities, how important sweetness is, where it occurs in a taste-preference hierarchy, or how it is thought of in relation to other tastes. Moreover, there is much evidence that people's attitudes toward foods, including sweet foods, have varied greatly with time and occasion. In the modern world, one need only contrast the frequency, intensity, and scale of sugar uses in the French diet with, say, the English or American, to see how widely attitudes toward sweetness vary. Americans seem to like meals to end with sweetness, in desserts; others also like to start with sweetness. Moreover, sweetness is important in what anthropologists call interval eating, or snacks, in American life. Other peoples seem less inclined to treat sweetness as a "slot taste," suitable in only one or several positions; for them a sweet food might appear at any point in the meal—as one of the middle courses, or as one of several dishes served simultaneously. The propensity to mix sweetness with other tastes is also highly variable.

The widely different ways that sweetness is perceived and employed support my argument that the importance of sweetness in English taste preferences grew over time, and was not characteristic before the eighteenth century. Though in the West sweetness now generally is considered by the culture (and perhaps by most scientists) a quality counterposed to bitterness, sourness, and saltiness, which make up the taste "tetrahedron,"[19] or is contrasted to the piquancy or hotness with which it is sometimes associated in Chinese, Mexican, and West African cuisines, I suspect that this counterposition—in which sweetness becomes the "opposite" of everything—is quite recent. Sweet could only be a countertaste to salt/bitter/sour when there was a plentiful enough source of sweetness to make this possible. Yet the contrast did not always occur when sugar became plentiful; Britain, Germany, and the Low Countries reacted differently, for instance, from France, Spain, and Italy.

That some built-in predisposition to sweetness is part of the human equipment seems inarguable. But it cannot possibly explain differing food systems, degrees of preference, and taxonomies of taste—any more than the anatomy of the so-called organs of speech can "explain" any particular language. It is the borderline between our human liking for sweetness and the supposed English "sweet tooth" that I hope to illuminate in what follows.

2 · Production

Sucrose—what we call "sugar"—is an organic chemical of the carbohydrate family. It can be commercially extracted from various plant sources, and it occurs in all green plants.[1] A plant food manufactured photosynthetically from carbon dioxide and water, sucrose is thus a fundamental feature of the chemical architecture of living things.

The two most important sources of processed sucrose—of the refined carbohydrate product we consume and call "sugar"—are the sugar cane and the sugar beet. Sugar beets were not economically important as a source of sucrose until the middle of the nineteenth century, but sugar cane has been the prime source of sucrose for more than a millennium—perhaps for much longer.

The sugar cane (*Saccharum officinarum* L.) was first domesticated in New Guinea, and very anciently. The botanists Artschwager and Brandes believe that there were three diffusions of sugar cane from New Guinea, the first taking place around 8000 B.C. Perhaps two thousand years later, the cane was carried to the Philippines and India, and possibly to Indonesia (though some authorities regard Indonesia as yet another locus of domestication).[2]

References to sugar *making* do not appear until well into the Christian era. There are some earlier references in Indian literature. The *Mahābhāshya* of Patanjali, for instance, a commentary on Panini's study of Sanskrit, the first grammar of a language ever written (probably around 400–350 B.C.), mentions sugar repeatedly in particular food combinations (rice pudding with milk and sugar; barley meal and sugar; fermented drinks flavored with ginger and sugar); if one assumes that what was meant was some nonliquid product as least partially crystallized from the juice of the sugar cane, this would be the earliest such mention we have. But it is open to doubt, because there is no sure evidence that the product was crystallized. A little later, in 327 B.C., Nearchus, Alexander's general, sailing from the mouth of the Indus River to the mouth of the Euphrates, asserted that "a reed in India brings forth honey without the help of bees, from which an intoxicating drink is made though the plant bears no fruit."[3] The sugar engineer and historian Noel Deerr accepts this as a reference to sugar cane, but his citations from Greek and Roman authorities are not entirely convincing. The term *sakcharon* or *saccharon*—σάκχαρον—used by Dioscorides, Pliny, Galen, and others, is not translatable as some single specific substance. The historian of food R. J. Forbes, carefully reviewing the evidence from pre-Christian Greece and from Rome, concluded that *saccharon* was available in India "and even known, though imperfectly, to the Hellenistic visitors to this country [India]"; and here he does mean sugar made from the juice of the sugar cane. He accepts Dioscorides, who wrote: "There is a kind of concreted honey, called *saccharon*, found in reeds in India and Arabia Felix, like in consistence to salt, and brittle to be broken between the teeth, as salt is. It is good for the belly and the stomach being dissolved in water and so drank, helping the pained bladder and the reins." To which Forbes adds: "Sugar was therefore produced, at least in small quantities, in India and was just becoming known to the Roman world in Pliny's day"—that is, during the first century A.D.[4] He reminds us, however, that terms like *saccharon* and even "manna" were used for a variety of sweet substances, including plant secretions, the excreta of plant lice, the mannite exudation of *Fraxinus ornus* (the so-called manna ash tree), etc.[5]

Some students of sugar history suppose that *saccharon* referred to an entirely different substance, the so-called sugar of bamboo, or *tabashir*, a gum that accumulates in the stems of certain bamboos and has a sweet taste.[6] Obscure though this controversy is, it highlights a vital feature in the history of sugar: sugar must be crystallized from liquid. What we call "sugar" is the end product of an ancient, complex, and difficult process.

One begins with the sugar-cane plant itself, a large grass of the family *Gramineae*. There are six known species of sugar cane, of which *Saccharum officinarum*—"sugar of the apothecaries"—has been important throughout history. Though other species besides *Saccharum officinarum* have been used to breed new varieties in recent decades, the source of genes for sucrose accumulation has continued to be this species above all, the so-called noble cane, with soft, sweet, juicy stalks that grow as thick as two inches, and twelve to fifteen feet high, when mature. Cane is propagated asexually from cuttings of the stem having at least one bud.[7] Once planted, the cane sprouts and with adequate heat and moisture may grow an inch a day for six weeks. It becomes ripe—and reaches the optimum condition for extraction—in a dry season after anywhere from nine to eighteen months. "Ratoon" cane, grown from the stubble of the preceding crop without replanting, is normally cut about every twelve months. Seed cane cuttings in the tropics take longer to reach maturity. In all cases cane must be cut when ready so as not to lose its juice or the proportion of sucrose in this juice; and once it is cut, the juice must be rapidly extracted to avoid rot, desiccation, inversion, or fermentation.

The intrinsic nature of sugar cane fundamentally affected its cultivation and processing. "Though we speak of sugar factories," writes one scholar, "what actually takes place there is not a manufacturing process but a series of liquid-solid operations to isolate the sucrose made by nature in the plant."[8] The practice of crushing or comminuting the cane fibers so their liquid content can be extracted must be almost as old as the discovery that the cane was sweet. This extraction can be accomplished in a number of different ways. The cane can be chopped, then ground, pressed, pounded, or soaked in liquid. Heating the liquid containing the sucrose causes evaporation and a resulting sucrose concentration. As the liquid becomes supersaturated, crystals begin to appear. In effect, crystallization requires the concentration of a supersaturated solution in which sucrose is contained in liquid form. While cooling and crystallizing, low-grade massecuites leave "final" or "blackstrap" molasses. This molasses, or treacle, cannot be crystallized further by conventional methods. It is, of course, quite sweet, and can be used for sweetening food; in the English diet, it was for more than a century at least as important as any crystalline form of sugar; in refined forms, it remains important to this day.

This much of the process is ancient. Supplementary steps leading to sugars that are less dark, chemically purer, or more refined (the latter two are not the same thing), and to an ever-increasing differentiation of final products, including alcoholic beverages and many different syrups, have developed over the centuries. But the basic process is very old. In fact, there is no other practical means by which to "make" sugar from the cane than by "a series of liquid-solid operations" accompanied by heating and cooling; and maintaining proper temperatures, while keeping the investment in heating methods and fuels affordable, has been a serious technical problem throughout most of sugar's history.

The sugar eventually fabricated from the sucrose magma differs strikingly from both sugar-cane juice and from the various sucrose-rich syrups used in candy making and food preparation. In certain respects there is nothing that refined white sugar resembles so much as salt: white, granular, brittle, and nearly 99 percent pure: "the only chemical substance to be consumed in practically pure form as a staple food."[9] Thus there are two remarkable different end products of sugar making. Even though both are sugars and nearly perfectly pure, one is liquid and usually golden, the other granular and usually white. Pure and refined sugars may be made in any color, of course. But at one time their whiteness served as evidence of their fineness and purity. The idea that the finest and purest sucrose would also be the whitest is probably a symbolically potent aspect of sugar's early European history; but the fact that sucrose can be prepared in many usable forms, one of which resembles honey, is also significant. The honeylike "treacle" or "golden syrup," so important in the making of the modern English diet, gradually won out over the ancient competitor, honey, which it mimicked. It even carried off some of the poetic imagery formerly associated with honey.[10] We shall have reason to return to both of these features of sugar's history.

It is not until about 500 A.D. that we get unmistakable written evidence of sugar making. The *Buddhagosa*, or *Discourse on Moral Consciousness*, a Hindu religious document, describes by way of analogy the boiling of juice, the making of molasses, and the rolling of balls of sugar. (It is likely that the first sugars—sufficiently crystallized to be nonliquid, but probably not yet intentionally crystallized into solids—were taffylike rather than brittle.[11]) But the references are few, and puzzling. In a report by the Byzantine emperor Heraclius in 627, when he seized a palace dwelling of the Persian king Chosroes II near Baghdad, sugar is described as an "Indian" luxury. Between the fourth and eighth centuries, the major sugar-fabrication centers seem to have been the coast to the west of the Indus delta (coastal Baluchistan), and the head of the Persian Gulf, on the Tigris-Euphrates delta. Only after the eighth century was sugar known and consumed in Europe itself; and only from that same time do references to cane growing and sugar making around the eastern Mediterranean begin to appear. Sucrose was practically unknown in northern Europe before perhaps 1000 A.D., and only barely known for another century or two. Still, sketching in some crude "periods" or "stages" may provide some guide to the discussion that follows.

The Arab expansion westward marked a turning point in the European experience of sugar. Between the defeat of Heraclius in 636 and the invasion of Spain in 711, in less than a single century, the Arabs established the caliphate at Baghdad, conquered North Africa, and began their occupation of major parts of Europe itself. Sugar making, which in Egypt may have preceded the Arab conquest, spread in the Mediterranean basin after that conquest. In Sicily, Cyprus, Malta, briefly in Rhodes, much of the Maghrib (especially in Morocco), and Spain itself (especially on its south coast), the Arabs introduced the sugar cane, its cultivation, the art of sugar making, and a taste for this different sweetness.[12] One scholar claims that sugar did not reach Venice until 996, whence it was exported northward; but this date is perhaps late.[13] By then sugar cane was being grown across North Africa and on several Mediterranean islands, including Sicily, as well as being the subject of agricultural experimentation in Spain itself. But before that, and even before Venice became a major re-exporting center for Europe, sugar in many forms was reaching Europe from the Middle East. Persia and India, the regions that had known sugar making for the longest time, were probably where the fundamental processes associated with sugar making had been invented. From the Mediterranean basin, sugar was supplied to North Africa, the Middle East, and Europe for many centuries. Production there ceased only when production in New World colonies became dominant, after the late sixteenth century. During the Mediterranean epoch, western Europe very slowly became accustomed to sugar. From the Mediterranean, the industry then shifted to the Atlantic islands of Spain and Portugal, including Madeira, the Canaries, and São Tomé; but this relatively brief phase came to an end when the American industries began to grow.

Only in recent years have the civilizational accomplishments of the Arab world begun to receive fair attention in the West. The Europe-centered historical view most of us share tends to exclude interest in the rest of the world's technical accomplishments, which we seem to recognize best when we "explain" them by reference to great inputs of labor (the Pyramids, the Great Wall, the Temple to the Sun, Machu Picchu, etc.); our warmest compliments are saved for the aesthetic, not the technical, achievements of those we regard as technically inferior, whether we admit it or not. Though we never quite bring ourselves to say so baldly, the western view is one of amazement that the aesthetic capacities of other peoples are not confined by their technical limitations. Yet anyone even casually interested in the history of southern Europe knows that the Moorish conquest of Spain was only the terminus of a brilliantly rapid westward expansion, as much technical and military as economic, political, and religious.

The Moors were not halted in their outward movement until they reached Poitiers in 732, where Charles Martel turned their flank. That year marked only the hundredth anniversary of the death of

Mohammed and of the installation of the first caliph, Abu Bakr. After 759, the Moors withdrew from Toulouse and southern France and entrenched themselves behind the Pyrenees; but it would be seven hundred years before the Spain they had conquered in only seven would once again become completely Christian. Some portions of the Mediterranean world fell to Islam after Spain herself had fallen. Crete, for instance, was not taken until 823; Malta not until 870. And wherever they went, the Arabs brought with them sugar, the product and the technology of its production; sugar, we are told, followed the Koran.

Though the unusual demands of sugar cultivation slowed its development as a commercial crop throughout the Islamic Mediterranean, its perfection as far north as central Spain was a great technical achievement. The Mediterranean's Arab conquerors were synthesists, innovators transporting the diverse cultural riches of the lands they subjugated back and forth across portions of three continents, combining, intermixing, and inventing, creating new adaptations. And many significant crops—rice, sorghum, hard wheat, cotton, eggplant, citrus fruits, plantains, mangoes, and sugar cane—were diffused by the spread of Islam.[14] But it was not so much, or exclusively, new crops that mattered; with the Arab conquerors there also traveled phalanxes of subordinate administrators (predominantly non-Arab), policies of administration and taxation, technologies of irrigation, production, and processing, and the impulses to expand production.

The spread of sugar cane and the technology required for its cultivation and conversion encountered obstacles—mostly rain and seasonal temperature fluctuations. As we have seen, sugar cane is a tropical and subtropical crop with a growing season that may be in excess of twelve months; it requires large amounts of water and labor. Though it can flourish without irrigation, it does far better (and increases its sugar content) when it is watered regularly and when its growing season is not subject to sharp and sudden declines in temperature.

Early Islam in the Mediterranean actually added to the agricultural seasons by producing crops like sugar cane in the summer, thereby altering the round of the agricultural year and the allocation of labor during it. By expanding the production of sugar cane on both southern and northern fringes of the Mediterranean—as far south as Marrakech and even Agadir and Taroudant in Morocco, for instance; and as far north as Valencia in Spain and Palermo in Sicily—the Arabs tested to their limits the potentialities of these newly conquered lands. On the one hand, the danger of frosts on the northern margins meant a shorter growing season—sugar planted in February or March had to be harvested in January. Such cane required just as much labor—from preparing the fields through processing the syrup—for less yield; this eventually counted against the Mediterranean industries when American sugar began to enter Europe in large quantities. On the other hand, the lack of adequate rainfall on the southern margins—as in Egypt—meant labor-intensive irrigation; in the Egyptian case, we are told, cane got twenty-eight wettings from planting to cutting.[15]

Sugar cane—if the crop is to be used to make sugar and not just for the extraction of juice, so that proper cultivation, prompt cutting and grinding, and skilled processing are involved—has always been a labor-intensive crop, at least until well into the twentieth century. Sugar production was a challenge not only in technical and political (administrative) terms, but also in regard to the securing and use of labor.

Everywhere, the Arabs showed a lively interest in irrigation, water use, and water conservation. They took with them, wherever they went, every watering device they encountered. To existing pre-Islamic forms of irrigation in the Mediterranean, they added the Persian bucket wheel (which the Spaniards call *noria*, from the Arabic term for "creaking sound"), the water screw, the Persian *qanat* (that remarkable labor-intensive system of engineered underground tunnels serving to carry ground water to arable fields by sheer gravity, apparently brought to Spain first and thence to North Africa), and many other devices. None of these innovations by itself could have made a decisive difference; what mattered was the energy and dedication of the conquerors and their apparently skillful use of local labor—in itself a subject of the greatest importance, but concerning which we still know relatively little.

Deerr tells us that there was "one great difference between the sugar industry founded by the Arabs and that developed by Christian Europeans. Although Islam recognized the status of slavery, the Mediterranean industry is free from that ruthless and bloody reproach, the curse of organized slavery that for 400 years tainted the New World production."[16] But this flat claim is unfounded. Slavery played a part in the Moroccan sugar industry[17] and probably elsewhere; a slave revolt involving thousands of East African agricultural laborers took place in the Tigris-Euphrates delta in the mid-ninth century, and they may even have been sugar-cane-plantation workers.[18] But slavery did grow more important as the European Crusaders seized the sugar plantations of the eastern Mediterranean from their predecessors; and its importance for sugar production did not diminish significantly until the Haitian Revolution, at the close of the eighteenth century.

The sugars of the Arabs were no single homogeneous substance; from the Persians and Indians, the Arabs had learned a variety of sugar types or categories. We know about these various sugars and even something about the processes of their manufacture, but the details remain vague. Milling also poses a question: some studies of the history of Arab milling have been made, but it remains an area of controversy.[19] In the extraction of juice from the cane, the more efficient the process, the greater the eventual yield. High-percentage yields of cane juice date only from the late nineteenth century, although there was improvement beginning at least in the seventeenth.

A decisive step in sugar technology came with the invention of the vertical three-roller mill, powered by either water or animal traction. This mill could be operated by two or three persons, who would pass the cane back and forth through the rollers (if animal-powered rather than hydraulic, the mill required a third worker to look after the animal or animals). The origins and exact ages of such mills remain obscure. Deerr (following Lippmann) attributes their invention to Pietro Speciale, prefect of Sicily, in 1449;[20] Soares Pereira doubts this—and with good reason, arguing instead that it was invented in Peru and came to Brazil between 1608 and 1612, then elsewhere.[21] But this controversy hardly concerns us, because the Arabs' Mediterranean sugar industry, some five centuries prior to Speciale's alleged invention, made do with other, less efficient systems. There is sure evidence of the use of water power for cane milling at an early time in Morocco and Sicily, even if beyond that we know little.

The Crusades gave many Europeans the opportunity—though not the first, as is sometimes claimed—to familiarize themselves with many new products, sugar among them. The Crusaders learned about sugar under pressing circumstances, we are told. Albert van Aachen, who collected the reminiscences of veterans of the First Crusade (1096–99), writes:

> In the fields of the plains of Tripoli can be found in abundance a honey reed which they call Zuchra; the people are accustomed to suck enthusiastically on these reeds, delighting themselves with their beneficial juices, and seem unable to sate themselves with this pleasure in spite of their sweetness. The plant is grown, presumably and with great effort, by the inhabitants.... It was on this sweet-tasting sugar cane that people sustained themselves during the sieges of Elbarieh, Marrah, and Arkah, when tormented by fearsome hunger.[22]

But it was not just that the Crusades taught the peoples of western Europe about sugar. Soon enough the Crusaders were supervising the production of that same sugar in the areas they had conquered, as in the kingdom of Jerusalem (1099–1187), until it fell to Saladin. They became the supervisors of sugar-cane cultivation and sugar production at the still-visible site called Tawahin A-Sukkar, "the sugar mills," scarcely a kilometer's remove from Jericho, where mills that were still in use in 1484 are documented as early as 1116.[23] (Though it is not certain they were used to grind cane at the earlier of these dates, they were surely so used later.)

When Acre fell to the Saracens in 1291, the Knights of Malta were planting cane there (at a later point in history, they sought to establish plantations in the Caribbean). Meanwhile, Venetian merchants were energetically developing sugar enterprises near Tyre, on Crete, and on Cyprus. In other words, Europeans became producers of sugar (or, better, the controllers of sugar producers in conquered areas) as a consequence of the Crusades.

The decline of the Mediterranean sugar industry has traditionally—and for the most part correctly—been attributed to the rise of a competing sugar industry on the Atlantic islands and, later, in the New World. But in fact, as the geographer J. H. Galloway pointed out, the eastern-Mediterranean industry lost ground a century before the first sugar was produced in Madeira, and sugar production in Sicily, Spain, and Morocco actually gained ground in the fifteenth century.[24] He believes that warfare and plague, with the resultant declines of population, hurt the sugar industry in Crete and Cyprus. Also, the prices of labor-costly goods like sugar rose after the Black Death. Indeed, in his opinion, it was the expanded use of slave labor to compensate for plague-connected mortality that initiated the strange and enduring relationship between sugar and slavery: "The link between sugar cultivation and slavery which was to last until the nineteenth century became firmly forged in Crete, Cyprus, and Morocco."[25]

The decline of the Mediterranean sugar industry that had been created by the Arabs was uneven and protracted. In some subregions, the successive contractions of Arab political control, often resulting in inferior local administration, put an end to effective irrigation and labor allocation. In others, the Christian challenge sometimes resulted in continued sugar production under the invader's auspices—for instance, in Sicily after the Norman conquest, and on Cyprus. Yet, though the Crusaders and the merchants from Amalfi, Genoa, and other Italian states divided among themselves the duties of administering production and trade, these arrangements did not last long. Portugal was not content to experiment with sugar-cane cultivation at home in the Algarve when better opportunities beckoned elsewhere, and Spain was not far behind.

The Christian continuation of Arab production in the eastern Mediterranean, on the one hand, and the experiments undertaken by Portugal (and soon by Spain) at the western end of that sea on the other, foretokened two rather different developments, however. In the eastern Mediterranean, production actually rose at first, even following the withdrawal of the Franks from Palestine in the thirteenth century, and the later Ottoman expansion. Crete, Cyprus, and Egypt continued to produce sugar for export.[26] Yet this region became less and less important as a source of sugar; and it was the development of the industry by the Portuguese and Spaniards on the Atlantic islands that changed forever the character of European sugar consumption. These were the stepping stones by which the industry would move from the Old World to the New; it was in the form perfected on them that the New World industry was to find its prototype.

Even before the New World industries were established, however, the sugar industry on the Atlantic islands damaged the competitive position of Malta, Rhodes, Sicily, and the other small Mediterranean producers. By 1580 the Sicilian industry, once flourishing, did little more than supply its domestic market, and in Spain itself, sugar production began to decline in the seventeenth century, though sugar did continue to be produced in the extreme south of the peninsula.

At the time that the Portuguese and the Spaniards set out to establish a sugar industry on the Atlantic islands they controlled, sugar was still a luxury, a medicine, and a spice in western Europe. The peoples of Greece, Italy, Spain, and North Africa were familiar with sugar cane as a crop and, to some extent, with sugar itself as a sweetener. But as sugar production in the Mediterranean waned, knowledge of sugar and the desire for it waxed in Europe. The movement of the industry to the Atlantic islands occurred when European demand was probably growing. Individual entrepreneurs were encouraged to establish sugar-cane (and other) plantations on the Atlantic islands, manned with African slaves and destined to produce sugar for Portugal and other European markets, because their presence safeguarded the extension of Portuguese trade routes around Africa and toward the Orient:

> In...a series of experiments, the plantation system, now com-
> bining African slaves under the authority of European settlers in
> a racially mixed society, producing sugar cane and other com-
> mercial crops, spread as island after island [the Madeira Islands,
> including Madeira, La Palma, and Hierro; the Canary Islands,
> including Tenerife, Gran Canaria, and Fuerteventura; the nine
> widely scattered islands that compose the Azores; the Cape Verde
> Islands, including Boa Vista, Sto. Antão, and São Tiago; São
> Tomé and Principe; etc.] was integrated as part of the expanding

kingdom. In only some of the islands did sugar cane plantations prosper....But overall, sugar cane and the plantation did enable the government of Portugal, once it had committed itself to the policy of commercially oriented expansion, to have settled, at the expense of private citizens, island bases that gave her control of the South Atlantic and made possible the rounding of Africa and trade in the East.[27]

There were intimate links between the Atlantic-island experiments of the Portuguese, especially São Tomé, and west European centers of commercial and technical power, especially Antwerp.[28] It is of particular significance that from the thirteenth century onward, the refining center for European sugar was Antwerp, followed later by other great port cities such as Bristol, Bordeaux, and even London. Control of the final product moved into European hands—but not, it bears noting, into those of the same Europeans (in this instance, the Portuguese) who pioneered the production of sugar overseas. The increasing differentiation of sugars, in line with the growing differentiation of demand, was another cause of growth. The descriptive lexicon for sugars expanded, as more and more sorts became familiar to the Europeans.[29]

Sugar itself was now known throughout western Europe, even though it was still a product *de luxe*, rather than a common commodity or necessity. No longer so precious a good as musk or pearls, shipped to the courts of Europe via intermediary countries and their luxury traders, sugar was becoming a raw material whose supply and refining were managed more and more by European powers, as European populations consumed it in larger and larger quantities. The political differentiation of the western states interested in sugar proceeded apace after the fifteenth century. To a surprising degree, the way sugar figured in national policies indicated—perhaps even exercised some influence over—political futures.

Portugal's and Spain's sugar experiments in the Atlantic islands had many parallels, though later they diverged sharply. In the fifteenth century both powers looked for favorable locales for sugar production: while Portugal seized São Tomé and other islands, Spain captured the Canaries. After about 1450, Madeira was the leading supplier, followed by São Tomé; by the 1500s, the Canary Islands had also become important.[30] And both powers experienced a growing demand for sugar (suggested, for instance, by the household accounts of Isabella the Catholic, queen of Castile from 1474 to 1504).

The sugar industries in the Spanish and Portuguese Atlantic islands were characterized by slave labor, a tradition supposedly transferred from the Mediterranean sugar plantations of the Arabs and Crusaders. But the Spanish scholar Fernández-Armesto tells us that the striking feature of the Canarian industry was its use of both free and enslaved labor, a combination that resembled more the pioneering mixed-labor systems of a later era: the seventeenth-century British and French Caribbean plantations, on which enslaved and indentured laborers would work alongside one another. Slaves were decidedly important, perhaps crucial; but a substantial amount of the labor was actually done by free wage earners paid partly in kind—some of them specialists, others temporary laborers. This system was probably not quite so atypical as it seems. But it is true that free wage earners hardly figure in sugar's history between the Atlantic island phase and the epoch of revolution and emancipation in the New World, from the start of the Haitian Revolution until emancipation in Brazil. "The Canarian system," Fernández-Armesto tells us, "evokes far more the methods of the Old World, and the equal sharing of produce between owners and workers is most akin to the farming *a mezzadria*, which developed in late medieval northern Italy and in some parts is still practised today."[31]

Sugar cane was first carried to the New World by Columbus on his second voyage, in 1493; he brought it there from the Spanish Canary Islands. Cane was first grown in the New World in Spanish Santo Domingo; it was from that point that sugar was first shipped back to Europe, beginning around 1516. Santo Domingo's pristine sugar industry was worked by enslaved Africans, the first slaves having been imported there soon after the sugar cane. Hence it was Spain that pioneered sugar cane, sugar making, African slave labor, and the plantation form in the Americas. Some scholars agree with Fernando Ortiz that these plantations were "the favored child of capitalism," and other historians quarrel with this assessment. But

even if Spain's achievements in sugar production did not rival those
of the Portuguese until centuries later, their pioneering nature has
never been in doubt, though scholars of New World sugar have
sometimes neglected Spain's early Caribbean accomplishments in
the sugar trade because their global significance was slight. Wallerstein and Braudel are cavalier in their disregard; Braudel has sugar
cane and sugar mills not reaching Santo Domingo until after 1654,
for instance.[32]

By 1526, Brazil was shipping sugar to Lisbon in commercial
quantities, and soon the sixteenth century was the Brazilian century
for sugar. Within the Spanish New World, the early achievements
in Santo Domingo and the rest of the Caribbean were outstripped
by developments on the mainland. In Mexico, Paraguay, the Pacific
coast of South America, and in fertile valleys everywhere, sugar
cane prospered.

Yet the very first experiments with sugar-cane growing and sugar
making on Santo Domingo had been doomed to failure. When two
planters there tried to make sugar—Aguilón in 1505–6 and Balles-
ter in 1512—Spain was not yet ready to support their ambitions,
nor were the skills extant in Santo Domingo able to sustain them.[33]
The only available milling techniques were probably modeled on
tenth-century Egyptian edge-roller mill designs, originally intended
for use as olive presses. Such devices were inefficient and wasteful
of labor. Another serious problem was the labor supply itself. The
rapid destruction of the indigenous Arawakan-speaking Taino Indians of Santo Domingo had left too little manpower even for the
gold mines, let alone for the experimental sugar plantations. The
first African slaves were imported before 1503, and in spite of local
fears of depredations by slave runaways (*cimarrones*), the importations continued. By 1509, enslaved Africans were being imported
to work the royal mines; others soon followed to power the sugar
industry.

When the surgeon Gonzalo de Vellosa—perhaps taking note of
the rising prices of sugar in Europe—imported skilled sugar masters
from the Canary Islands in 1515, he took the first step toward
creating an authentic sugar industry in the Caribbean. With the
Canary Island technicians, he (and his new partners, the Tapia

brothers) imported a mill with two vertical rollers, usable with either animal or water power and "patterned on that developed in 1449 by Pietro Speciale."[34] The gold deposits in Santo Domingo were soon nearly exhausted; labor was more and more likely to be African, as the vertiginous decline of the aboriginal population continued. But the price of sugar had become high enough in Europe to compensate partly for cost of transporting it, and to encourage additional risks in production, perhaps especially in Spain's settled Caribbean colonies, where alternative opportunities (such as mining) were shrinking.

One scholar has estimated that the mill fabricated by the Canary Island engineers in Santo Domingo could grind enough cane in one season to produce 125 tons of sugar a year if water-powered, and "perhaps a third of that tonnage" if powered by animals.[35] Vellosa and his associates lacked the capital to develop the infant industry by themselves. But they took advantage of the presence of three Jeronymite fathers, sent to Santo Domingo to supervise Indian labor policy, who eventually became the de facto governors of the colony. At first the Jeronymites merely endorsed the pleas of the planters for royal support. Soon, however, they made loans of state revenues they had collected to the planters.[36] When the new king, Charles I, ordered the replacement of the Jeronymites by the royal judge Rodrigo de Figueroa, the policy of state assistance continued and expanded. By the 1530s, the island had a "fairly stable total" of thirty-four mills; and by 1568, "plantations owning a hundred-fifty to two hundred slaves were not uncommon. A few of the more magnificent estates possessed up to five hundred slaves, with production figures correspondingly high."[37] One interesting feature of this development was the part played by the state and, indeed, by civil servants, who owned, administered, bought, and sold plantations. Not only was there no private and separate "planter class" at the outset; the commission merchants and other intermediaries who emerge in the Caribbean sugar colonies of other, rival powers were absent.

In the other Greater Antilles—Cuba, Puerto Rico, and Jamaica—Spanish settlers eventually brought in sugar cane, the methods for its cultivation, the technology of water- and animal-powered mills, enslaved labor, and the process for grinding, boiling, and fabricating sugars and molasses from extracted juice, as well as for distilling rum from the molasses. And yet this burgeoning Spanish American industry came to almost nothing—in spite of royal support, much intelligent experimentation, and successful production. The Portuguese planters in Brazil succeeded where the Spaniards in the Antilles failed. Within only a century, the French, and even more the British (though with Dutch help from the outset), became the western world's great sugar makers and exporters. One wonders why the early phase of the Hispanic sugar industry stagnated so swiftly after such promising beginnings, and the explanations we have are not entirely satisfactory. The flight of island colonists to the Mexican mainland after the conquest of Tenochtitlán (1519–21); the Spaniards' obsession with metallic riches; the excessively authoritarian controls imposed by the crown on all productive private enterprise in the New World; the chronic lack of capital for investment; the so-called *deshonor del trabajo* (ignobility of [manual] labor) supposedly typical of the Spanish colonists—these factors seem reasonable, but are not entirely convincing. Probably we will not learn why such important early experiments failed until we better understand the nature of the Spanish market for Caribbean sugars, and Spain's ability or inability to export a sugar surplus. With Spain's conquests of Mexico and the Andes, a basic shift was created in policy: for more than two centuries thereafter, the Caribbean possessions served primarily as way stations and fortresses along the trade routes, signaling Spain's unproductive, tribute-taking, labor-squandering role in the Americas. The pioneering opportunity was soon lost; from about 1580 in the Greater Antilles, until the French and the English began sugar-cane planting on the smaller islands (particularly Barbados and Martinique), after 1650, the Caribbean region produced little sugar for export. By that time the European market situation had modified, and the momentum of production had passed out of Spanish hands.[38]

Whereas the Spaniards (and, to a lesser extent, the Portuguese) concentrated their colonizing efforts in the New World on the extraction of precious metals, for their North European rivals trade and the production of marketable commodities mattered more, and plantation products figured importantly—cotton, indigo, and, soon enough, two beverage crops: cacao, a New World cultigen and more an indigenous food than a drink, and coffee, of African origin. The costs of labor and the lack of capital held down New World plantation production at first, and gains were made at the cost of production elsewhere. "To thrive, the colonists had to catch better or cheaper fish than the Dutch in the Baltic or the North Sea, to trap or persuade the Indians to trap better or cheaper furs than the Russians, to grow better or cheaper sugar than the Javanese or Bengalis."[39] The first crop in the New World to win a market for itself was tobacco, an American domesticate, swiftly transformed from a rare upper-class luxury into a working-class necessity. Tobacco made headway even against royal disapproval, and became part of the consumption of ordinary folk by the seventeenth century. But by the end of that century, sugar was outpacing tobacco in both the British and the French West Indies; by 1700, the value of sugar reaching England and Wales was double that of tobacco. The shift from tobacco to sugar was initially even more pronounced in the French Caribbean colonies than in the British, though in the long term the French market for sugar never attained the scale of the British market.

Certain facts stand out in the history of sugar between the early decades of the seventeenth century, when the British, Dutch, and French established Caribbean plantations, and the middle of the nineteenth century, by which time Cuba and Brazil were the major centers of New World production. Over this long period, sugar production grew steadily, as more westerners consumed sugar and each consumer used it more heavily. Yet technological changes in the field, in grinding, and even in refining itself were relatively minor. Generally speaking, the enlarged market for sugar was satisfied by a steady extension of production rather than by sharp increases in yield per acre of land or ton of cane, or in productivity per worker.

But the impulse to produce sugar, as well as to trade in it and consume it, can be traced further back in the record. Soon after Sir Walter Raleigh's first voyage to the Guianas in 1595, the English explorer Captain Charles Leigh attempted to start a settlement on the Waiapoco (Oyapock) River (now the border between Brazil and French Guiana). Though neither effort succeeded, both were connected with an interest in sugar and other tropical products. In 1607 Jamestown—the first English colony in the New World—was founded. Sugar cane was brought there in 1619—as were the first enslaved Africans to reach an English colony—but the cane would not grow. Three years earlier, sugar cane had been planted in Bermuda, but this tiny, arid island never produced sugar. These facts indicate that even before the seventeenth century there was a lively awareness of the desirability of sugar, and of at least some of its potential market—in short, of its long-term profitability as a commodity. The aim of acquiring colonies that could produce sugar (among other things) for the metropolis hence predates the seventeenth century. And before she was able to produce sugar in her own colonies, England was not above stealing it. In 1591 a Spanish spy reported that "English booty in West India [American] produce is so great that sugar is cheaper in London than it is in Lisbon or the Indies themselves."[40]

The turning point for British sugar was the settlement of Barbados in 1627, an island Britain claimed after Captain John Powell's landing there in 1625, while returning to Europe from Brazil. It was not until around 1655—the same year the British invasion of Jamaica was launched as part of the Western Design—that Barbadian sugar began to affect the home market, however. (In that year, 283 tons of "clayed" sugars and 6,667 tons of "muscovado" sugars were produced in Barbados;[41] meanwhile, other Caribbean acquisitions also began to contribute to homeland consumption, and to make of sugar an imperial source of profit.) After 1655 and until the mid-nineteenth century, the sugar supply of the English people would be provided substantially within the skein of the empire. From the establishment of the first British colonies that succeeded by exporting unfinished products—particularly sugar—to the metropolis, imperial laws were passed to control the flow of such goods, and of the goods for which they were exchanged.[42]

At the consumption end, changes were both numerous and diverse. Sugar steadily changed from being a specialized—medicinal, condimental, ritual, or display—commodity into an ever more common food. This insertion of an essentially new product within popular European tastes and preferences was irreversible, though the cost of sugar at times certainly braked consumption.

The seventeenth century was of course one of tremendous activity for English sailors, merchants, adventurers, and royal agents. Many more individual English colonies were established in the New World than Dutch or French; and the English settler population, including African slaves, far exceeded that of either of her two principal North European rivals. From 1492 until 1625, the Spanish Caribbean, though weakened by smuggling and raids, remained intact; but when St. Kitts was settled, an irreversible process of English territorial expansion began there, which reached its climax only thirty years later with the invasion of Jamaica. The seventeenth century was also the century of European naval wars in the Caribbean, as north European powers defined their stakes; their scale varied from hit-and-run piracy and town burning to large-scale naval encounters. Several different but related processes were occurring at once, but Spain was everyone's enemy, for it was upon her predefined colonial empire that they all fed.

England fought the most, conquered the most colonies, imported the most slaves (to her own colonies and, in absolute numbers, in her own bottoms), and went furthest and fastest in creating a plantation system. The most important product of that system was sugar. Coffee, chocolate (cacao), nutmeg, and coconut were among the other products; but the amount of sugar produced, the numbers of its users, and the range of its uses exceeded the others; and it remained the principal product for centuries. In 1625, Portugal was supplying nearly all of Europe with sugar from Brazil. But the English soon developed their sources in Barbados and then in Jamaica, as well as in other "sugar islands." The English learned methods of producing sugar and its kindred substances from the Dutch, whose experiments with plantation agriculture on the Guiana coast the Portuguese had thwarted. From humble beginnings on the island of Barbados in the 1640s, the British sugar industry expanded with astounding rapidity, engulfing first that island and, soon after, Jamaica—the first territorial conquest from Spain in the Greater Antilles, and nearly thirty times the size of Barbados. As English sugar became price-competitive with Portuguese sugar, England was able to drive Portugal out of the north European trade. From the resulting monopoly came monopoly prices, however, and then stiff competition from the French.[43] In 1660, sugar was enumerated (and taxed); but the West India colonies were given a virtual monopoly of Britain's national market. In France, restrictive policies kept English sugars competitive until about 1740, when French rivalry won out. Britain never again retrieved the European markets, but her planters and merchantmen consoled themselves with the domestic market. In 1660, England consumed 1,000 hogsheads of sugar and exported 2,000. In 1700, she imported about 50,000 hogsheads and exported about 18,000. By 1730, 100,000 hogsheads were imported and 18,000 exported, and by 1753, when England imported 110,000 hogsheads, she re-exported only 6,000. "As the supply from the British West Indies increased, England's demand kept pace with it, and from the middle of the eighteenth century these islands seem never to have been able to produce much more sugar than was needed for consumption in the mother country."[44]

The steps by which England shifted from buying modest quantities of sugar from Mediterranean shippers; to importing in her own bottoms a somewhat larger supply; to buying yet larger quantities from the Portuguese, first in the Atlantic islands and then in Brazil, but refined outside England; to establishing her own sugar colonies—first to feed herself and to vie with Portugal for customers and then, with time, simply to feed herself, finishing the processing in her own refineries—are complex, but they followed in so orderly a fashion as to seem almost inevitable. On the one hand, they represent an extension of empire outward, but on the other, they mark an absorption, a kind of swallowing up, of sugar consumption as a national habit. Like tea, sugar came to define English "character."

The vision of an expanding consumers' market at home was grasped quite early. Sir Josiah Child, a pioneering mercantilist ("That all Colonies or Plantations do endamage their Mother-Kingdoms, whereof the Trades of such Plantations are not confined by severe Laws, and good execution of those Laws, to the Mother-Kingdom"), stressed the need to control the colonies so that their trade could be confined to the profit of the metropolis:

> It is in his Majesty's power, and the Parliament's, if they please, by taking off all charges from Sugar, to make it more entirely an *English* Commodity, than White Herrings are a *Dutch* Commodity; and to draw more Profit to the Kingdom thereby, than the Dutch do by that. And that in consequence thereof all Plantations of other Nations, must in a few Years sink to little or nothing.[45]

Sir Dalby Thomas, governor of Jamaica and a sugar planter himself in the late seventeenth century, was an early booster of sugar production. He also envisioned how flourishing sugar colonies might be consumers of the mother country's products as well:

> 1. The greatest consumption of Sugar is made by themselves [the legislators of Parliament] and the rest of the rich and opulent People of the Nation.
> 2. The Quantity yearly produc'd is not less than 45,000 tuns [he is presumably speaking of all sugars produced in British colonies at the time, circa 1690].
> 3. The Moiety of this is consum'd in *England*, and amounts to about £800,000 in Value. The other Moiety is exported, and after it has employed Seamen, is sold for as much, and consequently brings back to the Nation in Money, or useful Goods, £800,000. Add to this, That before Sugars were produc'd in our Colonies, it bore four times the Price it does now; and by the same Consumption at the same Price, except we make it our selves, we should be forc'd to give in Money or Money's worth, as *Native* Commodities and Labour, £240,000 for the Sugar we spend.

To which the historian Oldmixon warmly adds, "'Tis certain we bought as much Sugar of Portugal as amounted to £400,000 yearly, which is sav'd by our making it."[46] Thomas continues: "We must consider too the Spirits arising from *Melasses*, which is sent from the Sugar Colonies to the other Colonies and to *England*; which if all were sold in England, and turn'd into Spirits, it would amount annually to above £500,000 at half the Price the like Quantity of Brandy from *France* would cost." He recognized not only the different sources of mercantile profit to be had from the sugar colonies, but also the vast and incompletely fulfilled promise of these colonies as buyers of the finished goods of the metropolis. In arguing that America's mainland southern colonies resembled more closely the Antilles than New England, he put this part of the case eloquently:

> ...could they readily get Negroes from Guinea, every one of which consumes yearly two Hilling-Hoes, two Weeding-Hoes, two Grubbing-Hoes, besides Axes, Saws, Wimbles, Nails, and other Iron Tools and Materials, consum'd in Building and other Uses, to the Value of at least £120,000 in only Iron-Work. The Cloaths, Guns, Cordage, Anchors, Sails, and Materials for Shipping, besides Beds and other Houshold Goods, consum'd and us'd by them is infinite: Nor is the Benefit of them to the Kingdom sufficiently to be explained, therefore, let it suffice, in a Word, to Say, that the Produce and Consumption, with the Shipping they give Employment to, is of an infinite deal more Benefit to the Wealth, Honour, and Strength of the Nation, than four times the same Number of Hands, the best employ'd at home can be.[47]

Thomas grasped the unfolding of what was to be Europe's greatest mass market for a foreign luxury. And he saw that because the whole process—from the establishment of colonies, the seizure of slaves, the amassing of capital, the protection of shipping, and all else to actual consumption—took shape under the wing of the state, such undertakings were at every point as meaningful politically as they were economically. Like all of the eloquent sugar touts to follow him, Thomas made his arguments both economic and political (he was not above making them medicinal and ceremonial as well):

> The Europeans 500 years since, were perfect strangers to the use of it [sugar], and scarcely knew its name...but the Physitians soon found [it] to answer all the ends of honey, without many of its ill effects: So that it quickly became a Commodity in mighty esteem, and though the price then was ten times more than now, yet it prevailed so fast, and the Consumption of it became so great....
> The Vertues of Mellasses formerly sold only in Apothecary's Shops by the name of Treacle being now so well known both to the Distiller and Brewer...nor can it be imagined how many new

ways are found dayly for Venting and Consuming usefully the various products of a Sugar-Plantation: The severall Shapes it appears in at Christenings, Banquets and Rich mens Tables, being but the least of its good qualities, tho' of great Delight as well as Ornament, and should the art of making it be so discouraged as to take its next flight to the *Dutch* or *French*, as it did from Portugall to Us, the loss would prove of the like Consequence, which is no less than the decay of the greatest part of their Shipping, and the fall of half their Revenues....[48]

We can see that Englishmen understood well the benefits of having their own sugar-producing colonies, and that they also understood better and better the growth potential of the British market for sugar. Hence it is no surprise that later centuries saw the production of tropical commodities in the colonies tied ever more closely to British consumption—and to the production of British shops and factories. Production and consumption—at least with regard to the product we are considering here—were not simply opposite sides of the same coin, but neatly interdigitated; it is difficult to imagine one without the other.

One hundred and fifty years after Thomas rhapsodized on sugar and the sugar trade, another Englishman commented on the colonies and their products in illuminating fashion. "There is a class of trading and exporting communities," John Stuart Mill wrote, "on which a few words of explanation seem to be required."

These are hardly to be looked upon as countries, carrying on an exchange of commodities with other countries, but more properly as outlying agricultural or manufacturing estates belonging to a larger community. Our West Indian colonies, for example, cannot be regarded as countries with a productive capital of their own ... [but are, rather,] the place where England finds it convenient to carry on the production of sugar, coffee and a few other tropical commodities. All the capital employed is English capital; almost all the industry is carried on for English uses; there is little production of anything except for staple commodities, and these are sent to England, not to be exchanged for things exported to the colony and consumed by its inhabitants, but to be sold in England for the benefit of the proprietors there. The trade with the West Indies is hardly to be considered an external trade, but more resembles the traffic between town and country.[49]

While it is true that these tropical commodities were not exchanged in the United Kingdom, but were sold instead for the profit of the plantation proprietors, it is also true that nearly everything consumed in the West Indian colonies came from England. There were no direct exchanges between the motherland and the colonies, but the patterns of exchange worked to the long-term benefit of imperial enterprise.

There grew up, in effect, two so-called triangles of trade, both of which arose in the seventeenth century and matured in the eighteenth. The first and most famous triangle linked Britain to Africa and to the New World: finished goods were sold to Africa, African slaves to the Americas, and American tropical commodities (especially sugar) to the mother country and her importing neighbors. The second triangle functioned in a manner contradictory to the mercantilist ideal. From New England went rum to Africa, whence slaves to the West Indies, whence molasses back to New England (with which to make rum). The maturation of this second triangle put the New England colonies on a political collision course with Britain, but the underlying problems were economic, taking on political import precisely because they brought divergent economic interests into confrontation.

The important feature of these triangles is that human cargoes figured vitally in their operation. It was not just that sugar, rum, and molasses were not being traded directly for European finished goods; in both transatlantic triangles the only "false commodity"— yet absolutely essential to the system—was human beings. Slaves were a "false commodity" because a human being is not an object, even when treated as one. In this instance, millions of human beings were treated as commodities. To obtain them, products were shipped to Africa; by their labor power, wealth was created in the Americas. The wealth they created mostly returned to Britain; the products they made were consumed in Britain; and the products made by Britons—cloth, tools, torture instruments—were consumed by slaves who were themselves consumed in the creation of wealth.

In the seventeenth century, English society was very slowly evolving toward a system of free labor, by which I mean the creation of a labor force that, lacking any access to productive property such as land, would have to sell its labor to the owners of the means of production. Yet in that same century, England was adapting a system of mostly coerced labor in her colonies to satisfy her needs there. These two radically different patterns of labor exaction were growing in two ecologically different settings and were critically different in form. Yet they served the same overarching economic goals, and were created—albeit in such different form—by the evolution of a single economic and political system.

So much has been written of the rise of British Caribbean sugar that no brief summary would be satisfactory. But enough should be said, at least, so that the qualitative changes that mark the differences between the Spanish plantation experiments of the late sixteenth century and the English achievements of the mid-seventeenth and eighteenth centuries can be grasped. Those differences have to do with changes in the scale not only of plantation operations, but also of the market. As we have seen, England's entry into the plantation production of sugar in its colonies first served to supply the domestic (British) consumers' market, but meant competing for the growing European market as well. After outselling the Portuguese (and later the French) on the Continent in the 1680s, the English soon relinquished the Continental market again, the better to supply their own growing needs. "After 1660, England's sugar imports always exceeded its combined imports of all other colonial produce."[50] These changes were paralleled by a steady expansion of plantation production, with more plantations in mature colonies, and added new colonies as well; and by a growing differentiation of the products themselves—first sugar and molasses; soon after, rum; then a multiplication of crystalline sugar varieties and of syrup types—redifferentiations that were accompanied by (or, better, responded to) more elaborate and heterogeneous consumer demand at home.

Meanwhile, the fates of individual sugar colonies (and even of different sectors of the plantation economy in any one colony) were anything but predictable. Plantations were highly speculative enterprises. While they eventuated in enormous profits for fortunate investors, bankruptcies were common; some of the most daring plantation entrepreneurs ended their days in debtors' prison. Sugar was never a sure thing, despite the unfailingly optimistic predictions of its protagonists. But the risks taken by individual investors and planters in particular colonies were counterbalanced, over time, by the unceasing increases in demand. Those who foresaw the increases included, as always, both eventual winners and losers. Overall, the British imperial system was able to gorge itself on an ever-growing demand for sugar that accompanied both a declining unit price for sugar and increases in worker productivity at home.

A mass market for sugar emerged rather tardily. Until the eighteenth century, sugar was really the monopoly of a privileged minority, and its uses were still primarily as a medicine, as a spice, or as a decorative (display) substance. "An entirely new taste for sweetness manifested itself," Davis declares, "as soon as the means to satisfy it became available...by 1750 the poorest English farm labourer's wife took sugar in her tea."[51] From the mid-eighteenth century onward, sugar production in the imperial economy became more and more important to England's rulers and ruling classes. This is only an apparent contradiction. As the *production* of sugar became significant economically, so that it could affect political and military (as well as economic) decisions, its *consumption* by the powerful came to matter less; at the same time, the production of sugar acquired that importance precisely because the masses of English people were now steadily consuming more of it, and desiring more of it than they could afford.

Not surprisingly, as the quantities of sugar consumed rose, the loci of production came into ever-closer alignment with the domestic British economy. Thus, for instance, until nearly the middle of the sixteenth century, sugar refining was carried on mainly in the Low Countries, especially in Antwerp, before it was sacked at the order of Philip II (1576). From 1544, England began refining her own sugar; "after 1585, London was the important refining center for the European trade."[52] The same shift occurred in shipping. The first documented shipload of sugar sent directly to England was in 1319. In 1551, however, Captain Thomas Wyndham, merchant-adventurer on the west African coast, returned to England from Agadir, Morocco, with a cargo of sugar, "perhaps being the first to be brought to England in an English ship without break of cargo and direct from country of origin."[53] By 1675, four hundred English vessels with average 150-ton cargoes were carrying sugar to England; at that time, as much as half was being re-exported.

Eventually the mercantilist viewpoint embodied in the imperial sugar trade was crushed by an aggressive new economic philosophy labeled "free trade." But the importance of the mercantilist dogma to Britain's development was at least threefold: it guaranteed her supply of sugar (and other tropical commodities) and the profits made from processing and re-exporting them; it secured a large overseas market for finished British goods; and it supported the growth of the civil (and military) marine. Buy no finished goods elsewhere, sell none of your (tropical) products elsewhere, ship everything in British bottoms: during nearly two centuries these injunctions, only slightly less sacred than Holy Writ, bound planters and refiners, merchantmen and dreadnaughts, Jamaican slave and Liverpudlian stevedore, monarch and citizen together.

But mercantilist injunctions did not always serve the same classes. If at one point mercantilism protected the planters' market from foreign sugar producers, at another it protected the factory owners from the foreign producers of finished goods. Overall, however, the two hundred years during which mercantilism persisted were marked by a gradual decline in the position of the planter classes, after their swift and early rise to power within the national state—and a more or less steady improvement in the position of the industrial capitalists and their interests at home. Mercantilism was finally dealt its quietus in the mid-nineteenth century, and the sugar market and its potential played a part. By then, sugar and consumer items like it had become too important to permit an archaic protectionism to jeopardize future metropolitan supplies. Sugar surrendered its place as luxury and rarity and became the first mass-produced exotic necessity of a proletarian working class.

Before turning to the last period in the history of sugar production, it might be useful to look more intently at the plantations, those tropical enterprises that were the seats of sugar production. These were, of course, agricultural undertakings, but because so much of the industrial processing of the cane was also carried out on the plantations, it makes good sense to view the plantations as a synthesis of field and factory. Thus approached, they were really quite unlike anything known in mainland Europe at the time.

We have already observed that sugar cane must be cut when it is ripe, and ground as soon as it is cut. These simple facts give a special character to any enterprise dedicated to the production of sugar, as opposed to the simple expression of cane juice. The history of sugar making and refining has been one of irregular improvement of the level of chemical purity, with many consumers (in different cultures, and in different historical periods) developing preferences for one or another degree of purity, color, form, granule size, and so on. But without boiling and skimming and reducing juice there is no way to make granular sugar. It cannot be done without solid technical mastery, particularly in the control of heat. Just as factory and field are wedded in sugar making, brute field labor and skilled artisanal knowledge are both necessary.

The early Spanish plantations of Santo Domingo probably consisted of about 125 acres of land, manned by as many as two hundred slaves and freemen. The needed technical skills were imported, principally from the Canaries. Perhaps only a tenth of the labor force was required in the mill and the boiling house, but their operations and those of the cutting crews had to be coordinated, while the field labor had to be divided not only seasonally but also between the cane and the subsistence crops. The specialization by skill and jobs, and the division of labor by age, gender, and condition into crews, shifts, and "gangs," together with the stress upon punctuality and discipline, are features associated more with industry than with agriculture—at least in the sixteenth century.

Most like a factory was the boiling house, where the juice from the crushed cane was transferred for reduction, clarification, and crystallization. The Barbadian colonist Thomas Tryon—whose complaints must be viewed with some skepticism, since he was a planter himself—nonetheless conveys well the modern-sounding quality of the mill in this seventeenth-century description:

> In short, 'tis to live in a perpetual Noise and Hurry, and the only way to render a person Angry, and Tyrannical, too; since the

Climate is so hot, and the labor so constant, that the Servants [or slaves] night and day stand in great Boyling Houses, where there are Six or Seven large Coppers or Furnaces kept perpetually Boyling; and from which with heavy Ladles and Scummers they Skim off the excrementitious parts of the Canes, till it comes to its perfection and cleanness, while other as Stoakers, Broil as it were, alive, in managing the Fires; and one part is constantly at the Mill, to supply it with Canes, night and day, during the whole Season of making Sugar, which is about six Months of the year; so that what with these things, the number of the Family, and many other Losses and Disappointments of bad Crops, which often happens, a Master Planter has no such easy life as Some may imagine, nor Riches flow upon him with that insensibility, as it does upon many in England.[54]

One supposes that the riches flowed even less abundantly upon the slaves and servants.

The seventeenth century was preindustrial; and the idea that there might have been "industry" on the colonial plantation before it existed in the homeland may seem heretical. First, it has been conceived of as predominantly agricultural because it was a colonial enterprise and manned mostly by coerced, rather than free, labor. Second, it produced a consumable food—rather than textiles, say, or tools, or some other machined nonfood. Finally, scholars interested in the history of western industry quite predictably began with the artisans and craftsmen of Europe and the putting-out shops that followed them, rather than with overseas ventures. It followed naturally that plantations were seen as by-products of European endeavor rather than as an integral part of the growth from shop to factory. But it is not clear why such preconceptions should interfere with a recognition of the industrial aspects of plantation development. It may seem a topsy-turvy view of the West to find its factories elsewhere at so early a period. But the sugar-cane plantation is gradually winning recognition as an unusual combination of agricultural and industrial forms, and I believe it was probably the closest thing to industry that was typical of the seventeenth century.

Strangely, historians have also paid insufficient attention to the scale of plantation enterprises. The planters of the British Caribbean certainly were large-scale entrepreneurs for their time: a "combination farmer-manufacturer" with a work force of perhaps a hundred could have eighty acres put to cane and expect to produce eighty tons of sugar after the harvest. To make sugar he needed one mill or two, a boiling house to clean and reduce the juice, a curing house to drain the molasses and dry the sugar heads, a distillery to make rum, and a storehouse to hold his raw sugar for shipment—representing an investment of thousands of pounds sterling.[55]

The subtropical environments of the plantation required planters to adjust to seasonal schedules wholly different from those of temperate climes. Sugar crops needed up to a year and a half to mature, so that planting and harvesting schedules were elaborate and novel for Englishmen. On Barbados, English planters soon divided their lands into equal portions of about ten acres each so that they could be planted and harvested *seriatim*, assuring a steady flow of cane to the mill.

Boiling and "striking"—transferring the liquid, and arresting its boiling when it was ready—required great skill, and sugar boilers were artisans who worked under difficult conditions. The heat and noise were overpowering, there was considerable danger involved, and time was of the essence throughout, from the moment when the cane was perfect for cutting until the semicrystalline product was poured into molds to drain and be dried. During the harvest the mills operated unceasingly, and the labor requirements were horrendous. Writing of the eighteenth-century picture, Mathieson tells us, "The production of sugar was the most onerous of West Indian industries."[56] From the first of the year until about the end of May, cane cutting, grinding, boiling, and potting were conducted simultaneously. Weather was a continuing concern—fear of droughts at the outset of the cutting season, when lack of rain reduced the sugar (or liquid) content of the cane, fear of heavy rain toward late spring, which could rot cane in the ground or immediately on cutting. But the work pressure also came from the somewhat misleading idea that sugar syrup, once boiling, should not be permitted to cool until "struck." The only break in the work week was from Saturday night till Monday morning. Otherwise, the twenty-five men and women in the factory worked continuously in shifts lasting all day and part of the night, or the whole of every second or third night:

So rapid was the motion of the mill, and so rapid also the combustion of the dried canes or "trash" used as fuel in the boiling house that the work of the millers and firemen, though light enough in itself, was exhausting. A French writer described as "prodigious" the galloping of the mules attached to the sweeps of the mill; but "still more surprising" in his opinion was the ceaseless celerity with which the firemen kept up a full blaze of cane-trash. Those who fed the mill were liable, especially when tired or half-asleep, to have their fingers caught between the rollers. A hatchet was kept in readiness to sever the arm, which in such cases was always drawn in; and this no doubt explains the number of maimed watchmen. The negroes employed as boilermen had a less exacting, but a heavier task. Standing barefoot for hours on the stones or hard ground and without seats for their intermissions of duty, they frequently developed "disorders of the legs." The ladle suspended on a pole which transferred the sugar from one cauldron to another was "in itself particularly heavy"; and, as the strainers were placed at a considerable height above the cauldrons, it had to be raised as well as swung.[57]

The relationship between the cultivation of cane and its mechanical/chemical transformation into sugar—the final steps of which have never been commonly undertaken in the tropical zone, where the plant itself is grown—springs from the inherent perishability of the crop. Because of the links between cutting and grinding, and between boiling and crystallization, land and mill must be coordinated, their labor synchronized. A major consequence is that sugar-cane plantations have not usually been divided upon inheritance, since their value (except under special conditions of change) depends upon keeping intact the land-and-factory combination. But other consequences have been careful scheduling at the top, and the application of iron discipline at the base. Without overall control of land and mill, such scheduling and discipline would not have been possible.

It is in terms like these that one can see that the sugar-cane plantation, very early in its career as a form of productive organization, was an industrial enterprise. When it is remembered that the plantation form probably first developed in the eastern Mediterranean, was perfected (mostly with enslaved labor) by the Crusaders after 1000, was transferred to (and in part, perhaps, reinvented on) the Atlantic islands by 1450, and was thereupon re-established in the New World colonies, the significance of their industrialism— at a time when industry itself was largely based on home labor, except for shipbuilding and some textiles in Europe itself—becomes more persuasive. Since cane growing and even sugar making were, at least until the nineteenth century, activities in which mechanical force was only an imperfect and incomplete substitute for manual labor, "industry" may seem a questionable descriptive term. Also, most plantation development was based on coerced labor of various sorts, which likewise seems to run counter to our ideas of industry. We are inclined instead to think of industry in postfeudal Europe, replacing the guild system and the artisan by the factory and by a free but unskilled labor force, divested of its tools and mass-producing commodities previously produced by hand.

All the more reason to specify what is meant by "industry" here. Today we speak of "agro-industry," and the term usually implies heavy substitution of machinery for human labor, mass production on large holdings, intensive use of scientific methods and products (fertilizer, herbicides, the breeding of hybrid varieties, irrigation), and the like. What made the early plantation system agro-industrial was the combination of agriculture and processing under one authority: *discipline* was probably its first essential feature. This was because neither mill nor field could be separately (independently) productive. Second was the organization of the labor force itself, part skilled, part unskilled, and organized in terms of the plantation's overall productive goals. To the extent possible, the labor force was composed of interchangeable units—much of the labor was homogeneous, in the eyes of the producers—characteristic of a lengthy middle period much later in the history of capitalism. Third, the system was time-conscious. This time-consciousness was dictated by the nature of the sugar cane and its processing requirements, but it permeated all phases of plantation life and accorded well with the emphasis on time that was later to become a central feature of capitalist industry. The combination of field and factory, of skilled workers with unskilled, and the strictness of scheduling together gave an industrial cast to plantation enterprises, even though the use of coercion to exact labor might have seemed somewhat unfamiliar to latter-day capitalists.[58]

There were at least two other regards in which these plantation enterprises were industrial: the separation of production from consumption, and the separation of the worker from his tools. Such features help us to define the lives of the working people, mostly unfree, who powered plantation enterprises between the sixteenth and the late nineteenth centuries in the New World. They call our attention to the remarkably early functioning of industry in European history (overseas colonial history, at that). They throw rather provocative light on the common assertion that Europe "developed" the colonial world after the European heartland. They also afford us an idea of the life of plantation laborers, to contrast with that of European agricultural workers and peasants of the same era.

Near the mid-seventeenth century, when British and French colonists first considered producing sugar in the Caribbean, the European market for tobacco had become saturated, and the price for this curious, addictive new commodity had fallen sharply. The colonists were, for the most part, small-scale cultivators of limited means. Many of them employed on their farms freshly arrived settlers from the mother countries who were contracted to labor for a fixed period of years. These workers were debt servants, petty criminals, political and religious nonconformists, labor organizers, Irish revolutionaries—political prisoners of different sorts. Many were simply kidnapped; to "barbadoes" someone became a seventeenth-century verb for stealing humans.[59] Both Britain and France used this system to rid themselves of "undesirables," in a period when there was more labor than the domestic economies could absorb.

These contracted English laborers, called indentured servants (in French *engagés*), represented a vital contribution to the labor needs of the colonies, on the mainland as well. At the termination of their contracts in the islands, such persons were to be given tracts of land of their own, and by this process, the new colonies would presumably fill up with settlers over time. But the colonists in places such as Barbados and Martinique needed more labor than they could readily obtain. Sometimes they were able to lay hands on some enslaved Native Americans who might work alongside the contracted Europeans. But soon enough, the island planters began to acquire enslaved Africans. Hence the early labor patterns in the so-called sugar islands were mixed, combining European smallholders, indentured laborers, and African and Indian slaves.

The shift to sugar production required substantial capital, which, as I have mentioned, was supplied by Dutch investors, men already familiar with the cultivation of sugar cane and the manufacture of sugar. In English Barbados, as the more successful planters bought their neighbors' lands and built new mills and boiling and drying houses, the shift from tobacco to sugar created larger estates. At the same time, the pattern enabling indentured servants to acquire land at the end of their terms disappeared. Small farms were replaced by plantations, and by the late seventeenth century and thereafter, the number of enslaved Africans rose sharply. Slavery emerged as the preferred form of labor exaction, even though it required substantial investment in human "stock." A young teacher named Downing, writing from Barbados in 1645 as the plantation system took hold there, recounted that the Barbadians "have bought this yeare no less than a thousand negroes, and the more they buie, the more they are able to buie, for in a yeare and a halfe they will earn with God's blessing as much as they cost." The success of slavery in pioneering islands like Barbados and Martinique marked the beginning of the Africanization of the British and French Caribbean. From 1701 to 1810 Barbados, a mere 166 square miles in area, received 252,500 African slaves. Jamaica, which in 1655 had been invaded by the British, followed the same pattern of "economic development"; in the same 109 years, it received 662,400 slaves.[60]

The eighteenth century was the apogee of the British and French slave-based sugar plantations. The first, Spanish period of Caribbean plantation history saw a "mixed" form of labor; the second, 1650–1850, with the Danes, Dutch, English, and French, embraced three quite different forms of labor exaction, and actually changed before the exclusively "slave" form ended with emancipation (1838 for the English, 1848 for the French). The third, "contract" form of plantation life in the Caribbean, which began with a new arrangement using imported labor to soften the effects of emancipation and to keep labor costs down, ended by the 1870s; in 1876, slavery ended in Puerto Rico and, in 1884, in Cuba. Thereafter Caribbean labor (with few exceptions) was entirely "free."

From the point of view of the English consumers of commodities like sugar, such changes were perhaps not of great importance. Yet changing metropolitan attitudes toward the treatment of labor in the colonies certainly had an economic coefficient. When slave-based plantations were evolving on the Caribbean islands, Europe itself was witnessing the emergence of free proletarian labor, along the very lines Karl Marx employed in describing capitalism. "We have seen," he writes, "that the expropriation of the mass of the people from the soil forms the basis of the capitalist mode of production." And "so-called primitive accumulation...is nothing less than the historical process of divorcing the producer from the means of production."[61] The European laborers who had been dispossessed by profound social and economic alterations of their countrysides would eventually become the urban factory workers—the proletariat—whose emergence so fascinated Marx when he was writing in the mid-nineteenth century. But in the seventeenth century that transformation had but barely begun.

At the same time, in the newly acquired Caribbean colonies of Britain and France, labor was being exacted from massive populations of similarly dispossessed persons. But they were slaves, not free landless workers. These displaced and enchatteled Africans, who did not own their own bodies, let alone their own labor, were being reunited with the means of production, from which enslavement and transportation had separated them, but by the lash, rather than through the operation of the market. The differences between these laboring populations give rise to odd questions. Were those Caribbean colonies, the planters who ran them and the slaves who worked them, part of the same system that embraced the free and dispossessed workers of western Europe? In the period before factory capitalism had become typical of western Europe, how do we describe the Caribbean plantations and their mode of operation?

What sort of economic system were they part of, since capitalism, as it is commonly conceived, had not yet even appeared?

Most students of capitalism (though not all) believe that capitalism itself became a governing economic form in the late eighteenth century and not before. But the rise of capitalism involved the destruction of economic systems that had preceded it—notably, European feudalism—and the creation of a system of world trade. It also involved the creation of colonies, the establishment of experimental economic enterprises in various world areas, and the development of new forms of slave-based production in the New World, using imported slaves—perhaps Europe's biggest single external contribution to its own economic growth. The Caribbean plantations were a vital part of this process, embodying all of these features, and providing both important commodities for European consumption and important markets for European production. As such they were crucial to profit making for Europe herself, even before capitalism—in the opinion of most authorities—had emerged there.

The reader may see that this line of argument harks back to my discussion of the plantation as an early form of industrial organization, for it, too, stresses a precocious development outside the European heartland. Both in its labor forms and in its organization, then, the plantation is an oddity. Yet its existence was predicated on European intent, and in its own way it became vital to European development over time. If it was not "capitalistic," it was still an important step toward capitalism.

The early sugar planters of Barbados and then Jamaica measured their worth in the profit their plantations brought them; their plantations were judged in the same way by their creditors. The owners of these plantations were usually businessmen, often absentee, and the capital they invested was commonly borrowed, mostly from metropolitan banks.

> These planters were in every way of great financial benefit to England. The mortgages on their estates, because of the high rate of interest which they paid for the loan of capital, were a most desirable investment for English capitalists. Money invested in

the plantations, moreover, was of much more value to the mother country than if it had been put out at interest at home, for it became a means of retaining settlers in the colonies who in every way increased the consumption of English manufactures. One thousand pounds spent by a planter in Jamaica produced in the end better results and greater advantages to England than twice that sum expended by the same family in London.[62]

Though a few students of the imperial economy have concluded that the West Indian colonies represented a net loss to Britain because of the costs of protectionism to the consumers, it must be remembered that the sugar eater's loss was the sugar planter's gain—while the duties enriched the crown, no matter who paid them. At the same time, these colonies were an enormous market for finished goods. During the eighteenth century, English combined exports to the North American and West Indian colonies expanded by 2,300 percent! As Thomas and McCloskey point out, there is a difference between social and private profitability:

> It is obvious that the colonial plantations and farms were privately profitable to their owners. The costs of the sugar preferences were borne by the British consumer and the costs of administration and protection by the British tax payer. The costs were widely diffused, but the benefits accrued to a small group of owners who happened to be well represented in Parliament. British mercantilism during the eighteenth century was not a consistent national policy designed to maximise the wealth of Britain; nor was it a preview of the alleged enrichment of capitalist nations by nineteenth-century empires. It was instead, as Ralph Davis suggests, a means to provide revenue to the government and a device to enrich special interest groups. The truth of the matter is that what was in the interest of the Manchester textile manufacturer or the Bristol slave trader or the West Indian planter was usually not in the interest of the British economy as a whole.[63]

That early prophet of free trade, Adam Smith, understood this well: "To found a great empire for the sole purpose of raising up a people of customers, may at first sight appear a project fit only for a nation of shopkeepers. It is, however, a project altogether unfit for a nation of shopkeepers; but extremely fit for a nation whose government is influenced by shopkeepers."[64] But it was the "shopkeepers" who won out, and sugar was one of their favorite weapons. To understand them, we need to understand the peculiar appeal of sugar. It then becomes important both to explain how and why the market for sugar and like commodities grew at such a pace in the homeland between 1650, when the first "sugar islands" were acquired, and the mid-nineteenth century; and to describe a little more fully what this odd colonial agricultural system had to do with capitalism.

But first some more must be said of the plantation system itself, grounded as it was in the use of forced labor, even though the stimulus to its growth originated with far-off European entrepreneurs. Like proletarians, slaves are separated from the means of production (tools, land, etc.). But proletarians can exercise some influence over where they work, how much they work, for whom they work, and what they do with their wages. Under some conditions, they may even possess a great deal of influence. Of course, slaves, too, may have some freedom of maneuver, depending upon the nature of the system they live in. Yet because they were themselves chattels—property—slaves in the New World during the period when plantations operated with feverish intensity could exercise their will only in the interstices of the system. Slaves and forced laborers, unlike free workers, have nothing to sell, not even their labor; instead, they have themselves been bought and sold and traded. Like the proletarians, however, they stand in dramatic contrast to the serfs of European feudalism, and they are propertyless.

These two great masses of workers had noticeably different histories, and the forms of labor exaction they embodied, during most of the 380-year period concerning us here, evolved in different parts of the world. At the same time, their economic functions in the world trade system, especially from the mid-seventeenth to the mid-nineteenth century, were overlapping, even interdependent. The linkage between Caribbean slaves and European free laborers was a linkage of production and hence also of consumption, created by the single system of which they were both parts. Neither group had much to offer productively but its labor. Both produced; both consumed little of what they produced. Both were divested of their tools. In the views of some authorities, they really form one group, differing only in how they fit into the worldwide division of labor others created for them.[65]

Putting things this way may oversimplify what was the complex evolution of a modern world labor force, let alone the diversified capitalistic economy that both created it and was serviced by it. The maturing of a plantation system based on slavery in the Caribbean region came with, and was partly preconditioned on, the development of powerful commercial and military navies in western Europe. It meant the funneling of great quantities of commodities (rum, arms, cloth, jewelry, iron) into Africa for the purchase of slaves— an investment that did nothing for Africa's development but only stimulated more slave raiding. It led to enormous outputs of wealth in the metropolises to garrison the colonies and to ensure the coercion and control of the slaves. To maintain the mercantilist premises of the system—that the colonies buy from and sell to the motherland only, and that trade be carried only in the motherland's ships— was expensive for each national system, though of course certain groups inside each system profited greatly from it, as we have seen. The creation and consolidation of a colonial, subordinate plantation economy based on coerced labor stretched over four centuries. But the system in the colonies changed little, relative to the tremendous changes in the European centers that had created it.

It is common to describe the period 1650–1750 as one of mercantile, trading, or commercial expansion, and to treat only the industrial phase beginning with the late eighteenth century as "real capitalism."[66] But would this mean that capitalism somehow existed before the capitalist mode of production? The plantations that supplied Europe with sugar, tobacco, etc., were presumably noncapitalist, for their labor force was enslaved, not proletarian. But this way of putting things is not entirely satisfactory, either, for it leaves us in the uncomfortable position of being unable to specify what sort of economic order gave rise to the plantation system.

Banaji, in a stimulating critique, points out that many Marxist writers, even including some classical figures such as Lenin and Kautsky, had trouble making sense of modern slave economies and their place in world economic history.[67] Marx himself did not always seem to know how to fit slave plantations into his picture of capitalism. Of the West Indian colonies, he wrote that their settlers acted "like people who, driven by motives of bourgeois production, wanted to produce commodities...."[68] The plantations were enterprises of "commercial speculation," in which "a capitalist mode of production exists, if only in a formal sense.... The business in which slaves are used is conducted by capitalists."[69] Yet elsewhere he wrote, "The fact that we now not only call the plantation owners in America capitalists, but that they *are* capitalists, is based on their existence as anomalies within a world market based on free labour."[70] Later writers attacking the same issue showed some of the same uncertainties. Eugene Genovese, for instance, says at one point that "the slave regime in the British Caribbean bore the clear stamp of capitalist enterprise," and that sugar was grown on "large plantations of a decidedly bourgeois type" operated by "capitalist slaveholders."[71] But Genovese's earlier work (dealing, to be sure, not with West Indian plantation sugar makers but with U.S. plantation cotton growers) says "the planters were not mere capitalists, they were pre-capitalist, quasi-aristocratic landowners who had to adjust their economy and ways of thinking to a capitalist world market."[72]

One might ask what difference it makes whether one calls the plantation system "capitalistic" or not. The question matters because it has to do with the ways economic systems grow and change, and with the chain of causation that leads from one stage of development to another. I have argued that the plantations were themselves precocious cases of industrialization. But this does not necessarily mean that the European economy that gave rise to these plantations was capitalist. As we have seen, slave labor is so contrary a form of labor power to be associated with "the capitalist mode of production," which is always described as based on free labor, that even Marx himself seems uncertain how to treat it. Yet there is no question of the importance of plantations to the metropolitan economies, or of the tremendous economic activity they stimulated, both by their production and by the market their consumption needs afforded the metropolis.

In Banaji's view, plantations were capitalist enterprises, all right—linked to European centers, fueled by European wealth, returning some portion of that wealth to metropolitan investors in various forms, and functioning as centers of "commercial speculation," in Marx's words. Yet the investment they represented took a fairly static form—so much for land, for slaves, for equipment—that did not significantly vary for centuries. They generated profit, which could be increased by increasing the scale of the enterprise—two produce twice as much as one, or possibly more—but only in very limited fashion by improving the technology or by raising productivity. Hence they were at once speculative enterprises and conservative enterprises: one gambled on making money from sugar production, but the way one produced sugar was virtually unchanged, including the coercion of the labor force, for centuries. Of this curious blend of slavery and the expanding world market for plantation commodities—what the Trinidadian historian Eric Williams once called a system combining the sins of feudalism with those of capitalism, and without the virtues of either[73]—Banaji writes, "This heterogeneous and, as it appears, disarticulated nature of the slave plantation generated a series of contradictory images when the early Marxist tradition, not equipped with the same abundance of material available today, attempted its first characterizations."[74]

My own sense of it is that those "contradictory images" persist. It is true that much of the wealth invested in the plantation system did not result in high levels of accumulation, and that for centuries the relations among land, labor, and technology on the estates did not much vary. In these ways the plantation system surely differed from capitalism in its late, productive, and industrial phase. It is also true that the plantation mode of production before 1850, based as it was on slave labor, differs greatly from the so-called capitalist mode of production, the labor power of which is purchased on an impersonal market, as are the other factors of production, and it would be wrong to treat the plantation system as "capitalistic" in the same way that the British factory system of the nineteenth century was capitalistic. Yet to detach the plantations from the emergent world economy that spawned them, or to rule out their contribution to the accumulation of capital in world centers, would be equally mistaken, I believe. Scholars who demonstrate that the European capital invested in the West Indies might actually have earned more if invested elsewhere or otherwise—who conclude that the whole plantation phenomenon ended up losing money for the English economy, say—are usually ready to admit that this phenomenon nonetheless made an immense amount of money for some Englishmen, even if it proved prohibitively expensive for others.[75] Nor did that money stop "working" once it was made. And perhaps that is the principal point. Early in the seventeenth century, some people in power in Britain became convinced that commodities like sugar mattered so much to their well-being that they would politick fiercely for the rights of capital invested in developing the plantations and all that went with them. If these people were not capitalists, if the slaves were not proletarians, if mercantilism rather than a free economy prevailed, if the rate of accumulation of profit was low and the organic composition of capital static—if all of these things were true, it also remains true that these curious agro-industrial enterprises nourished certain capitalist classes at home *as they were becoming more capitalistic*. Later we shall see how they also nourished the emerging proletarian classes, who found sugar and kindred drug foods profound consolations in the mines and in the factories.

The English connection between sugar production and sugar consumption was welded in the seventeenth century, when Britain acquired Barbados, Jamaica, and other "sugar islands," vastly expanded her trade in African slaves, made inroads into the Portuguese domination of the Continental sugar trade, and first began to build a broad internal consumer market. That connection, once created, survived most attacks by other classes in the metropolis, at least until the mid-nineteenth century. Thereafter it was supplanted by arrangements that could guarantee an abundant but cheaper supply of the same goods to English consumers, without special West Indian privileges. The middle of the nineteenth century was a period of important transition from the so-called protectionism under the Navigation Acts to so-called free trade. Actually, this transition began before 1850, and was not wholly accomplished, as far as sugar was concerned, until the 1870s.

The debates that marked this transition are tangled and difficult to summarize, because many different motives lay behind the positions taken by the protagonists. Some were concerned mainly with preventing any economic encouragement to those foreign colonies where slavery still obtained, and hence opposed the admission of slave-grown produce into Britain without penalties. Yet others— the "Manchester School"—were unconcerned with slavery but wanted the indiscriminate admission of the cheapest produce to Great Britain at any cost. The West Indian planters, of course, demanded special-entry privileges for their sugars against all sugars produced either within or outside the empire, as well as the right to import contracted labor to the colonies, once slavery ended (1834–38). It would be foolish to suppose that these and the many other contending interest groups were prepared to be candid about why they wanted one or another outcome; the debates over free trade made a parliamentary high-water mark for disingenuousness. Viscount Palmerston's concluding ironies in the 1841 debates on a government initiative to lower the duties on foreign sugars in order to raise revenues by encouraging increased consumption of sugar— that is, to push down the price of sugar for the British consumer to the benefit of the exchequer—are deliciously revealing:

> We say to these Brazilians we can supply you with cotton goods cheaper than you can buy them elsewhere. Will you buy them? By all means, say the Brazilians, and we will pay you with our sugar and coffee. No, say we, your sugar and coffee are produced by slave labour; we are men of principle and our consciences will not allow us to consume the product of slave labour. Well, anyone would imagine that the matter ended there, and we left the Brazilians to consume their own sugar and coffee. No such thing. We are men of principle, but we are also men of business, and we try to help the Brazilians out of their difficulty. We say to them: Close to us and near at hand live some 40,000,000 industrious and thriving Germans, who are not as conscientious as we are; take your sugar to them; they will buy it from you, and you can pay us for our cottons with the money you thus receive. But the Brazilians represent that there will be some difficulty with this. The Germans live on the other side of the Atlantic; we must send them our sugar in ships; now our ships are few and ill-fitted to cope with the waters of the great ocean. Our reply is ready. We have plenty of ships and they are at your service. It is true

that slave-labour sugar would contaminate our warehouses, but ships are different things. But the Brazilians have another difficulty. They say the Germans are particular and have a fancy for refined sugar. It is not easy to refine sugar in Brazil, and these Germans do not like the trouble of refining it themselves. Again we step in with an expedient. We will not only carry your sugar but we will refine it for you too. It is sinful to consume slave-grown sugar, but there can be no harm in refining it, which in fact is to cleanse it from part of its original impurity. The Brazilians are at us again. Say they, we produce a great deal of sugar more than the Germans will buy. Our goodness is infinite; we ourselves will buy your surplus. It cannot be consumed at home, because the people of this country are men of conscience, but we will send it to the West Indies and Australia. The people who live there are only negroes and colonists, and what right have they to consciences? And now that you may plague us no more about these matters, we tell you at once, that, if the price of our own sugar should rise above a certain value, we will buy more of your slave-grown sugar and we will eat it ourselves.[76]

The hottest debates came in the 1840s, as the West Indian planters, fattened on slavery and protectionism, found themselves unable to compete in a widening market, while the free-trade advocates at home saw a chance that the government's motives and their own might coincide for a change.

Between 1660—when Barbados was already producing considerable sugar and Jamaica had fallen into British hands—and 1700, English foreign trade had been transformed, as woolen cloth was displaced by other products. A re-export trade, based largely on tropical commodities, had begun to take over, with 30 percent of imports coming from either the East or the New World. Such expansion occurred partly because new sources of supply had been opened up, but also because "vast new sources of demand were being opened in England and Europe—demand created by a sudden cheapness when these English plantation goods brought a collapse in prices which introduced the middle classes and the poor to novel habits of consumption; demand which, once realized, was not shaken by subsequent vicissitudes in prices, but continued to grow rapidly throughout the century."[77] This change was seen perhaps most dramatically in the case of tobacco. A luxury at the end of the sixteenth century, in a hundred years it had become "the general solace of all classes." The case of sugar was similar:

> The development of English production was part of an international movement which brought prices down. At the beginning of the seventeenth century Portuguese (i.e., Brazilian) production was already growing fast and reducing prices sharply and the English West Indian islands, when they turned to sugar production, had this large established New World producer to contend with. They came late into the field—Barbados in the 1640s, Jamaica, as a substantial grower, after 1660—and in the early 1660s they were still contending with the Portuguese, even for the English market. But already their competition had caused a considerable decline in prices, and prices continued to fall, on the whole, until about 1685, by which time the English product had driven Brazilian sugar from the North European as well as from the English market. West Indies sugar imports to London, negligible before the Civil War, rose from 148,000 cwt. in 1663/69 to 371,000 cwt. in 1699/71—and a third of this latter total was re-exported. The plantation price of sugar reached a low point in 1685 of 12s. 6d. per cwt.; the retail price was halved between 1630 and 1680.[78]

Davis argues convincingly that it was not only the establishment of English colonies and entrepôts outside Europe that mattered, but the sudden cheapness of the commodities they dealt in. "In this respect," he says, this expansion "bears a striking similarity to the technological revolution which, getting under way a century later, developed new consumption habits in English and foreign populations with the cheap product of the machine."[79] In terms of production, these changes were only analogous; sugar-producing plantations are not the same as steam-driven textile mills. But in terms of consumption, they were homologous, because they made visible, perhaps for the first time in history, a critical connection between the will to work and the will to consume. The introduction of growing quantities of consumer goods to masses of people who had never had them before gave the privileged classes the opportunity to imagine that such people might respond to the promise of enlarged consumption with more effort.

Before the diversification of industry had made a substantial impact on foreign trade, and four generations before technical changes created an entirely new basis for commercial expansion, the English merchant class was able to grow rich, to accumulate capital, on middlemen's profits and on the growing shipping industry which was needed to carry cheap sugar and tobacco, pepper and saltpetre on the ocean routes. Because these sources made their great contribution to English foreign trade in the century after 1660, and in that century made great demands on the nation's capital, perhaps we should look with a little more favour on those historians of the past who dubbed this century with the title of "The Commercial Revolution."[80]

This so-called Commercial Revolution, which many Marxist writers have refused to consider fully capitalistic, nonetheless plainly underlay the events that followed it a century later. For Marx, this was the process of accumulation that would make capitalism possible:

> The different momenta of primitive accumulation distribute themselves now, more or less in chronological order, particularly over Spain, Portugal, Holland, France and England. In England at the end of the seventeenth century, they arrive at a systematical combination, embracing the colonies, the national debt, the modern mode of taxation, and the protectionist system. These methods depend in part on brute force, e.g., the colonial system. But they all employ the power of the State, the concentrated and organised force of society, to hasten, hothouse fashion, the process of transformation of the feudal mode of production into the capitalist mode, and to shorten the transition....
> The veiled slavery of the wage-workers of Europe needed, for its pedestal, slavery pure and simple in the new world.[81]

How intimately related to what was to come were the slave-labor plantations of the New World, producing their shiploads of stimulants, drugs, and sweeteners for the growing urban populations of Europe, is suggested by another assertion of Marx:

> Freedom and slavery constitute an antagonism.... We are not dealing with the indirect slavery, the slavery of the proletariat [sic], but with direct slavery, the slavery of the black races in Surinam, in Brazil, in the Southern States of North America.

Direct slavery is as much the pivot of our industrialism today as machinery, credit, etc. Without slavery, no cotton; without cotton, no modern industry. Slavery has given their value to the colonies; the colonies have created world trade; world trade is the necessary condition of large-scale machine industry. Before the traffic in Negroes began, the colonies only supplied the Old World with very few products and made no visible change in the face of the earth. Thus slavery is an economic category of the highest importance.[82]

Hobsbawm has shown how increases in the consumption of sugar and like commodities were predicated upon a basic structural realignment of European economic activity. In his view, a lengthy period of economic contraction in Europe—a "general crisis"—marked the seventeenth century. This crisis, a last phase of the transition from feudalism to capitalism, wrecked the earlier Mediterranean and Baltic trade systems, and they were soon replaced by North Atlantic centers. This shift meant a fundamental reordering of the flow patterns of world exchange. "The powerful, growing and accelerating current of overseas trade which swept the infant industries of Europe with it—which, in fact, sometimes actually *created* them—was hardly conceivable without this change."[83] Such a change, Hobsbawm argues, rested on three new conditions: the growth of an expandable consumers' market in Europe itself, tied to changes in production elsewhere; the seizure of colonies abroad for European "development"; and the creation of colonial enterprises (such as plantations) to produce consumer goods (and to soak up a substantial portion of the products of the homeland). As the organization of European economic activity shifted toward the United Kingdom and away from both the Mediterranean and the Baltic, the upward spurts in the production and consumption of tropical commodities like sugar were both a consequence and a cause of the growing importance of the United Kingdom in world trade.

By the early eighteenth century, the pioneering overseas economic expansion of the preceding fifty years began to be reflected in the form of changes in homeland consumption. To be sure, the consumption of imported commodities like sugar remained modest by modern (even by nineteenth-century) standards. But the meanings of sugar in the life of the British people changed radically. Statistics on British trade compiled by Elizabeth Boody Schumpeter and interpreted by Richard Sheridan show that the percentage of imports in the "groceries" category (tea, coffee, sugar, rice, pepper, etc.), as a fraction of the total value of imports, more than doubled during the eighteenth century—from 16.9 percent in 1700 to 34.9 percent by 1800:

> None of the other eight groups exceeded six per cent of total imports in 1800. Among grocery items brown sugar and molasses were the most prominent. They made up, by official value, two-thirds of the group in 1700 and two-fifths in 1800.... English sugar consumption probably increased about four-fold in the last four decades of the next century [1700–40] and more than doubled again from 1741–45 to 1771–75. If it is assumed that one-half of the imports were retained in 1663, *the consumption of England and Wales increased about twenty-fold in the period from 1663 to 1775.* The fact that the population increased from 4½ million to only 7½ million in the same period is indicative of a marked increase in per capita consumption.[84]

Sugar and related imports (rum, molasses, syrup) were among the leaders. Indeed, the English economic historian D. C. Coleman believes per-capita sugar consumption rose more rapidly than bread, meat, and dairy consumption between 1650 and 1750;[85] Deerr estimates British per-capita annual consumption, 1700–1800, as follows:[86]

1700–1709	4 lbs.
1720–1729	8 lbs.
1780–1789	12 lbs.
1800–1809	18 lbs.

To be sure, eighteen pounds of sugar a year was still not very much.[87] But how much that meager quantity mattered to how many people was the important thing; it represented more than a 400-percent increase in one century, and now sugar mattered to many more than before.

The nineteenth century dawned for a population already accustomed to sugar—if only in small amounts—and eager for more. That century saw the end of slavery in the British Empire; soon thereafter, protectionism for sugar began to lose out to free trade. These events occurred only after pitched battles between different sectors of Britain's capitalist classes; and though sugar by itself neither caused nor explains these battles entirely, its production and consumption were important aspects of what happened.[88] The slave trade to the British colonies ended in 1807; slavery itself was abolished in 1834–38; and the future of the sugar colonies (hence of sugar production itself) figured in the debates over both. It was becoming steadily clearer that the closed trade circuits typical of the previous century were not going to last forever. Though the Anglo-Caribbean sugar industry continued to supply much of Britain's sugar, its dominance shrank, because of many factors: the perfection of beet-sugar extraction on the Continent as part of Napoleon's politics, after the loss of Saint-Domingue, and the spread of the beet-sugar industry across Europe; the rise of new and competing intraimperial sugar colonies within the British system, such as Mauritius (and later Fiji, Natal, and others); and the growing production of sugar elsewhere, much of it slave-produced (as in Cuba) and often available at better prices than the sugars of the British West Indies.

More, perhaps, than any other tropical commodity, sugar became a signal of the struggles among different sectors of British capitalism, and a symbol of the dangers of a doomed commercial exclusivism. The West Indian colonies continued to be subject to the metropolis, and their populations were still compelled to provide labor to the plantations; but the metropolis soon freed itself to buy sugar when and where it wished. Whatever archaism the use of slave labor had made for in the production of sugar, after 1838 it had to be rooted out; otherwise the industry would be kept alive only by subsidies and immobilized (if "free") labor. Eventually the Anglo-Caribbean sugar industry, the oldest in the empire, had to choose between stagnation and expensive, large-scale expansion. In most cases, it was not free to choose. As I have argued elsewhere,

The post-slavery aftermath was, in general, a period of intensified competition on the world sugar market. Ultimately—that is, in the very long run—the victors of this rivalry would be the planter groups who could successfully underwrite and incorporate large-scale technical improvements. But this is viewed from a very broad perspective. On the local level—that is, colony by colony—it is true that the planter groups were substantially united in their hostility to any changes that might improve the bargaining position of labour. But of course within such groups there was competition for that labour—and there were differing capacities to reduce the dependence on that labour by technical advance.... [We] may really have to deal with two intersecting and chronologically overlapping processes, which take for granted the internal differentiation of each planter group. One such process is the struggle to contain and to supplement the labour power of the "potential" peasantry; the other is the movement toward technical improvement, based on the pace of technical achievement and on availabilities of intensified capital inputs.[89]

On the one hand, the relatively minor technological changes that had typified the history of the sugar industry for centuries were now supplanted by important and sweeping alterations. Immense improvements in grinding capacity, cane varieties, pest-control and cultivation methods, increasing use of machinery, and revolutionary changes in transportation eventuated in vast new agro-industrial complexes, completely different from the smaller enterprises that preceded them. The Caribbean cane-sugar industry, which had been colonial, industrial, and export-oriented ever since the Hispanic expansion, was now unquestionably absorbed into expanding overseas European capitalism. After the abolition of slavery in Cuba in 1884, all Caribbean sugar was made by proletarian labor.[90]

Though some comments have been made about the curious association between sugar and slavery, little attention has been given to the "labor problems" created by successive emancipations in the Caribbean region. Throughout, emancipation (and, in the case of Haiti, revolution) meant a sharp decrease in sugar production, as those who had been freed sought to create new ways of life independent of the plantation. As the slaves were freed (by Denmark in 1848, England in 1834–38, France in 1848, Netherlands in 1863, Puerto Rico in 1873–76, Cuba in 1884), on the one hand, competition from imported contracted laborers forced the freedmen to work harder and for less money; on the other, since access to idle land and other local resources was shut off, the freedmen were prevented from developing alternative sources of livelihood. In effect, the planter classes sought to re-create pre-emancipation conditions—to replace the discipline of slavery with the discipline of hunger. They believed they were forced into this position—at least in the British sugar colonies—by the successive ends of the slave trade, of slavery, and of protection for their sugars. Naturally, they felt betrayed by their class equals at home.

But another way to say this would be to argue that sugar consumption, and the government income it provided, had finally become so important to British capitalist development that sugar production was no longer allowed to depend upon the mercantilist-nationalist arrangements that had formerly controlled it. By removing barriers to "free" trade—in other words, by making it possible for the world's cheapest sugars to reach the widest possible market in Britain—the leading sectors of British capitalism sold out their planter-capitalist fellows. This was precisely what the West India interest accused them of doing.

As the world sugar market opened up, labor still needed to be found, both for the more ancient colonial areas where slavery had now ended (Jamaica, Trinidad, British Guiana), and for those newer, pioneering areas (Mauritius, Natal, Fiji) that were now becoming producers. The political struggle between the metropolitan capitalist classes and the colonial planters was partly eased by recourse to external but politically accessible labor pools. In fact, the defeat of protectionism in the form of differential duties for West Indian sugar was accompanied by a victory in regard to labor importation—easier regulations, as well as funds for financing immigration. West Indian sugar was thus indirectly protected, even if West Indian working people were not. (Some cynics might see a parallel to events in the United States after the Civil War.)

At any rate, migrant labor moved within the bounds of empire.

A portion of the contracted Indian labor in the French West Indies, for instance, came from French India, a portion of the contracted Indian labor in the British West Indies came from British India, and so on. But because many of the new sugar-producing areas needed labor as well, not all the movement was of this sort. During the nineteenth century, perhaps a hundred million people migrated in the world at large. About half came from Europe and about half from the "nonwhite" world, including India. The Europeans moved principally to areas of prior European settlement outside Europe itself, including Canada, Australia, New Zealand, South Africa, southern South America, and, especially, the United States, while the nonwhites moved to other places. As I have already observed,

> Sugar—or rather, the great commodity market which arose demanding it—has been one of the massive demographic forces in world history. Because of it, literally millions of enslaved Africans reached the New World, particularly the American South, the Caribbean and its littorals, the Guianas and Brazil. This migration was followed by those of East Indians, both Moslem and Hindu, Javanese, Chinese, Portuguese, and many other peoples in the nineteenth century. It was sugar that sent East Indians to Natal and the Orange Free State, sugar that carried them to Mauritius and Fiji. Sugar brought a dozen different ethnic groups in staggering succession to Hawaii, and sugar still moves people about the Caribbean.[91]

Several factors can be seen here. For one, the link between sweated, tropical colonial labor and nonwhite labor was preserved, largely undisturbed by the end of slavery. For another, the relationship between sugar and the subtropical colonial regions was likewise maintained (though beet-sugar extraction, important from about the mid-nineteenth century onward, was a temperate-zone development—marking the first time that a temperate-zone commodity would make a serious dent in the market for subtropical and tropical production). The product in question continued to flow to the metropolises, while the products obtained in exchange—food, clothing, machinery, and nearly everything else—continued to flow to the "backward" areas. It can be contended that the "backward" areas became less backward through their economic dependence on the developed areas, but this assertion is vulnerable. Most less developed societies of this sort have been able to industrialize only feebly (cement, glass bottles, beer, and soft drinks are often their major "industries"). They continue to import the bulk of their finished goods and, often, have even increased their importations of food.

Also problematic is the divided migrant flow of the nineteenth century. The economist Sir W. Arthur Lewis links this two-sided demographic picture to the relatively lower productivity of tropical agriculture in the countries of origin of the migrants, when compared with the agricultural productivity of the temperate lands from which the white migrants came (Italy, Ireland, Eastern Europe, Germany, etc.).[92] Presumably, migrants from the more productive countries would not be prepared to migrate for promised wages as low as those that could attract migrants from the less productive countries. But the exclusion of nonwhites from the temperate world was the clear consequence of racist policies in such countries as Australia, New Zealand, Canada, and the United States. It is not merely ironical to point out that the white migrants would soon be eating more sugar, produced by the nonwhite migrants at lower wages, and producing finished goods at higher wages, to be consumed by the nonwhite migrants.

So the production of sugar continued to rise, and at a dizzying rate, even while the loci of production increased in number and dispersion, techniques of labor coercion became somewhat less naked, and the uses to which sugars were put in the developed world became steadily more differentiated. The upward climb of both production and consumption within the British Empire must be seen as part of an even larger general movement. Figures for world sugar production before the mid-nineteenth century are unreliable, and there is no way of judging the quantities of sugars produced and consumed without reaching the market. Thus we know that sugar consumption in the old sugar colonies like Jamaica was always very substantial—indeed, that slaves were given sugar, molasses, and even rum during the slavery period as part of their rations. In countries like India, the ancient hearth of sugar making, and Russia (the Soviet Union), where beet-sugar production was established within a decade of its achievement in western Europe, our knowledge of quantities produced and consumed is uncertain. But even if we limit ourselves to what can be confidently estimated, the figures on world production and consumption of sugar during the past two centuries or so are still quite astounding.

In 1800—by which time, as we have seen, British consumption had probably increased some 2,500 percent in 150 years—perhaps 245,000 tons of sugar reached consumers through the world market. Nearly all of those consumers were Europeans. By 1830, before beet sugar had begun to reach the world market, total production had risen to 572,000 tons, an increase of more than 233 percent in thirty years. Another thirty years later, in 1860, by which time beet-sugar production was growing rapidly, total world production of sucrose (both beet and cane) stood at an estimated 1.373 million tons, or another increase of more than 233 percent. By 1890, world production exceeded six million tons, representing a percentage increase of nearly 500 over that of thirty years earlier. It is not surprising that Dr. John (Lord Boyd) Orr should have concluded, looking back at the nineteenth century, that the single most important nutritional datum on the British people was their fivefold increase in sugar consumption.[93]

The actual details of consumption are, of course, much more complex. But for the present, it may be enough to say that probably no other food in world history has had a comparable performance. Why this should be so is not, however, a simple question. To get some sense of how sugar gained its place in the English diet, it will be necessary to turn back again to the beginning of the story.

3 · Consumption

For people living today in societies like Britain or the United States, sugar is so familiar, so common, and so ubiquitous that it is difficult to imagine a world without it. People now in their forties or older may recall the sugar rationing of World War II, of course, and those who have spent time in poorer societies may have noticed that some peoples seem to experience even greater pleasure than we when consuming sugar.[1] So plentiful and important is this substance in our lives today that it has become notorious: campaigns are waged against it, eminent nutritionists attack and defend it, and battles for and against its consumption are waged in the daily press and in Congress. Whether the discussions concern baby food, school lunches, breakfast cereals, nutrition, or obesity, sugar figures in the argument. If we choose not to eat sugar, it takes both vigilance and effort, for modern societies are overflowing with it.

Only a few centuries ago it would have been equally difficult to imagine a world so rich in sugar. One writer tells us that when the Venerable Bede died in 735 A.D., he bequeathed his little treasure of spices, including sugar, to his brethren.[2] If true, this is a remarkable reference, for there follow many centuries during which sugar in the British Isles remained unmentioned and, one supposes, virtually unknown.

The presence of sugar was first acknowledged in England in the twelfth century. What was most striking about the English diet at that time was its complete ordinariness and meagerness. Then and for long thereafter, most Europeans produced their own food locally, as best they could. Most basic foods did not move far from where they were produced; it was mainly rare and precious substances, principally consumed by the more privileged groups, that were carried long distances.[3] "Bread made in the home almost everywhere in the country," write Drummond and Wilbraham of England in the thirteenth century, was "indeed the staff of life in those days."[4] Wheat was particularly important in England, but in the north of the country other grains were grown and eaten more: rye, buckwheat, oats, barley, and important pulses and legumes such as lentils and many kinds of beans. In poor areas throughout Europe, these carbohydrates were likely to be primary, since they were more plentiful and cheaper than wheat.

All other foods, including meats, dairy products, vegetables, and fruits, were subsidiary to grains. It was poverty of resources, not plenty, that made them accessories to the starch-based diet. "Judging from the controls and regulations that all authorities throughout Western Europe set to cover virtually every transaction, grain was the core of the diet of the poor," one scholar has written.[5] When the wheat harvest failed, people in southern England switched to rye, oats, or barley; in the north, these were already the mainstay. "They stretched their bread grain with peas and beans and apparently consumed some milk, cheese, and butter in normal years," but in the worst years—such as the so-called dear years of 1595–97—even dairy products were priced out of the reach of the poorest people.[6] In times of want, said William Harrison, writing in the late sixteenth century, the poor "shifted from wheat to Horsse corne, beanes, peason, otes, tare and lintels."[7] Such people probably forwent their skimpy consumption of dairy products and the like, if it meant they could obtain more of the bulkier legumes. Often enough, it seems, many Englishmen had not enough of anything to eat; but they ate as much bread as they could, when harvests permitted.[8] One can assume a meager supply of protein from domesticated fowl and animals, probably eked out with wild birds, hares, and fish, both fresh and preserved, and some vegetables and fruit.

Working people, however, greatly feared the effects of fresh fruit, supposedly dangerous when eaten in quantity. The resistance to fresh fruit harks back to Galenic biases against it,[9] and infantile diarrhea, frequent in the summertime, which was a great killer as late as the seventeenth century, doubtless reinforced the fear of fresh fruit. Sir Hugh Platt (who reappears later in these pages as a gourmet and *bon vivant*) had grim advice for his countrymen on the occasion of the 1596 famine: when flour supplies were short, he advised the poor to "boil your beanes, pease, beechmast, &c. in faire water... and the second or third boyling, you shall finde a strange alteration in taste, for the water hath sucked out & imbibed the greatest part of their ranknesse, then must you drie them... and make bread thereof."[10] Even when cultivated flour substitutes were exhausted, Platt writes consolingly, the poor could turn to "excellent bread of the rootes of Aaron called Cuckow pot, or starch rootes" (the cuckoopint, *Arum maculatum*).[11] If the picture is not one of chronic or countrywide need, it is also certainly not one of general dietary adequacy.

Between the onset of the bubonic plague in 1347–48 and the early fifteenth century, the population of Europe decreased sharply and did not begin to climb again until after about 1450; the plague continued to disrupt economic life until the mid-seventeenth century. These were centuries when European agriculture wanted for labor, but even when population increased again, English agriculture remained inadequately productive. Of the production of grains for making bread, the economic historian Brian Murphy writes: "The harvest of the years 1481–82, 1502, 1520–21, 1526–29, 1531–32, 1535, 1545, 1549–51, 1555–56, 1562, 1573, 1585–86, 1594–97, 1608, 1612–13, 1621–22, 1630, and 1637, could be said to have been such that the average wage earner with a family to support can have had little left over after buying bread."[12] Though they were irregularly spaced, the bad years averaged one every five during this 150-year period. Murphy believes the bad years reflect "the varying encroachment of animals on breadgrain"—which is to say, the competition between the production of wool and of grain foods, a critical economic problem in sixteenth-century England.

The seventeenth century seems to give evidence of significant change. Between 1640 and 1740, the English population rose from about five million to slightly more than five and one-half million, a rate of growth, lower than in the preceding century, that may have reflected greater disease vulnerability brought about by bad nutrition and/or the spread of gin drinking. There were poor harvests in 1660–61, 1673–74, 1691–93, 1708–10, 1725–29, and 1739–40—a worsening to a one-bad-year-in-four ratio over eighty years. Yet, as Murphy points out, by then there seems to have been enough grain, if export figures mean anything. Between 1697 and 1740, England became a net exporter of grain, exporting more than she imported in all but two years (1728 and 1729). Yet even as grain exportation continued, "There were still plenty of people with empty stomachs, but who, even at low bread prices, lacked the money to fill them."[13] Grain production might appear to have yielded a surplus, but Murphy shows that it was rather a matter of grossly inadequate income among the laboring classes.

During the centuries when sugar and other unfamiliar substances were entering into the diet of the English people, then, that diet was still meager, even inadequate, for many if not most people. It is in the light of these dietary, nutritive, and agricultural practices that sugar's place at the time can best be understood.

From the first known introduction of sugar to England until the late seventeenth century, when it became a desired good—consumed frequently by the wealthy, and soon to be afforded by many who would forgo important quantities of other foods in order to have it—we are dealing with limited agricultural production and a narrow diet. And even as consumption of sugar rose, there is no conclusive evidence that the basic diet of most people was otherwise improving. Indeed, for a long time sugar and a few other new substances were the only major additions to the English diet. Explaining this particular addition requires first some attention to the ways Englishmen learned to use sugar.

Cane sugar—sucrose—is a versatile, one might say protean, substance. During the early centuries of north European usage, however, it was not some single undifferentiated good. It was already possible to obtain sugars varying from syrupy liquid to hard crystalline solid, from dark brown ("red") in color to bone white (as well as many other brilliant colors), and in degree of purity from slight to nearly 100 percent. Purer sugars were prized for aesthetic reasons, among others, and reference has already been made to the preference for fine white varieties, particularly in medico-culinary usage. The purer the sugar, generally, the better it combines with most other foods, and the more easily it can be preserved. The history of sugar is marked by culturally conventionalized preferences for one or another such variety, and many different sugars evolved over time to satisfy particular preferences.

For our purposes here, sucrose can be described initially in terms of five principal uses or "functions": as medicine, spice-condiment, decorative material, sweetener, and preservative. These uses are often difficult to separate from one another, however. Sugar used as a spice or condiment, for instance, differs from sugar used as a sweetener largely in terms of the quantities used, relative to other ingredients. Moreover, the different uses of sugar did not evolve in any neat sequence or progression, but overlapped and intersected; that sugar commonly serves more than one such purpose at a time is considered one of its extraordinary virtues. Only after these various uses had multiplied, had become differentiated, and were firmly embedded in modern life would it be appropriate to add to them the use of sugar as a *food*. This final change did not begin before the late eighteenth century. By that time sugar had moved beyond its traditional uses, and—in Britain, at least—was actually altering the ancient core-fringe, complex-carbohydrate–flavoring pattern of the human majority, in a revolutionary fashion.

Disentangling sugar's various uses is nearly impossible; yet it is a worthwhile task. To some extent, one can learn in this way how the users themselves became more aware of sugar's versatility, and how they reacted creatively to it. Most sugar uses arrived in England together with particular sugars, from regions long familiar with this rare and unusual substance. But it was inevitable that, in the hands of new users, the uses and meanings of sugar would change in some ways, becoming what they had not been before. A sketchy overview of major uses, then, plotted against a background of change, may suggest how this happened.

A Negro Servant from America Cutting Sugar Cane first appeared in Father
J.-B. Labat's *Nouveau voyage aux isles d'Amérique* (1722). The artist's choice
of exotic costume was a common affectation of the time. In fact, cane-cutting
gangs worked in rags, under the direction of a "driver" who held a whip in his
hand. The illustration from *Ten Views of Antigua*, on the following page,
provides a more realistic view of field labor on a sugar plantation.
(Bibliothèque Nationale, Paris)

This careful display of tropical plants, from William Rhind's *A History of the Vegetable Kingdom* (1865), includes sugar cane, somewhat exaggerated in height and thickness but otherwise accurately illustrated. Interestingly, the only human figures are shown next to the cane; one appears to be cutting cane, and both are depicted as black.

One of W. Clark's *Ten Views of Antigua* (1823), which shows a slave gang hoeing and planting sugar cane. Though this drawing was made only a few years before the Emancipation in the British West Indies, the highly organized, almost industrial character of field labor probably typified the slave-based Caribbean plantation from its very beginnings more than three centuries earlier. *(British Library)*

This fanciful drawing, from *De Americae* (Part V, 1595), by the engraver Theodor de Bry, illustrates a text by Girolamo Benzoni on the sugar-cane industry in Santo Domingo. Benzoni, an Italian adventurer, visited the New World in the years 1541–55, and his account, *La Historia del mondo nuovo* (1565), is one of the earliest we have for the Caribbean. In this depiction the workers resemble Classical Greeks more than Africans or Indians, and the cane processing is confusingly presented: a "mill" at the upper right shows only a sluice and a water wheel, while the device inside the shed is an edge-roller, long employed in Europe to crush olives and apples and in India and elsewhere to crush cane, but whose use is not documented for the New World.

This engraving, from César de Rochefort's *Histoire naturelle et morale des Antilles* (1681), is signed "A.W. delin" (presumably *delineavit*), but A.W. is unidentified. The kind of sugar mill design it shows was retained for centuries.

Two interior views of nineteenth-century sugar boiling-houses, by R. Bridgens (above) and W. Clark (below). Once again, the time-conscious, disciplined, industrial character of sugar manufacture is suggested.
(*British Library*)

A contemporary sugar mill in the Dominican Republic. Closely resembling their predecessors going back several centuries, such mills are still to be found in the Caribbean, as well as on the South American mainland. The final product is a coarse brown sugar popular in the traditional cuisines of many regions. *(Bonnie Sharpe)*

The Sugar Hogshead, by E. T. Parris (1846). Sugar shipped in great barrels such as this was dispensed by local grocers. Parris, a sentimental and rather undistinguished artist, painted many such London scenes. The children, drawn like flies to the now-empty barrel, reveal nicely how important sugar had become in the nineteenth-century British diet.

These elegant nineteenth-century desserts, illustrations from the cookbooks of the French bakers Dubois and Bernard, reveal the niche in *haute cuisine* that developed after sugar lost its special symbolic potency and became a relatively inexpensive commodity. *(Centre de Documentation du Sucre)*

Sugar as a spice or condiment alters the flavor of food as does any other spice—saffron, say, or sage, or nutmeg—but without clearly sweetening it. So much sucrose is now used in the modern world that such restricted use may seem unlikely, but any experienced cook is familiar with this archaic practice. Sugar as a decorative material must first be mixed with other substances, such as gum arabic (extracted from the trees *Acacia senegal* and *Acacia arabica*, among others), oil, water, or, often, ground nuts (particularly blanched almonds); it can then be made into a pliable, claylike or pastelike solid, which can be molded before hardening; once firm, it can be decorated, painted, and displayed before being eaten. Such derivative practices may well have first arisen from sugar's uses in medicine, and the observations of its nature recorded by physicians. It seems certain that sugar was first known in England as spice and as medicine, however, and its medicinal usefulness persisted for centuries—indeed it has never been entirely lost, though it figures far less importantly in modern practice. Sugar as sweetener seems glaringly obvious to us; but the shift from spice to sweetener was historically important, and sugar use in Britain changed qualitatively when this became economically possible. Finally, preserving may have been one of sugar's oldest purposes, and in English history this function was always important, but became qualitatively and quantitatively different in modern times.

A moment's reflection shows why these uses overlap. While sugar used decoratively was usually eaten after display, that used to coat medicines was both preservative and medicinal. Fruit preserved in syrup or in semicrystalline sugar was eaten together with its coating, which of course was sweet as well. Yet we can still observe that uses were added on and occasionally discarded as the volume of sugar consumed steadily increased. Differences in quantity and in form of consumption expressed social and economic differences within the national population.

When it was first introduced into Europe around 1100 A.D., sugar was grouped with spices—pepper, nutmeg, mace, ginger, cardamom, coriander, galingale (related to ginger), saffron, and the like. Most of these were rare and expensive tropical (and exotic) imports, used sparingly by those who could afford them at all.[14] In the modern world, sweetness is not a "spice taste," but is counterposed to other tastes of all kinds (bitter as in "bittersweet," sour as in "sweet and sour," piquant as in "hot sausage" and "sweet sausage"), so that today it is difficult to view sugar as a condiment or spice. But long before most north Europeans came to know of it, sugar was consumed in large quantities as a medicine and spice in the eastern Mediterranean, in Egypt, and across North Africa. Its medical utility had already been firmly established by physicians of the time— including Islamized Jews, Persians, and Nestorian Christians, working across the Islamic world from India to Spain—and it entered slowly into European medical practice via Arab pharmacology.

As a spice sugar was prized among the wealthy and powerful of western Europe, at least from the Crusades onward. By "spice" is meant here that class of "aromatic vegetable productions," to quote Webster's definition, "used in cooking to season food and flavor sauces, pickles, etc." We are accustomed not to thinking of sugar as spice, but, rather, to thinking of "sugar *and* spice." This habit of mind attests to the significant changes in the use and meanings of sugar, in the relationship between sugar and spices, and in the place of sweetness in western food systems that have occurred since 1100.

In the fourteenth century—by which time we can detail with some confidence the place of sugar in English households—Joinville's *Chronicle* touchingly betrays European ignorance of the origin and nature of spices, among which sugar was then still included. Impressed by the Nile, which he believed to originate in some far-off earthly paradise, Joinville describes it thus:

> Before the river enters into Egypt, people who are accustomed to do so, cast their nets outspread into the river, at night; and when morning comes, they find in their nets such goods as are sold by weight, and brought into the land, viz., ginger, rhubarb, wood of aloes, and cinnamon. And it is said that these things come from the earthly Paradise, just as the wind blows down the dry wood in the forests of our own land; and the dry wood of the trees in Paradise that thus falls into the river is sold to us by the merchants.[15]

Whether or not this friend and biographer of Saint Louis truly believed that spices were fished out of the Nile, his description charmingly confirms the exotic character of spices, which were (like sugar) mostly tropical in origin.

Various explanations have been advanced for the popularity of spices among the privileged of Europe, particularly the chronic scarcity of winter fodder before about 1500, which led to heavy fall butchering and the consequent need to eat meats that were cured, salted, smoked, spiced, and sometimes rotten. But perhaps it is enough simply to remind ourselves how pleasantly aromatic, pungent, and salty, sour, bitter, oily, piquant, and other tasty substances can relieve a monotonous diet. And spices can also aid in digestion. Even when people do not have enough to eat, they can become bored with their food. The rich and powerful of Europe gave evidence of their desire to make their diet digestible, varied, contrastive, and—in their own view of things—savory:

> The reason for the immoderate use of spices may be found in part in the current opinions on diet in the Middle Ages. Most men know that the enormous amount of meat served for a feast, or even for an ordinary meal, imposed a heavy burden upon the digestion, and hence they used cinnamon and cardamom and ginger and many other spices to whip up the action of the stomach. Even when not at table they made free use of spiced comfits, partly for the sake of aiding digestion and partly to gratify the appetite. One may well believe, too, that at a time when overkept meats and fish were freely used, spice was employed to cover up the incipient decay. At all events, whatever the reason, most dishes were smothered in spices, whether needed or not. As a rule, possibly because of its provenance from the East, sugar was classed with spices.[16]

Sugar figures importantly in these usages. Adam de Moleyns's *Libelle of Englyshe Polycye* (1436), a paean to English sea power, belittled most imports via Venice—but not sugar:

> *The grete galees of Venees and Florence*
> *Be wel ladene wyth thynges of complacence,*
> *All spicerye and other grocers ward,*

Wyth swete wynes, all manere of chaffare,
Apes and japes and marmusettes taylede,
Niffles, trifles that litell have availed,
And thynges wyth whiche they fetely blere oure eye,
Wyth thynges not endurynge that we bye.

Even the imported drugs were unessential, thought de Moleynes; but he adds:

And yf there shulde excepte by ony thynge,
It were but sugre, trust to my seyinge.[17]

In the earliest English cook books of which we have record, the place of sugar as flavoring or spice is unmistakable, and that use can be documented in some detail. But the first written mention of sugar, if we omit the Venerable Bede, is in the pipe rolls—the official records of royal income and expenditures—of Henry II (1154–89). This sugar was used as a condiment in cooking and was purchased directly for the court. The quantities involved must have been very small: only royalty and the very rich could have afforded sugar at the time. In 1226, Henry III requested the mayor of Winchester to get him three pounds of Alexandrian (Egyptian) sugar, if so much could be had at one time from the merchants at the great Winchester fair.[18]

During the thirteenth century, sugar was sold both by the loaf and by the pound, and though its price put it beyond the reach of all but the wealthiest, it could be procured even in remote towns.[19] The sugar of Beza, we are told, was the kind most commonly in use; "that from the marts of Cyprus and Alexandria was in higher esteem."[20] But sugar names in those early centuries were also attributions, such as the "Zuker Marrokes" of the account rolls for 1299, the "sugre of Sicilis," and "Barbarye sugar"—all among the Oxford Dictionary citations. By 1243, Henry III was able to order the purchase of 300 pounds of "zucre de Roche," presumably lump sugar, among other spices.[21] By 1287, during the reign of Edward I, the royal household used 677 pounds of ordinary sugar, as well as 300 pounds of violet sugar and 1,900 pounds of rose sugar.[22]

The following year the sugar consumption of the royal household climbed sharply, to 6,258 pounds.[23]

Precious though it was, sugar's popularity as a spice was already spreading. The countess of Leicester's remarkable seven-month account in 1265, which the historian Margaret Labarge used in her rich description of a baronial household, mentions sugar frequently. "It used to be thought," writes Labarge, "that sugar was unknown until later in the Middle Ages, and that only honey was employed for sweetening; but a close study of accounts shows that sugar was in continuous use in wealthy households by the middle of the thirteenth century."[24] Bishop Swinfield's household account for 1289–90 mentions the purchase of "more than one hundred pounds of sugar—mostly in coarse loaves—and also of liquorice and twelve pounds of sweetmeats."[25] The bishop of Hereford's household roll for the same year shows sugar purchased in Hereford and Ross-on-Wye.[26]

The countess's records note both "ordinary sugar" and powdered white sugar. The "ordinary sugar" was presumably in crystalline loaves, only imperfectly refined; the whiter the product, the more expensive it was. During those seven months in 1265 for which we know the countess's household expenditures, fifty-five pounds of sugar (of both types) were purchased. But the countess's household also used fifty-three pounds of pepper (presumably *Piper nigrum*, or Indian peppercorns) during the same period, which may support the view that sugar was used as a condiment.

The quantities of various sugars imported gradually increased during the subsequent century, but it seems certain that this was because the privileged classes were consuming more, not because its uses were spreading downward. By the early fifteenth century, sugar cargoes had become substantial—Alexander Dordo's galley brought twenty-three cases in 1443, some more refined ("kute"—later, "cute," from the French *cuit*) than the rest. Less refined brown sugar, partially cleaned and crystallized, was imported in chests—the "casson sugar," later called "cassonade," one finds in the inventory lists of grocers in the mid-fifteenth century. This sugar could be refined further, but commercial refineries do not appear in England for another century.

Molasses, which apparently reached England by the late thirteenth century, was distinguished from other sugar forms. It came from Sicily, where it was fabricated together with brown and other sugars; it had begun to be shipped by Venetian merchants on the Flanders galleys making their annual voyages.[27] (Of rum manufactured by distilling from molasses there is no mention before the early seventeenth century.[28])

Toward the end of the fifteenth century, when Atlantic-island sugar production was supplanting North African and Mediterranean sugars, there was some price decline, but prices rose again in the mid-sixteenth century. At best, sugars were still costly imports; and though they were becoming important in the feasts and rituals of the powerful, they were still beyond the reach of nearly everyone—luxuries, rather than commodities. A shopkeeper whose stock has been described for the year 1446 carried saffron, saunders (powdered sandalwood, used as a spice more than as a scent), and sugar, as well as spectacles, caps for chaplains and priests, and the like—hardly everyday necessities.[29] But that sugars were already of substantial importance to the wealthy and powerful is easily documented. The first English cook books to provide recipes date from the late fourteenth century, by which time sugar was known among the privileged classes in England and used by them. These recipes make clear that sugar was perceived as a segment of a taste spectrum—not a quadrangle or tetrahedron—that might enhance or conceal the underlying tastes of the food. The somewhat indiscriminate use of sugar in flesh, fish, vegetable, and other dishes is evidence that sugar was regarded as a spice at the time.

William Hazlitt, who read and interpreted many early cook books, shows his disdain for "the unnatural union of flesh with sweets," the source of which he locates (probably inaccurately) in "the prehistoric bag pudding of King Arthur": "That wedlock of fruit with animal matter—fat and plums—which we post-Arthurians eye with a certain fastidious repugnance, but which, notwithstanding, lingered on to the Elizabethan or Jacobean era—nay, did not make the gorge of our grandsires turn rebellious."[30] Hazlitt confesses that this "wedlock" never wholly vanished from English cuisine. But he was wrong to treat it as some continuous tradition traceable to a semimythical past, and to suppose, as he puts it, that "it survives among ourselves only in the modified shape of such accessories as currant jelly and apple sauce."[31]

A striking feature of the sugar uses of the late fourteenth century is sugar's frequent combination with honey, as if the tastes of the two substances were not only different (which, of course, they are) but also mutually beneficial. Here again, however, the condimental character of these sweet substances is revealed in the recipes themselves, which call for sauces used on fish or meat; salted, heavily spiced solids whose base is rice flour; spicy drinks that are to be "allayed" with refined sugar if they are overspiced; and so on.[32]

Sugar and other spices were combined in dishes that tasted neither exclusively nor preponderantly sweet. Often, food was reduced by pounding and mashing, and so heavily spiced that its distinctive taste was concealed: "Nearly every dish, whatever its name, was soft and mushy, with its principal ingredients disguised by the addition of wine or spices or vegetables. Practically everything had to be mashed or cut into small pieces and mixed with something else, preferably of so strong a flavour as to disguise the taste of most of the other ingredients."[33] Perhaps this was because of the absence of forks at the table; but that hardly explains the seasoning. In his discussion of medieval English cuisine, the British historian William Mead lists few recipes without sugar, and, like Hazlitt, he seems offended by the presence of sugar. "Everyone is aware," he tells us, "that nothing is more sickening than an oyster sprinkled with sugar. Yet we have more than one old receipt recommending such a combination."[34] The recipe he cites, however ("Oyster in gravy Bastard"), combines the oyster liquor, ale, bread, ginger, saffron, and powdered pepper and salt, along with sugar; since the proportions are unspecified, there is no certainty that the oysters actually tasted sweet. Admittedly, they must have tasted little like oysters as we know them. But admirers of Oysters Rockefeller and kindred wonders may not be quite so shocked as Mead.

Perhaps authors such as Hazlitt and Mead are objecting not so much to the taste of sweetness as to the conjunction of sweetness with other tastes. That such preferences can change over time and even at a very rapid rate seems certain. Whereas Mead deplores the use of sugar with fried pork—"Such delicacies," he says, "are not for our time"[35]—Thomas Austin's late-nineteenth-century notes to *Two Fifteenth-Century Cookery-Books* recount that pork "was quite lately taken with it [sugar] at St. John's College, Oxford."[36] From *The Forme of Cury*, compiled around 1390 by the master cooks of Richard II, come scores of recipes that illustrate well the spice character of sugar. "Egurdouce" (*aigredouce* in French) was made using rabbit or kid with a sweet-and-sour sauce, as follows:

> Take conynges or kydde and smyte hem on pecys rawe; and frye hem in white grece. Take raysons of corannce and fry hem, take oynonns parboile hem, and hewe hem small and fry him; take rede wyne, sugar, with powdor of pepor, of gynger, of canel, salt, and cast thereto; and let it seeth with a gode quantite of white grece, and serve it forth.[37]

Even more illustrative is the recipe for "Chykens in cawdel":

> Take chykenns and boile hem in gode broth, and ramme him up [bruised, and pressed close together]. Thenne take zolkes of ayren[eggs], and the broth, and alye [mix] it togedre. Do thereto powdor of gynger, and sugar ynowh [enough], safronn and salt; and set it over the fyre withoute boyllynge, and serve the chykens hole, other ybroken [or cut up], and lay the sowe [sauce] onoward.[38]

Though there are many recipes in which sugar figures as a principal ingredient, especially for pastries and wines, those based on meat, fish, fowl, or vegetables usually list sugar with such ingredients as cinnamon, ginger, saffron, salt, galingale, and saunders, if they include it at all.

This usage of sugar as spice may have reached some sort of peak in the sixteenth century. Soon thereafter, prices, supplies, and customary uses began changing rapidly and radically. It is not surprising that the spice use of sugar tended to disappear as sugar itself became more plentiful. But the condimental use of sugar survives in a number of fringe areas that deserve mention in passing. Cookies or biscuits associated with the holiday seasons commonly combine sugar and spices (ginger, cinnamon, and pepper, for instance) in ancient ways; similar usages apply to holiday fowl, such as ducks or geese, with which fruit jams, brown sugar, and sweet sauces are combined; and to hams, commonly prepared with cloves, mustard, brown sugar, and other special flavorings for festive treats. Yet this apparent gravitation of sugar to ceremonial usages is deceptive. Rather than being some shift in usage, these condimental associations merely demonstrate what anthropologists have long contended—that holidays often preserve what the everyday loses. The world in which sugar was used primarily as a spice is long vanished; now sugar is all about us. Like tipping one's hat or saying grace, baking and eating gingerbread is a way of reaching back.

By the sixteenth century, the habit of using sugar as decoration, spreading through continental Europe from North Africa and particularly Egypt, began to percolate downward from the nobility. To understand this decorative use, we need to touch briefly on two aspects of sugar making. First, pure sucrose is white. To make modern white sugar, one boils off water until the sucrose crystallizes and impurities are removed; after a few more (complex) steps, the molasses is removed from the brown crystals by centrifugation. But early sugars could not be refined to the whiteness of modern sugars, since the refining techniques were limited. They weren't very white, and the whiter, the more expensive. European preferences for the whitest sugars may have been imitations of the tastes of the Arabs, among whom sugar consumption was already an ancient habit. But the association between whiteness and purity was also ancient in Europe. Because of it, white sugar was commonly prescribed in medicines, and combinations of white foods (chicken, cream, etc.) at times enjoyed a popularity out of all proportion to their therapeutic efficacy.

Second, sugar is preservable, the more so when it is highly refined. Insects and animals may eat it, of course, and it cannot withstand long exposure to moisture, but it bears remembering that under favorable circumstances substances made with sugar can be durable.

To these two features of sugar we may add another: the relative ease with which other edibles can be combined with it, whether in solid or in liquid form. Among these, one additive of the greatest importance in European usage, and clearly diffused from the Middle East and North Africa, was the almond. Though marzipan in Europe cannot be documented earlier than the end of the twelfth century,[39] it was known and fabricated in the Middle East before then. Sugar was also combined with oil of almonds, with rice, with scented waters, and with various gums. Recipes for these combinations abound in sixteenth- and seventeenth-century texts; though they are not readily traceable to specific Egyptian recipes, a connection (via Venice in particular) seems likely.

The important feature of these recipes is that the resulting pastes were used to sculpture forms—forms having an aesthetic aspect but also preservable and edible. The eleventh-century caliph al-Zahir, we are told, in spite of famine, inflation, and plague, celebrated the Islamic feast days with "art works from the sugar bakers," which included 157 figures and seven large (table-sized!) palaces, all made of sugar. Nasir-i-Chosrau, a Persian visitor who traveled in Egypt in 1040 A.D., reports that the sultan used up 73,300 kilos of sugar for Ramadan—upon his festive table, we are told, there stood an entire tree made of sugar, and other large displays. And al-Guzuli (d. 1412) gives a remarkable account of the caliph's celebration, at which a mosque was built entirely of sugar and beggars were invited in at the close of the festivities to eat it.[40]

Not surprisingly, analogous practices soon spread to Europe. Marchpane (marzipan) and marchpanelike pastes were used at royal French feasts in the thirteenth century.[41] Soon continental waferers and confectioners crossed from France to England, to practice their arts there. The confections were based primarily on the combination of sugar with oil, crushed nuts, and vegetable gums, to make a plastic, claylike substance. It was possible to sculpture an object out of this sweet, preservable "clay" on any scale and in nearly any form, and to bake or harden it. Such displays, called "subtleties," served to mark intervals between banquet "courses," but each such course actually consisted of several different dishes. Thus, for instance, at the marriage of Henry IV and Joan of Navarre in 1403, three courses of "meat" (each consisting of several dishes, in fact, not all of them meat) were followed by three courses of "fish," and each set concluded with a "sotelte," as follows:

First Course

Fylettes in galentyne.—Vyand ryall [a dish prepared with rice, spices, wine, and honey]—Gross chare: [beef or mutton]—Sygnettes—Capoun of haut grece:—Chewetys [pudding]—a sotelte.[42]

The subtleties were in the form of animals, objects, buildings, etc., and because sugar was desirable and expensive, they were admired and eaten. But the preciousness of the ingredients, and the large quantities required, confined such practices at first to the king, the nobility, the knighthood, and the church. Initially, the displays were important simply because they were both pretty and edible. But over time, the creative impulses of the confectioners were pressed into essentially political symbolic service, and the subtleties took on greater significance. "Not only compliments," writes one commentator, "but even sly rebukes to heretics and politicians were conveyed in these sugared emblems."[43] For royalty, what had begun as "Conserves and marchpanes made in sundry shapes, as castles, towers, horses, bears and apes," were transformed into message-bearing objects that could be used to make a special point. At the coronation of Henry VI, two quite different subtleties, fully described in the literature, dramatize the strange significance of a food that could be sculptured, written upon, admired, and read before it was eaten. One was:

A sotyltie of Seynt Edwarde and Seynt Lowys armyd, and upon eyther his cote armoure, holdynge atwene them a figure lyke unto kynge Henry, standynge also in his cote armour, and a scripture passynge from them both, sayinge: "beholde ii. parfyght kinges under one cote armour."

The other was a "warner"—one of the names used for a subtlety, usually when it preceded a "course"—directed against the Lollards, religious dissenters. This was "of the emperor and the kynge that ded is, armed, and their mantels of garters, and the king that now is, kneeling before them with this reason":

Ayeinst miscreants the emperor Sigismund
Hath shewid his myghte, which is Imperial;

Sithen Henry V. so noble a knyght was founde
For Christ's cause in actis martial.
Cherisshyng the chirch, Lollardes had a falle,
To give example to kynges that suited....[44]

Similar displays followed each course, their accompanying texts confirming the king's rights and privileges, his power, and sometimes his intent. The highly privileged nature of such display rested on the rarity of the substances used; almost no one except a king could afford such quantities. But to be able to provide one's guests with attractive food, which also embodied in display the host's wealth, power, and status, must have been a special pleasure for the sovereign. By eating these strange symbols of his power, his guests validated that power.

The connection between elaborate manufactures of sweet edibles and the validation of social position is clear. Before too long, one commentator was at pains to explain that merchants now picked and chose the foods they would serve at their feasts with such care that they were "often comparable to the nobility of the land":

> In such cases also, jellies of all colours, mixed with a variety in the representation of sundry flowers, herbs, trees, forms of beasts, fish, fowl, and fruits, and thereunto marchpane wrought with no small curiosity, tarts of divers hues and sundry denominations, conserves of old fruits, foreign and home bred, suckets, codinacs, marmalades, marchpane, sugarbread, gingerbread, florentines, wild fowls, venison of all sorts, and sundry outlandish confections, altogether sweetened with sugar.[45]

By the sixteenth century, merchants as well as kings were showmen and consumers.

As a still-scarce substance associated with foreign trade, the nobility, and sumptuary distinction, sugar had become desirable almost as soon as its importation was stabilized in the fourteenth century. But it was not simply as a spice or as an item of direct consumption that sugar was appealing. At the same time that sugars were becoming more commonly used by the powerful, the links between such consumption and the mercantile sinews of the kingdom were becoming more intimate. And as sugar came closer to the ceremonial nexus of certain forms of consumption, it acquired greater symbolic weight or "voltage" in English life.

Thomas Warton's *History of English Poetry* incidentally documents the growing importance of the feast as a form of symbolic validation of powers and authority, even among scholars and clerics, as early as the fifteenth century:

> These scholastic banquets grew to such excess that it was ordered in the year 1434, that no inceptor in arts should expend more than "3000 grossos Turonenses." ... Notwithstanding, Neville, afterwards Bishop of York, on his admission to the degree of master of arts in 1452, feasted the academics and many strangers for two successive days, at two entertainments, consisting of nine hundred costly dishes.... Nor was this reverence to learning, and attention to its institutions, confined to the circle of our universities.
>
> Such was the pedantry of the times, that in the year 1503, archbishop Wareham, chancellor at Oxford, at his feast of inthronisation, ordered to be introduced in the first course a curious dish, in which were exhibited the eight towers of the university. In every tower stood a bedell; and under the towers were figures of the king, to whom the chancellor Wareham, encircled with many doctors properly habited, presented four Latin Verses, which were answered by his majesty.

The "curious dish" was a subtlety constructed entirely of sugar.[46]

Certainly by the late sixteenth century, and probably even earlier, the creation of subtleties—however modest—occurred in families that, though still well within the upper stratum of English society, were neither noble nor exceedingly wealthy. Partridge's classic sixteenth-century cook book (1584), devoted largely to recipes in which sugar figures as a condiment (to bake chicken, fry vegetable marrow, season a roast rabbit, or bake an ox tongue), also contains recipes such as that for marchpane, which appears more or less completely plagiarized in many other cook books thereafter:

> Take...blanched almonds...white suger...Rosewater...and Damask water.... Beate the Almondes with a little of the same water, and grind them till they be small: set them on a few coales of fyre, till they waxe thicke, then beate them again with the sugar, fine.... mix the sweet waters and them together, and...

fashion your Marchpane. Then take wafer cakes.... Have redy
a hoope of greene Hazell wand.... Lay this hoope upon your
wafer cakes.... Cut away all the parts of the Cakes.... Set it upon
a warm hearth... and ye maye while it is moysse stiche it full of
Comfets, of sundrie colours. If it be thorough dryed...a Marchpane will last many yeares. It is a comfortable meate, meete for
weake folkes, such as have lost the taste of meates by much and
long sicknesse....[47]

Here sugar is combined with other substances in a decorative
sweetmeat that will keep indefinitely, and supposedly possesses special medicinal qualities—enough to suggest why a simple classification of sugar by its different uses is difficult. In later chapters,
Partridge makes more explicit his stress on decoration. Sweetmeats
are decorated with animal forms and words, cut from gold leaf (the
link between sugar and gold, in combination with such rarities as
almonds and rosewater, is significant). He instructs his readers to
combine gum dragant with rosewater, to which is added lemon
juice, egg white, and "fine white suger, well beaten to powder," to
make a soft paste. "This can then be formed into objects—all manner of fruites and other fine things, with their forme, as platters,
dishes, glasses, cuppes, and suchlike things wherewith you may
furnish a table." Once made and admired, these objects can then
be eaten by the guests: "At the end of the Banquet, they maye eate
all, and breake the platters, Dishes, Glasses, Cups, and all things,
for this paste is very delicate and savourous."[48]

Cook books in succeeding decades enlarged upon Partridge's techniques. Sir Hugh Platt's *Accomplisht ladys delight in preserving,*
physick and cookery first appeared soon after Partridge's book, and
went through at least eleven highly successful editions. It provides
detailed instructions for making "conceits in sugar-works," including "Buttons, Beakes, Charms, Snakes, Snailes, Frogs, Roses, Chives,
Shooes, Slippers, Keyes, Knives, Gloves, Letters, Knots, or any other
Iumball for a banquet quicklie."[49]

By 1660, subtleties were being prescribed for the wealthy on a
scale that dwarfed the "Buttons, Beakes, Charms, and Snakes."
Robert May was a professional cook who lived during the reigns
of Elizabeth, James I, Charles I, Cromwell, and Charles II, when

subtleties were an unfailing accompaniment to every feast. May wrote for wealthy commoners, and his recipes suggest a real attempt to ape the pretensions of royalty—a kind of confectioner's *lèse majesté*. "Make the likeness of a ship in paste-board," he advises those who, while rich, still cannot afford to make their subtleties entirely of marzipan. Then he maps out in exquisite detail an astounding display of sugar sculpture, complete with a stag that "bleeds" claret wine when an arrow is removed from its flank, a castle that fires its artillery at a man-of-war, gilded sugar pies filled with live frogs and birds, and much else. May's display ends with the ladies' tossing eggshells full of scented water at one another to counteract the smell of gunpowder. "These were formerly the delights of the Nobility," he tells his readers, "before good-housekeeping had left England, and the sword really acted that which was only counterfeited in such honest and laudable Exercises as these."[50]

While kings and archbishops were displaying magnificent sugar castles and mounted knights, the aspiring upper classes began to combine "course paste" men-of-war with marzipan guns to achieve analogous social effects at their festive tables. Some of these people were probably only newly ennobled; others were prosperous merchants or gentry. The techniques used to impress their guests and validate their status through consumption continued on a downward percolation—even though most of the creations lacked the majesty of an earlier era. By 1747, when the first edition of Mrs. Hannah Glasse's famous *The Art of Cookery* appeared, at least two recipes are included in the category of subtlety—though properly modified to fit the means of her customers. The first, for what are called "jumballs" (Sir Hugh Platt's "Iumball" of more than a century earlier), combines flour, sugar, egg whites, butter, and almonds, kneaded with rosewater and baked. Jumballs were then cut into the desired shapes: "cut your Jumball in what figures you fancy.... If you make them in pretty figures, they make a fine little dish."[51] Mrs. Glasse's other recipe is for "Hedgehog"—a marzipan confection meant to be admired before it is eaten, composed of crushed almonds, orange-flower water, egg yolks, sugar, and butter, made into a paste, and molded into the form of a hedgehog: "Then stick it full of blanched almonds slit, and stuck up like the Brissels of a Hedge-Hog." A yet more elaborate version, made with saffron, sorrel, nutmeg, mace, citron, and orange peel (cochineal in place of saffron, if saffron is too dear), was sent "hot to Table for a first course"!

Mrs. Glasse's special confectionery cookbook of 1760 included elaborate displays, graced with as many as ten different dessert items. The tables were decorated with ornaments "bought at the confectioners, and will serve year after year." There are hedges, gravel walks, "a little Chinese temple," and the top, bottom, and sides of the display were arrayed with "fruits, nuts of all kinds, creams, jellies, syllabubs, biscuits, etc., etc. and as many plates as you please, according to the size of the table." This all seems a far cry from the festive tables of Henry IV or Archbishop Warham. But it was also a good while later, when sugar had become relatively cheaper and more plentiful, and its function as a marker of rank had descended to the middle classes.

The Reverend Richard Warner, who compiled several early cookery tracts in his *Antiquitates Culinariae*, was keenly aware of the transformation of regal subtleties into bourgeois entertainments. "It seems probable," he writes, "that the splendid desert frames of our days, ornamented with quaint and heterogeneous combinations of Chinese architecture, Arcadian swains, fowl, fish, beasts, and fanciful representations drawn from Heathen mythology, are only the *remains of*, or, if more agreeable to the modern ear, *refinements on*, the Old English Sotiltees."[52]

It is no longer considered a sign of elevated rank to stuff one's guests with sugar—at least in most social groups and on most social occasions in the western world. Few allegories are any longer created at table, and writing in sugar is largely confined to Saint Valentine's Day, Christmas, birthdays, and weddings. But the confinement of sugar to somewhat narrower symbolic spheres was accompanied by its permeation of everyday life in other forms, attesting to the increased significance of sugar rather than the opposite. And sugars in such archaic forms as gingerbread houses, candy hearts, candy corn, and molded chickens and rabbits, once the playthings of the court and the wealthy, have now become the playthings of children.

The decline in the symbolic importance of sugar has kept almost perfect step with the increase in its economic and dietary importance. As sugar became cheaper and more plentiful, its potency as a symbol of power declined while its potency as a source of profit gradually increased. Hence, to speak of the decline of its symbolic importance is, in one sense, to speak in riddles. One must add a query: *for whom* has its symbolic importance declined? Without projecting symbols against the differentiated class structures of the societies within which they are being manipulated, we cannot illuminate the link between sweetness and power.

The frogs and birds that once sprang out of hot pies are no more; the famous dwarf who stepped forth from a cold pastry brandishing a sword and saluting Charles I and his new queen was the last of his kind; with four-and-twenty blackbirds there went the castles of marzipan. By the nineteenth century, culinary drama of this sort had lost most of its appeal, even for the middle classes. But old meanings diffused downward in society and new ones emerged.

As the spread of sugar downward and outward meant that it lost some of its power to distinguish those who consumed it, it became a new substance. In the eighteenth century, producing, shipping, refining, and taxing sugar became proportionately more effective sources of power for the powerful, since the sums of money involved were so much larger. Almost inevitably, sugar lost many of its special meanings when the poor were also able to eat it. But later, making sugar available in ever-larger quantities to the poor became patriotic as well as profitable.

Recent writers have emphasized the luxury status in England of early imports like sugar, which were eventually supplemented by the mass importation of more familiar food staples, such as fruits and grains.[53] In reaction, others have argued that the luxury/staple contrast tends to gloss over the great social importance of the so-called luxuries in establishing and maintaining social links among the powerful. "The relationship of trade to social stratification," the anthropologist Jane Schneider writes, "was not just a matter of an elevated group distinguishing itself through the careful application of sumptuary laws and a monopoly of symbols of status; it further involved the direct and self-conscious manipulation of various semiperipheral and middle level groups through patronage, bestowals, and the calculated distribution of exotic and valued goods."[54] This point is well taken, for the importance of a "luxury" like sugar cannot be judged by its bulk or weight, or without attention to the part it played in the social life of the powerful. The particular nature and the specific, culturally conventionalized uses of each such luxury are thus highly relevant to its importance. To put it differently, sugar and gold were both luxury imports; as medicines, they even overlapped slightly in use. But it was not possible to produce them in like quantities or to confine their uses to the same sphere. And while it is true that gold would one day be bought and sold in somewhat humbler strata, it can neither be produced nor be consumed as sugar is. Unless we look at the intrinsic—the "culturally usable"—character of a luxury, its meaning cannot be fully understood. As for sugar, it was *transformed* from a luxury of kings into the kingly luxury of commoners—a purchased luxury that could be detached from one status and transferred in use to another. Thus understood, sugar became, among other things, a spurious leveler of status. As this was occurring, of course, the rich and powerful were beginning to repudiate their consumption of a product the older symbolic meaning of which was being steadily emptied of its potency.

Sugar's special status as a medicine was largely incidental to the transmission of medicinal lore concerning it from classical texts to medieval Europe by way of Islam. The relatively meager reference to sugar in Greek texts is of interest, given that Galenic theory prevailed in European medicine for centuries after the Crusades. As far as the actual substances the terms were meant to stand for are concerned, there is uncertainty, and Greek knowledge of sugar— sucrose fabricated from the juice of the sugar cane—is questionable. But there is no doubt that the Moslem, Jewish, and Christian physicians from Persia to Spain who were the major interpreters of humoral medicine to the Europeans knew sucrose. (Spain [especially Toledo], Salerno [Sicily], and Gondeshapur [in deltaic Khuzestan, Persia] were the principal centers.) Certainly it was they, most of all, who brought sugar and its medicinal uses into European practice, incorporating sucrose into the Greek medical system they had adopted and adapted, in which it had figured only obscurely.

Because sugar has become controversial in modern discussions of health, diet, and nutrition, it may be difficult to imagine its having once been a wonder drug or panacea. But that epoch is not so remote. A ninth-century Arab manuscript from Iraq (*Al-Tabaṣṣur bi-l-tiğāra*: Concerning Clarity in Commercial Matters) documents the production of sugar from cane in Persia and Turkestan.[55] It describes musk and sweet sugar cane carried from the city of Khiva, in Khwarizm (Chorasmia); sugar candy from the Persian Gulf city of Ahwaz; fruit syrups, quince, and saffron from Isfahan, in central Persia; rosewater, syrups, water-lily ointment, and jasmine ointment from the province of Fars (probably Shiraz); even candied capers, from Bushari (Bushehr), near Ahwaz. Carried westward by the Arabs along with the cane itself, these products entered Europe as spices or *materia medica* via Spain, together with other innovations, including the lime, bitter orange, lemon, banana, tamarind, cassia, and myrobalan. All figured in medical preparations, but among them sugar stands out conspicuously. In the works of al-Kindi, al-Tabari, Abu'l-Dasim, and other writers in Arabic between the tenth and fourteenth centuries, sugar figures as one of the most important medicinal ingredients.

Arabic pharmacology was organized in terms of the medical formulary (*aqrābādhīn*), divided into sections or chapters on different sorts of pharmaceuticals. "The aqrābādhīn," writes the historian of Arab pharmacology Martin Levey, "may be considered to have had its organizational origin in Galen's *De Compositione medicamentorum*; surprisingly, it persisted well into the nineteenth century as a form of pharmacological literature."[56] Classified by type of preparation, these formularies provide a remarkable view of the medical role of sugar. One category was the syrup (*shurba* in Arabic): "a juice concentrated to a certain viscosity so that when two fingers were dipped into it, it behaved as a semi-solid when the digits were opened. Very often sugar and/or honey were added as thickeners and sweeteners."[57] Another category, the rob (*rubb* in Arabic), was similar: to prepare it, fruits and flower petals were immersed in hot water to which sugar was added, and the whole preparation was boiled down until it was concentrated. The julep (Arabic *julāb*, from the Persian gul + āb ["rose" + "water"]) was less thick than the rob—"Frequently, sugar was added to it."[58] Other categories included lohochs, decoctions, infusions, fomentations, powders, confections, electuaries, hieras, trypheras (aromatic electuaries), theriacs, etc. Sugar figures in some specific compounds in *every category*, and importantly so in many of them.[59]

We have seen that a term for what may be sugar is present in the original texts of Galen and Hippocrates, but mention is rare and vague enough to raise questions about its specific identity. Hence the introduction of sugar into Galenic practice—at least on a substantial scale—probably meant a significant addition to the Greco-Roman pharmacology that Islamic doctors were busily transmitting. Europe's acceptance of Arab science was considerable, by way of Latin translations of Arab texts, through the traditions of the School of Salernum (Salerno) via Spain, especially in the period 1000–1300 A.D., and through the Byzantine Empire. Scholars like the Persian Avicenna (ibn-Sina, 980–1037)—known for his assertion *"apud me in eis, quae dulcia sunt, non est malum!"* ("As far as I am concerned, sweetmeats are [always] good!")—who wrote the *Canon medicinae Avicennae* (*Qanun fi'l-tibb* in Arabic), remained authoritative in the practice of European medicine until nearly the seventeenth century.

After additional knowledge of sugar was borne back to Europe by the Crusaders, its medicinal and other uses spread. The Greek physician Simeon Seth (c. 1075) wrote of sugars as medicines; and Synesios, the eleventh-century court physician of the Byzantine emperor Manuel Comnenus, recommended rose sugar to break fever. In Italy, Constantinus Africanus (b. 1020) described medical uses for sugar, both internal and external, employing solid and liquid sugars. The *Circa Instans*, which he translated (and may have composed) while at the School of Salernum in the mid-eleventh century, epitomizes the changing medical picture in Europe itself. Western Latin translators who knew Arabic and/or Persian were beginning to make more available to northern Europe the collected medical beliefs of the Islamic world, as well as of the Greco-Roman predecessors they had inherited. In later editions of *Circa Instans* (1140–50), sugar is prescribed for fever, dry coughs, pectoral ailments, chapped lips, and stomach diseases. At this time sugar would have been available, even in the smallest quantities, only to the very rich. Honey was used in its stead for those somewhat poorer patients who could nevertheless afford some similar medication.

Not long afterward—in the thirteenth century, when some of the earliest written mentions of sugar turn up in England—prescriptions of medicinal tonics containing sugar also begin to appear. Aldebrando di Siena (d. 1287) and Arnaldus Villanovanus (1235?–1312?) both prescribed sugar frequently. It is Arnaldus who speaks of the uncommon healthfulness of *alba comestio*, which closely resembled Spain's traditional *majar blanco*, made of rice flour, milk, chicken breasts, and sugar.[60] The French *le grand cuisinier*, composed of white bread, almond milk, breast of capon, sugar, and ginger, was, similarly, food and medicine at once. Arnaldus also provides recipes for candying lemons and lemon slices, preserving pine kernels, almonds, hazelnuts, anise, ginger, coriander, and roses—all of which, he says, require the finest sugar. Again we see the differentiated uses of sugar intersecting—preservation, food, spice, decor, and medicine are tangled. The concept of sugar as medicine remained sturdy for centuries more.

In the twelfth century, the medicinal nature of sugar became the pivot upon which an important theological question turned—and this gives us an early glimpse of sugar's near invulnerability to moral attack. Were spiced sugars food? Did eating them constitute a violation of the fast? None other than Thomas Aquinas found them medicinal rather than foods: "Though they are nutritious themselves, sugared spices are nonetheless not eaten with the end in mind of nourishment, but rather for ease in digestion; accordingly, they do not break the fast any more than taking of any other medicine."[61] Aquinas thus endowed wondrous sucrose—all things to all men, protean and subtle—with a special advantage. Of all of the major tropical commodities—what I have called "drug foods"—whose consumption rose so sharply among European populations from the seventeenth to the twentieth centuries, including tea, coffee, chocolate, tobacco, rum, and sugar, only sugar escaped religious proscription. this special "secular" virtue of sucrose requires a further word.

That sugars, particularly highly refined sucrose, produce peculiar physiological effects is well known. But these effects are not so visible as those of such substances as alcohol; or caffeine-rich beverages like tea, coffee, and chocolate; or tobacco, the first use of which can trigger rapid changes in respiration, heartbeat, skin color, and so on. Though conspicuous behavioral changes occur when substantial quantities of sucrose are given to infants, particularly for the first time, these changes are far less dramatic in the case of adults. And all of these substances, sucrose included, seem to have a declining and less visible effect after prolonged or intensified use. This has nothing to do with their long-term nutritive or medical significance, but with visible, directly noticeable consequences. In all likelihood, sugar was not subject to religion-based criticisms like those pronounced on tea, coffee, rum, and tobacco, exactly because its consumption did not result in flushing, staggering, dizziness, euphoria, changes in the pitch of the voice, slurring of speech, visibly intensified physical activity, or any of the other cues associated with the ingestion of caffeine, alcohol, and nicotine.[62]

The medicinal attributes of sugar were expounded upon by other famed philosophico-medical figures besides Aquinas. Albertus Magnus, in his *De Vegetabilibus* (c. 1250–55), uses the language of humoral medicine to express a generally favorable opinion: "It is by nature moist and warm, as proved by its sweetness, and becomes dryer with age. Sugar is soothing and solving, it soothes hoarseness and pains in the breast, causes thirst (but less than honey) and sometimes vomiting, but on the whole it is good for the stomach if it is in good condition and free of bile."[63] Sucrose figured importantly in all of the supposed remedies for the Black Death. From Carl Sudhoff's essays on the Pest Books of the fourteenth century we learn, "In none of the prescriptions is sugar lacking, added as it is to the medicines of the poor, as a substitute for the costly electuaries, the precious stones and pearls to be found in the remedies for the rich."[64]

The identification of sugar with precious stones and metals reverberates with echoes of the "subtleties." What more pointed way of dramatizing privilege than the literal bodily consumption of preciosities? That one might seek to cure a physical ailment by the ingestion of crushed precious stones probably should not cause surprise. But consider this in the light of what we already know about the subtleties. To be able to destroy—literally, by consuming it—something that others desire is not a privilege alien to contemporary life and values. What may seem slightly offensive to modern bourgeois morality is its literalness. The egalitarian view is that invidious consumption ought not to be explicit, perhaps because it casts so bright a light upon the nonegalitarian motives of the consumer. When hierarchy is firm and acknowledged—when the rights of kings are considered rights by commoners—the excesses of nobility are not usually regarded as excesses. Indeed, the excesses of both nobility and poor seem more explicable, in terms of who they are, than do those of the ascendant middle classes. Inevitably, the crumbling of ancient hierarchy will affect the received morality of certain forms of consumption. Will those who have no chance of eating crushed diamonds resent the rights of those who do? Eating sugar might eventually bridge the distance between such groups. For this reason, what the consumption of sugar permits us to understand about how societies change may matter more than the consumption itself.

So useful was sugar in the medical practice of Europe from the thirteenth through the eighteenth centuries that the expression "like an apothecary without sugar" came to mean a state of utter desperation or helplessness. As sugar became more commonplace and honey more costly, the permeation of the pharmacopoeia by sucrose grew more pronounced. (The switching of honey and sugar was not limited to medicine; later their use as foods and preservatives would also be exchanged.)

But the spread of sugar as medicine also involved some important controversies. In a concise modern summary of sugars in pharmacy, Paul Pittenger, biochemist and pharmacologist, lists twenty-four uses for sucrose alone; of these, at least sixteen were almost certainly known to, and employed by, physicians of the Islamic world before the fourteenth century.[65] Given this intensive and varied use of one "medicine," first borrowed from an increasingly suspect foreign civilization, the rise of more independent medical perspectives among the physicians and pharmacists of Europe eventually led to some questioning of sugars as remedies. While European physicians never emerged as consistently antisucrose before this century, there were debates about the extent to which sugar should be relied upon in everyday medical practice. In some instances, arguments developed over the interpretations of Galenic medicine itself. Sixteenth-century criticisms of sugar by medical authorities may even have formed part of fashionable, anti-Islamic *partis pris*, common in Europe from the Crusades onward.

Miguel Serveto (Michael Servetus, 1511–53) and Leonhard Fuchs (1501–56) were the principal antagonists. Serveto, a precocious and overconfident young Spanish theologian who was to end his life at the stake (after having quite innocently turned to John Calvin for protection), was a critic of the medical syrups of the Arab world. Though he never practiced medicine, he served as an assistant in dissection, attended lectures at the University of Paris, and wrote two essays attacking the "Arabists." In the second, *On Syrups*, he charged the so-called Arabist School (especially Avicenna and Manardus) with distorting Galenic teaching.[66]

Paracelsus (1493?–1541) was also critical of the wide use of sucrose and syrups, and perhaps of their presence in Islamic formularies, but his hostility seems to have been directed more toward the doctors than toward sugar itself: "creating mixtures of good and bad, sugar combined with gall ... and their friends the apothecaries, those swill-makers who do an idiot's job by mixing drugs with sugar and honey."[67] Yet he also considered sugar "one of nature's remedies," recognized its utility as a preservative, and objected principally to its being combined with bitter medicines such as aloes or gentian, the effectiveness of which he thought it reduced. Some authorities argued that since sugar was capable of masking some poisons by its sweetness, it could be used sinfully.

Other authorities were not so much opposed to sugar as reserved about its therapeutic qualities. Hieronymus Bock's *New Herb Book* (1539) considers sugar "more as an extravagance for the rich than as a remedy," a truth many of his contemporaries would not acknowledge. He mentions sugar's usefulness for candying anise and coriander, violets, roses, and peach blossoms, and orange peel, which are items "good for ailments of the stomach," but he adds, rather offhandedly, that "he who cannot pay for the sugar may boil [such other ingredients] in water."[68]

Nevertheless, by the sixteenth century the medical uses of sugar had become widely established in Europe. Writers specified those uses. Tabernaemontanus (c. 1515–90) gave sugar a generally good assessment, even while identifying one of its disadvantages:

> Nice white sugar from Madeira or the Canaries, when taken moderately cleans the blood, strengthens body and mind, especially chest, lungs and throat, but it is bad for hot and bilious people, for it easily turns into bile, also makes the teeth blunt and makes them decay. As a powder it is good for the eyes, as a smoke it is good for the common cold, as flour sprinkled on wounds it heals them. With milk and alum it serves to clear wine. Sugar water alone, also with cinnamon, pomegranate and quince juice, is good for a cough and a fever. Sugar wine with cinnamon gives vigor to old people, especially a sugar syrup with rose water which is recommended by Arnaldus Villanovanus. Sugar candy has all these powers to higher degree.[69]

From the late sixteenth century, medical references to sugar occur commonly in English texts. According to Vaughan's *Naturall and Artificial Directions for Health*, "it mitigateth and openeth obstructions. It purgeth fleagme, helpeth the reines, and comforteth the belly."[70] Rice, "sodden with milke and sugar qualifieth wonderfully the heat of the stomake, increaseth genitall seede, and stoppeth the fluxe of the belly." Strawberries "purified in wine, and then eaten with good store of sugar doe assuage choler, coole the liver, and provoke appetite."[71] Still, Vaughan had some of the same reservations as Tabernaemontanus:

> Sugar is of a hot quality, and is quickly converted to Choler; for which cause I cannot approve the use thereof in ordinary meates, except it bee in vinegar or sharpe liquor, specially to young men, or to them which are of hot complexions: for it is most certain that they which accustome themselves unto it, are commonly thirsty and dry, with their bloud burned, and their teeth blackened

and corrupted. In medicine-wise, it may be taken either in water,
for hot Feavers, or in syrups, for some kinde of diseases. In beer
I approve it most wholesome.[72]

Vaughan goes on to recommend sugar for "noises and soundes in
the Eares," dropsy, ague, cough, flux, melancholia, and much else.

Tobias Venner, writing in 1620, provides an illuminating opinion,
first by comparing sugar medically to honey, second by distinguishing among sugar's then-used varieties. Whereas honey is "hot and
dry in the second degree, and of an abstersive and soluble facultie"—
more Galenical (humoral) shoptalk of the time—

> Sugar is temperately hot and moyst, of a detersive facultie, and
> good for the obstructions of the breast and lungs; but it is not so
> strong in operation against phlegm as honey.... Sugar agreeth with
> all ages, and all complexions; but contrariwise, Honie annoyeth
> many, especially those that are cholerick, or full of winde in their
> bodies.... Water and pure Sugar onely brewed toegether, is very
> good for hot, cholericke, and dry bodies, that are affected with
> phlegme in their breast.... Sugar by how much the whiter it is, by
> so much the purer and wholsomer it is, which is evident by the mak-
> ing and refining of it. It is made much after the same manner and
> forme as white salt is. The Sugar is nothing else but the iuyce of
> certain canes or reeds, which is extracted by boyling them in water,
> even after the same manner and fashion as they do salt. This first
> extracted Sugar is grosse, and of red colour: it is hot and dry, some-
> what tart in taste, and of a detersive facultie: by longer boyling it
> becometh hard, which we call Red Sugar Candie, which is only good
> in glysters, for to clense and irritate the expulsive facultie. This grosse
> reddish Sugar is againe mixed with water, and boyled, and cometh
> to be of an whitish colour, less hot, more moyst, and more ac-
> ceptable to the taste and stomacke. This kinde of second Sugar, we
> call common or kitchen Sugar. This being the third time diluted,
> and decocted, is of excellent temperament, most white, and of a
> singular pleasant taste. This is the best, purest, and wholsomest
> sugar... by further boyling becommeth hard, and of a resplendent
> white colour, which we commonly call white Sugar Candie: this is
> the best sugar for diseases of the breast, for it is not altogether so
> hot as the other Sugar, and is also somewhat of a more pure and
> subtile moysture. Wherefore it excellently assuageth and moy-
> stneth the asperitie and siccitie of the tongue, mouth, throat, and
> winde-pipe; and is very good for a dry cough, and other infirmities

of the lungs; it is most accommodate for all hot and dry constitutions.[73]

Most such home-physician books of the seventeenth century do not differentiate among sugar's possible medical uses, contenting themselves instead with discussions of sugar's place in humoral medicine, followed by various specific (and usually exotic) "prescriptions." Among the uses that seem to appear with considerable regularity are prescriptions for chest coughs, sore throat, and labored breathing (some of which uses persist to this day); for eye ailments (in the care of which sugar now appears to have completely disappeared); and a variety of stomachic remedies.

Not surprisingly, perhaps, an antisugar school of medicine arose anew, in the seventeenth and eighteenth centuries. In the same year that the seventh edition of Vaughan's work appeared, James Hart's *Klinike or the Diet of Diseases* raised some of the questions that were occurring to physicians of the time. Though the humoral context that would continue to dominate European medical thinking for another 150 years was plainly still very strong, Hart had some serious questions about sugar:

> Sugar hath now succeeded honie, and is become of farre higher esteem, and is far more pleasing to the palat, and therefore everywhere in frequent use, as well in sicknesse as in health.... Sugar is neither so hot nor so dry as honie. The coursest, being brownest, is most cleansing and approacheth neerest unto the nature of hony. Sugar is good for abstersion in diseases of the brest and lungs. That which wee commonly call Sugarcandie, being well refined by boiling, is for this purpose in most frequent request, and although Sugar in it Selfe be opening and cleansing, yet being much used produceth dangerous effects in the body: as namely, the immoderate uses thereof, as also of sweetconfections, and Sugar-plummes, heateth the blood, ingendreth the *landise obstructions, cachexias, consumptions*, rotteth the teeth, making them look blacke, and withall, causeth many time a loathsome stinking-breath. And therefore let young people especially, beware how they meddle to much with it.[74]

Until late in the eighteenth century, the prosugar and antisugar authorities would engage in serious argument about sugar's medicinal properties. But the medical and nutritional aspects of sugar's role were never far apart, any more than they are today. Whereas the Frenchman de Garancières thought that overconsumption of sugar by the English led to their melancholic dispositions, the Englishman Dr. Frederick Slare found sugar a veritable cure-all, its only defect being that it could make ladies too fat.

Slare's work is one of the most interesting of its time (1715), even to its title: *A Vindication of Sugars Against the Charge of Dr. Willis, Other Physicians, and Common Prejudices: Dedicated to the Ladies*.[75] Slare lost his quarrel with Dr. Willis, though he never knew it. Dr. Willis was the discoverer of diabetes mellitus, and his anti-sugar views arose from his study of the disease. Slare was eager to prove that sugar was beneficial to everyone, and could cause no medical harm. But his book does much more. Its dedication is accompanied by the assertion that female palates were more refined than males', "not being debauch'd by sowre or uncouth values, or Drams, or offensive Smoak, or the more sordid juice of the Indian Henbane, which is Tobacco, or vitiated by salt and sowre Pickles, too much the delight of our Coarser Sex."[76] That women would become "Patronesses of the Fair SUGAR" Slare fully expected, since they "of late had more experience of it, in a more liberal use than formerly."

Slare's encomia to sugar are accompanied by his recommendations to women to make their "Morning Repasts, call'd Break-fasts" consist of bread, butter, milk, water, and sugar, adding that coffee, tea, and chocolate are similarly "endowed with uncommon vertues." His message concerning sugar, he says, will please the West Indian merchant,

> who loads his Ships with this sweet treasure. By this commodity have Numbers of Persons, of inconsiderable Estates, rais'd Plantations, and from thence have gain'd such Wealth, as to return to their native Country very Rich, and have purchas'd, and do daily purchase, great Estates.
>
> The Grocer, who retails what the Merchant furnishes by wholesale, is also concerned for the Credit and Good Name of his defam'd and scandaliz'd Goods, out of which he has also made his Fortune, his Family Rich and Wealthy. In short, there is no

Family through the Kingdom but would make use of it, if they can get it, and would look upon it as a Matter of great Complaint, and a Grievance to be depriv'd of the use of it."[77]

Having dwelled upon these somewhat tangential aspects of sugar's virtues, however, Slare turns to its medical utility, offering the reader almost immediately a prescription from "the famous oculist of Sarum, Dr. Turberville," for ailments of the eye: "two drams of fine sugar-candy, one-half dram pearl, one grain of leaf gold; made into a very fine and impalpable powder, and when dry, blow a convenient quantity into the eye."[78] We see here anew the mixture of sugar and preciosities to be consumed in medication, harking back both to the medicine of the plague and the subtleties of earlier centuries. Mixing sugar, pearls, and gold leaf to produce a powder in order to blow it into one's ailing eye may seem bizarre in the extreme. It is necessary to keep in mind both the trustfulness born of desperation, and the power we invest in the things we hold dear.

Slare piles wonder upon wonder. We are instructed next on the value of sugar as a *dentifrice* (Slare prescribed it for his patients with great success, he says); as a hand lotion also helpful for external lesions; as snuff in place of tobacco; and for babies: "For I have heard many Ladies of the better Rank, who read Books of some learned Persons, condemn Sugar, and denied it to their poor Babes very injuriously."[79] "You may soon be convinc'd of the satisfaction a Child has from the Taste of Sugar," he writes, "by making two Sorts of Water-Paps, one with, and the other without Sugar, they will greedily suck down the one, and make Faces at the other: Nor will they be pleas'd with Cow's Milk, unless that be bless'd with a little Sugar, to bring it up to the Sweetness of Breast-Milk."[80]

Slare's enthusiasm is highly suspect but his work is much more than a mere curiosity, because it touches on so many aspects of what was even then a relatively new commodity for most people. The consumption of sugar in England was rising rapidly, and production of it in the British West Indies, following the conquest of Jamaica and steady increases in the slave trade, was keeping pace. By stressing its uses as medicine, food for persons of all ages, preservative, etc., Slare was simultaneously reporting on the success of sugar while attracting additional attention to it. "I forbear," he writes,

> to enumerate one Half of the Excellency of Sugar. I will refer the Reader to Confectioners Shops, or the Stores for Sweet-meats in the Places of the Rich, or rather to a Banquet, or Dessert serv'd up at a generous Feast, with the Encomium of Eloquent Ladies at the End of a Treat, upon every charming Sweet, which is purely owing to the artful Application of Sugar, being first the Juice of the Indian Cane, more grateful and more delicious than the mel- liflous Liquid of the Honey-comb.[81]

John Oldmixon, a contemporary, expressed similar sentiments:

> One of the most pleasant and useful Things in the World, for besides the advantage of it in Trade, Physicians and Apothecaries cannot be without it, there being nearly three Hundred Medicines made up with Sugar; almost all Confectionery Wares receive their Sweetness and Preservation from it, most Fruits would be per- nicious without it; the finest Pastries could not be made nor the rich Cordials that are in the Ladies' Closets, nor their Conserves; neither could the Dairy furnish us with such variety of Dishes, as it does, but by their Assistance of this noble Juice.[82]

As medicine it would become less uncritically prescribed in the late eighteenth and nineteenth centuries, and its medical role steadily diminished as it was transformed into a sweetener and preservative on a mass basis. Yet it mattered little whether people continued to use it medically, since they were already consuming it in substantial quantities. The former medicinal purposes of sugar were now as- similated into a new function, that of a source of calories.

Sugar as sweetener came to the fore in connection with three other exotic imports—tea, coffee, and chocolate—of which one, tea, became and has since remained the most important nonalco- holic beverage in the United Kingdom. All are tropical products, all were new to England in the third quarter of the seventeenth century, all contain stimulants and can be properly classified as drugs (to- gether with tobacco and rum, though clearly different both in effects and addictiveness). All began as competitors for British preference, so that the presence of each probably affected to some extent the fate of the others.

All three beverages are bitter. A liking for bitterness, even extreme bitterness, falls "naturally" within the range of normal human taste response and can be quickly and firmly developed. The popularity of such diverse substances as watercress, beer, sorrel, radishes, horseradish, eggplant, bitter melon, pickles, and quinine, to name only a few, suggests a broad human tolerance for bitterness. Turning this into a preference usually requires some culturally grounded habituation, but it is not difficult to achieve under certain circumstances.

Sweet-tasting substances, however, appear to insinuate themselves much more quickly into the preferences of new consumers. The bitter substances are "bitter-specific"—liking watercress has nothing to do with liking eggplant, for instance. But, in contrast, liking sucrose seems to be "sweet-general." Added to bitter substances, sugar makes them taste alike, at least insofar as it makes them all taste sweet. What is interesting about tea, coffee, and chocolate—all harshly bitter substances that became widely known in Great Britain at approximately the same time—is that none had been used exclusively with a sweetener in its primary cultural setting. To this day tea is drunk without sugar in China and by overseas Chinese. (Tea usage in India poses somewhat different problems, deeply influenced as it was by the export of British customs, and intensely developed in India only under British stimulus.) Coffee is often drunk with sugar, but not everywhere, and not always, even within areas of ancient usage such as North Africa and the Middle East. Chocolate was commonly (though not invariably) used as a food flavoring or sauce without sweetener in its original tropical American home.[83]

Though it is possible to date the first appearance of coffee, tea, and chocolate in Britain with fair confidence, documentation for the custom of adding sugar to such beverages during the early period of their use in the United Kingdom is almost nonexistent. Since the combination of a nonalcoholic, bitter, calorie-empty stimulant, heated and in liquid form, with a calorie-rich and intensely sweet substance came to mean a whole new assemblage of beverages, the lack of detailed information on how such combinations were first formed and received is frustrating. More than a century after coffee and tea habits were well established, Benjamin Moseley, a physician who practiced in the West Indies, tells us, "It has long been a custom with many people among us, to add mustard to their coffee.... The Eastern nations add either cloves, cinnamon, cardamoms, etc., but neither milk, or sugar. Milk and sugar, without the aromaticks, are generally used with it in Europe, America, and the West India islands."[84] But by this time the English people had been drinking these beverages for more than a century. In his treatise on beverages, however, John Chamberlayn asserts that sugar was taken with all three by the time he was writing (1685).[85]

Tea eventually supplanted home-brewed small beer almost entirely, even contested the popularity of sugar-flavored wines (such as hippocras), as well as gin and other strong alcoholic intoxicants. But at first, all three new beverages were drunk only by the wealthy and powerful, slowly becoming desired by the poor, and later preferred by them to other nonalcoholic drinks. By the time that tea and its sister drinks were taken up by working people, they were being served hot and sweetened. Well suited to the needs of people whose caloric intake may actually have been declining during the eighteenth century, and for whom a hot, sweet beverage must have seemed especially welcome given their diet and England's weather, these drinks swiftly became popular. As the English drank more and more of the new substances, the beverages themselves became more and more English in two senses: by the process of ritualization, on the one hand; and by being produced more and more in British colonies—at least for another century or two—on the other.

Catherine of Braganza, the Portuguese bride of Charles II, who reigned from 1649 to 1685, was "England's first tea-drinking queen. It is to her credit that she was able to substitute her favorite temperance drink as the fashionable beverage of the court in place of the ales, wines, and spirits with which the English ladies, as well as gentlemen 'habitually heated or stupefied their brains morning, noon and night.'"[86] As early as 1660, tea was being touted in London advertising: a famous broadside distributed by Garway's beverage house vaunts tea's supposed medicinal virtues. Before 1657, we are told, tea had been used only "as a regalia in high treatments and entertainments, and presents made thereof to princes and grandees."[87] But the Sultaness Head Coffee House had already advertised tea in the London newspaper *Mercurius Politicus* on September 30, 1658: "That excellent and by all physicians approved *China* drink, called by the Chineans *Tcha*, by other nations *Tay*, alias *Tee*, is sold at the Sultaness Head Cophee House...."[88]

Little more than a year later, *Mercurius Politicus Redivivus*, edited by Thomas Rugge, reports: "Theire ware also att this time a turkish drink to bee sould, almost in every street, called Coffee, and another drink called Tee, and also a drink called Chocolate, which was a very harty drink." The first London coffeehouse appears to have been opened by a Turkish merchant in 1652, and the institution grew with amazing rapidity, both on the Continent and in England. The late-seventeenth-century French traveler Misson was favorably impressed by London's coffeehouses: "You have all Manner of News there: You have a good Fire, which you may sit by as long as you please: You have a Dish of Coffee; you meet your Friends for the Transaction of Business, and all for a Penny, if you don't care to spend more."[89]

Arnold Heeren, the German historian, writing of the eighteenth century, tells us:

> The mercantile system lost none of its influence.... This was a natural consequence of the ever increasing importance of colonies, from the time that their productions, especially coffee, sugar, and tea, began to come into more general use in Europe. The great influence which these commodities have had, not only on politics, but also on the reformation of social life, is not easily calculated. Apart from the vast gains resulting to the nations at large from commerce, and to the governments from duties—what influence have not coffee-houses exercised in the capitals of Europe, as central points of political, mercantile, and literary transactions? In a word without those productions, would the states in the west of Europe have acquired their present character?[90]

Chocolate soon followed tea and coffee; it was more expensive than coffee, and gained greater favor with the rich. Chamberlayn's 1685 tract on the preparation of these three beverages indicates that they were already being taken with sugar ("small quantities") and makes clear that their use was slowly spreading throughout society.

In terms of drinkable beverage rendered per pound, tea soon emerged as the most economical. But its growing popularity cannot be so much attributed either to its relative price or to any intrinsic superiority to these other exotic stimulants, as to the way it is used. Tea can be more successfully adulterated than either coffee or chocolate,[91] apparently because it can be tolerated, even when very diluted, more readily than those other beverages. Perhaps weak sweet tea tastes more satisfying than equally weak, equally sweet coffee or chocolate. At any rate, such possible virtues of tea were revealed only when imperial protection for its cultivation and production was turned toward India by the machinations of the importers.

The Honourable East India Company was chartered in 1660, one of what were eventually sixteen such companies—Dutch, French, Danish, Austrian, Swedish, Spanish, and Prussian—competing for trade in the Indies. None was so powerful or successful as the John Company, as this British chartered body was also called, which made its start importing pepper, but grew important because of tea.

> Its early adventures in the Far East brought it to China, whose tea was destined later to furnish the means of governing India. ...During the hey-day of its prosperity John Company...maintained a monopoly of the tea trade with China, controlled the supply, limited the quantity imported into England, and thus fixed the price. It constituted not only the world's greatest tea monopoly but also the source of inspiration for the first English propaganda on behalf of a beverage. It was so powerful that it precipitated a dietetic revolution in England, changing the British people from a nation of potential coffee drinkers to a nation of tea drinkers, and all within the space of a few years. It was a formidable rival of states and empires, with power to acquire territory, coin money, command fortresses and troops, form alliances, make war and peace, and exercise both civil and criminal jurisdiction.[92]

As tea drinking became popular in England, the smuggling of tea grew into a major business and, for the tax agents of the crown, a major headache. In 1700, England received legally about twenty thousand pounds.[93] By 1715, Chinese green tea was flooding the London market (thanks to the John Company), and by 1760, duty was paid on more than five million pounds. By 1800, the legally imported total alone was more than twenty million pounds. In 1766, however, the government was estimating that as much smuggled as legally introduced tea was reaching England. In that year the Honourable East India Company carried more tea away from China— six million pounds—than any of its competitors. Not until 1813 did the government intercede in the company's administrative and commercial activities, and not until 1833 was its monopoly to China—largely consisting of tea—finally terminated.

There is no comparable story for either coffee or chocolate; nor is any such monopoly to be found in the history of West Indian sugar, where different sugar colonies vied with one another. But the relationship among these four products—together with rum (molasses) and tobacco—was intimate and entangled. Tea won out over coffee and chocolate and, in the long run, even over beer and ale (though by no means altogether over rum and gin!)—for many different reasons. But the East India Company's monopoly, which led in turn to the complete domination of tea growing in India by British capital—and with total governmental support—played an important part. India tea (usually combining leaves from both Indian and Chinese plants) was much delayed by the antagonism of the selfsame East India Company. By 1840, however, it was in production, which

> marked the beginning of the end of China tea in England.... Within six years from the time Lord Bentinck had appointed his tea committee, the Government had demonstrated that *British grown tea* could be produced in marketable quantities.... Within the span of three generations British enterprise carved out of the jungles of India an industry that covered over two million acres, representing a capital investment of £36,000,000 with 788,842 acres under tea producing 432,997,916 lbs. annually, giving employment to one and a quarter million people; at the same time creating one of the most lucrative sources of private wealth and government tax returns in the British Empire [italics added].[94]

The success of tea, like the less resounding successes of coffee and chocolate, was also the success of sugar. In the view of the West Indian interest, increasing consumption of any of these exotic liquid stimulants was highly desirable, for sugar went with them all. Tea was pushed hardest by British trade, and its victory over competing beverages was conditioned by factors quite unrelated to its taste. That it was a bitter stimulant, that it was taken hot, and that it was capable of carrying large quantities of palatable sweet calories told importantly in its success. But unlike that of coffee and chocolate, the production of tea was developed energetically in a single vast colony, and served there as a means not only of profit but also of the power to rule. The same could not really be said of chocolate or coffee at the time; the better analogy, if any, would be with sugar.

Tea's success was phenomenally rapid. Before the midpoint of the eighteenth century, even Scotland had become a land of tea addicts. The Scottish jurist and theologian Duncan Forbes looked back in time to write:

> But when the opening [of] a Trade with the East-Indies... brought the Price of Tea...so low, that the *meanest* labouring Man could compass the Purchase of it;—when the Connection which the Dealers in their Country had with many *Scotsmen* in the Service of the *Swedish* Company at *Gottenburg*, introduced the Common Use of that Drug among the *lowest* of the People;— when *Sugar*, the inseparable Companion of Tea, came to be in the possession of the very poorest Housewife, where formerly it had been a great Rarity,—and therby was *at hand*, to mix with Water and Brandy, or Rum;—and when Tea and Punch became thus the *Diet* and *Debauch* of all the Beer and Ale Drinkers, the effects were very suddenly and severely felt.[95]

And the historian of Scotland David MacPherson, writing at the beginning of the nineteenth century, looked back to the lowering of the duties on tea in 1784, and the even sharper increase in use that followed upon it:

> Tea has become an economical substitute to the middle and lower classes of society for malt liquor, the price of which renders it impossible for them to procure the quantity sufficient for them

as their only drink.... In short, we are so situated in our commercial and financial system, that tea brought from the eastern extremity of the world, and sugar brought from the West Indies and both loaded with the expense of freight and insurance... compose a drink cheaper than beer.[96]

Cheapness was important, but it does not by itself explain the growing tendency toward tea consumption. The cleric David Davies, an important observer of rural life at the end of the eighteenth century, discerned the combined circumstances leading to a deepening preference for tea and sugar over other items of diet at the time. Davies insisted that the rural poor would produce and drink milk if they could afford to keep a cow, but that this was beyond the means of most, and his detailed budgetary records support his view. Then, because malt was a taxed item, it was too costly to enable the poor to make small beer:

> Under these hard circumstances, the dearness of malt, and the difficulty of procuring milk, the only thing remaining of them to moisten their bread with, was *tea*. This was their last resource. Tea (with bread) furnishes one meal for a whole family every day, at no greater expense than about one shilling a week, at an average. If any body will point out an article that is cheaper and better, I will venture to answer for the poor in general, that they will be thankful for the discovery.[97]

Davies was sensitive to the arguments against tea:

> Though the use of tea is more common than could be wished, it is not yet general among the labouring poor: and if we have regard to numbers, their share of the consumption is comparatively small; especially if we reckon the *value* in money.
> Still, you exclaim *tea is a luxury*. If you mean fine hyson tea, sweetened with refined sugar, and softened with cream, I readily admit it to be so. But *this* is not the tea of the poor. Spring-water, just coloured with a few leaves of the lowest-priced tea, and sweetened with the brownest sugar, is the luxury for which you reproach them. To this they have recourse of necessity; and were they now to be deprived of this, they would immediately be reduced to bread and water. Tea-drinking is not the cause, but the consequence of the distresses of the poor.

> After all, it appears a very strange thing, that the common people of any European nation should be obliged to use, as part of their daily diet, two articles imported from opposite sides of the earth. But if high taxes, in consequence of expensive wars, and the changes which time insensibly makes in the circumstance of countries, have debarred the poorer inhabitants of this kingdom the use of such things as are the natural products of the soil, and forced them to recur to those of foreign growth; surely this is not *their* fault.[98]

Of course it was remarkable that, so early in England's history, "the common people ... should be obliged to use, as part of their daily diet, two articles imported from opposite sides of the earth." It was remarkable not only for what it shows us about the English economy, already in large measure a nation of wage earners, but also for what it reveals about the intimacy of the links between colony and metropolis, fashioned by capital. So vital had sugar and tea become in the daily lives of the people that the maintenance of their supply had by then become a political, as well as an economic, matter.

Other observers of English rural life, such as Sir Frederick Eden, also noted the growing consumption of tea and sugar in the countryside. Eden collected large numbers of individual family budgets, two of which, dating from 1797, are illustrative of the trend in sugar consumption. The first, a southern family of six, had a cash income of forty-six pounds per year; their calculation of money spent on food actually exceeds that figure slightly. This family's purchases were estimated to include two pounds of sugar weekly, or about a hundred pounds per year, which would give a per-capita average consumption of nearly seventeen pounds—a startlingly high figure for the time. The northern family had a more modest income. There were five, rather than six, members and they spent disproportionately less on food. Nonetheless, of the twenty pounds estimated to have been expended for food annually, tea and sugar cost £1 12s., and treacle 8s. more—in all, 10 percent of the cash purchases of food.[99]

Jonas Hanway, the eighteenth-century social reformer, was intensely hostile to the consumption of tea by the poor. The richness of his feelings can be conveyed by the following:

It is the curse of this nation that the labourer and mechanic will ape the lord. . . . To what a height of folly must a nation be arrived, when the common people are not satisfied with wholesome food at home, but must go to the remotest regions to please a vicious palate! There is a certain lane . . . where beggars are often seen . . . drinking their tea. You may see labourers mending the roads drinking their tea; it is even drank in cinder-carts; and what is not less absurd, sold out in cups to haymakers. . . . Those will have tea who have not bread. . . . Misery itself has no power to banish tea.[100]

John Burnett, a painstaking modern student of the history of British nutrition, reproaches Hanway gently. "Contemporary writers," he tells us, "are unanimous in blaming the labourer for his extravagant diet, and tireless in demonstrating that by better management he might have more meat and more variety in his meals. None of them seemed . . . to recognize that white bread and tea were no longer luxuries, but the irreducible minimum below which was only starvation. . . . Two ounces of tea a week, costing 8d. or 9d., made many a cold supper seem like a hot meal."[101] A number of scholars note that the substitution of tea for beer was a definite nutritional loss; tea was bad not only because it was a stimulant and contained tannin, but also because it supplanted other, more nutritious foods: "The poor people found that they could enjoy a quite deceptive feeling of warmth after drinking hot tea, whereas, in fact, a glass of cold beer would have given them far more real food."[102]

It was not simply as a sweetener of tea that sucrose became an item of mass consumption between the late seventeenth century and the end of the eighteenth. Mrs. Hannah Glasse's special confectionery cook book (1760), probably the first of its kind, appeared in more than a dozen editions and was widely read (and plagiarized); it probably contributed to the behavioral bridging between matron and drudge that accompanied the emergence of newer middle-class segments. It offers good evidence of how comprehensively sugar was entering the English diet. This pathbreaking work dealt not only with sugar-sculpture frames and mini-subtleties, but also with sweetened custards, pastries, and creams, the recipes for which required port, madeira, sack (sweet sherry), eggs, cream, lemons, oranges, spices, and immense quantities of sugar of many sorts. By instructing the rising middle classes in the fabrication of pastries and other desserts, Mrs. Glasse provides rich documentation that sugar was no longer a medicine, a spice, or a plaything of the powerful—though of course the powerful would continue to play with sugar, in new ways.

For the poor, probably the next most important use of sugar after sweetening tea was in supplementing the consumption of complex carbohydrates, particularly porridges and breads, with treacle (molasses). "Hasty pudding," so called, was in fact oatmeal porridge, commonly eaten with butter, milk, or treacle.[103] In the eighteenth century, treacle apparently dislodged the older combinations. Though molasses served as a sweetener in this instance, the taste of sweetness it afforded the porridge was probably more pronounced than in the case of tea, though tea was commonly drunk very sweet.

The first half of the eighteenth century may have been a period of increased purchasing power for laboring people,[104] even though the quality of nutrition probably declined at the same time. Innovations like the liquid stimulants and the greatly increased use of sugar were items for which additional income was used, as well as items by which one could attempt emulation of those at higher levels of the social system. But labeling this usage "emulation" explains very little. The circumstances under which a new habit is acquired are as important as the habits of those others from whom the habit is learned. It seemes likely that many of the new tea drinkers and sugar users were not fully satisfied with their daily fare. Some were doubtless inadequately fed; others were bored by their food and by the large quantities of starchy carbohydrates they ate. A hot liquid stimulant full of sweet calories doubtless "hit the spot," perhaps particularly for people who were already undernourished.

C. R. Fay, a sometimes mordant commentator on English social history, writes: "Tea, which refreshes and quietens, is the natural beverage of a taciturn people, and being easy to prepare, it came as a godsend to the world's worst cooks."[105] It is true that tea is easier to prepare (and soon became cheaper) than either coffee or chocolate. But the East India Company had much to do with which of these beverages would win out ultimately; and sugar may have helped as much as tea did to transform the English diet. It surely provided more calories.

These additions to the diet of the English people signaled the linkage of the consumption habits of every Englishman to the world outside England, and particularly to the colonies of the empire. For many people this widening of food choices was a distinct advantage, sometimes displayed with charm and wry humor:

> I am heartily glad that we shall keep Jamaica and the East Indies another year, that one may have time to lay in a stock of tea and sugar for the rest of one's days. I think only of the necessaries of life, and do not care a rush for gold and diamonds, and the pleasure of stealing logwood. The friends of government, who have thought on nothing but reducing us to our islandhood and bringing us back to the simplicity of ancient times, when we were the frugal, temperate, virtuous old England, ask how we did before tea and sugar were known. Better, no doubt; but as I did not happen to be born two or three hundred years ago, I cannot recall precisely whether diluted acorns, and barley bread spread with honey, made a very luxurious breakfast [letter of Horace Walpole to Sir Horace Mann, 15 November 1779].[106]

The uses of sugar as a sweetener for beverages grew in the company of ever more common pastries, often eaten with the beverages or in place of bread. This use would not reach its fullest development until the mass production of fruit preserves, conditioned by big drops in the price of sugar, was mastered in the nineteenth century. But as the use of tea and the other exotic beverages increased, so did the consumption of breads baked outside the home, which were often sweetened. Misson, the late-seventeenth-century French traveler who had rhapsodized about the coffeehouses, thought well of English puddings, too. Of "Christmas Pye," he writes, "It is a great Nostrum the composition of this Pastry; it is a most learned Mixture of Neats-tongues, Chicken, Eggs, Sugar, Raisins, Lemon and Orange Peel, various Kinds of Spicery, &c."[107] Of course such treats were not yet for the frequent delectation of the poorest segments of English society in the early eighteenth century. But as sugar became better known and more familiar, pastries and puddings became more widespread. "Red" (brown) sugar and treacle were now widely used in baking, in puddings, with cereals, spread upon bread, and in other ways.

Elisabeth Ayrton deals at length with the English sweet tooth in her sprightly and literate *The Cookery of England* (1974):

> Sugar had been a luxury too expensive for many until the beginning of the eighteenth century, when the price dropped to about 6d. per pound. Once it had done so, the practice of "scraping" the conical sugar-loaf over the crust of a pie and of supplementing sugar in the contents with raisins, was enlarged to a fuller use of sugar in pies and tarts and to its use with "flower" to make puddings.
>
> At first the puddings formed part of the second or third course, which might also consist of fish, some lighter meat dishes, pies, tarts, vegetables or fruit. By the beginning of the nineteenth century they often, though not invariably, followed the savoury dishes as a separate course. In the first part of the eighteenth century a "pudding" almost always meant a basis of flour and suet with dried fruit, sugar and eggs added. As the century went on, hundreds of variations were evolved, recipes multiplied; even the plainest dinner served above the poverty line was not complete without its pudding.
>
> Hot puddings, cold puddings, steamed puddings, baked puddings, pies, tarts, creams, moulds, charlottes and bettys, trifles and fools, syllabubs and tansys, junkets and ices, milk puddings, suet puddings: "pudding" used as a generic term covers so many dishes traditional in English cookery that the mind reels as it dwells on these almost vanished splendours of our tables.[108]

New foods and beverages were incorporated into daily life with unusual rapidity, and sugar had an important role in nearly all of these new items. But people do not simply add such important things to their diets without noticing what they are and how they can be used. Drinking tea, eating bread smeared with treacle or porridge sweetened with it, baking sweet cakes and breads were all acts that would gradually be assimilated into the calendar of work, recreation, rest, and prayer—into the whole of daily life, in sum—as well as into the cycle of special events such as births, baptisms, marriages, and funerals. In any culture, these processes of assimilation are also ones of appropriation: the culture's way of making new and unusual things part of itself.

In complex hierarchical societies, "the culture" is never a wholly unified, homogeneous system, however. It is marked by behavioral and attitudinal differences at different levels, which are expressed and reflected in the differing ways ideas, objects, and beliefs are used, manipulated, and changed. Cultural "materials"—including material objects, the words for them, ways of behaving and of thinking, too—can move upward or downward, from lord to commoner, or vice versa. But when they do so, they are not unaltered or unchanged in meaning. And it would be naïve to assume that such diffusion occurs as readily or as often in an upward direction as in a downward. Wealth, authority, power, and influence surely affect the ways diffusion occurs.

Substances such as sugar, tea, and tobacco, their forms and uses, became embedded somewhat differently in different portions of the English social system, and the meanings attached to them varied as well. At each level, moreover, differences of age, sex, and the norms of social assortment affect the ways new usages are institutionalized and relearned. Sometimes old men, sometimes young wives, sometimes infants of both sexes will be most affected by one or another such substance. In the case of sugar, the downward movement that typified its spread was accompanied, as we have seen, by changes in what it meant or could mean to those who used it. Since it took many forms, the meanings attachable to sugar would vary depending on whether it was a spice, a medicine, a form of decoration, a sweetener, or whatever—and also depending on the social group employing it.

In general terms, sugar's use as a spice and a medicine declined as its use as a decoration, a sweetener, and a preservative increased. In these latter categories, its availability for new meanings broadened, as its nature was more fully grasped by those who used it. It formed part of a "tea complex" (the term is used with some hesitancy) that gradually came to characterize British society top to bottom—though intricately and profoundly differentiated at different levels. Here it was both a sweetener of the tea itself and a fundamental ingredient of many of the foods that accompanied the tea. As a decoration, sugar was obviously important in ceremonial contexts, such as weddings, birthday parties, and funerals, where sculptured sugar could serve to memorialize—though of course the events in question were no longer matters of state or the appointments of church dignitaries. As a preservative, it had additional potentialities.

Two somewhat different processes were occurring as these uses became more or less standard, both of them aspects of what, for lack of a better term, may be called "ritualization"—the incorporation and symbolic reinvestment of new materials. (Because ritual has to do with regularity and with a sense of fitness, rightness, and validation, its meaning here is not confined to so-called religious behavior.) One such aspect may be called "extensification": larger numbers of persons were becoming familiar with sugar on a regular, perhaps even daily, basis. The regular consumption of sugar, particularly of cheap brown sugar or treacle, even in modest quantities, gradually reduced sugar's status as a glamorous luxury and a precious good. As a sweetener of tea, coffee, chocolate, and alcoholic drinks, and as an ingredient of bakery and fruit desserts, sugar acquired a more everyday, down-to-earth character in the eighteenth century. More frequent and greater consumption—with the addition of new food uses and new occasions for consumption, each of which forged and consolidated particular meanings—would deepen this everyday quality. A treat, perhaps, but a familiar, reliable, and expected treat—the analogy with tea itself, say, or even with tobacco may be persuasive. As sugar became more known, more "homey," it was endowed with ritual meanings by those who consumed it, meanings specific to the social and cultural position of the users. This is a part of the extensification itself: a recasting of meanings, now detached from the past, and from those given by other social groups.

In contrast, "intensification" involved more continuity with past usage, more fidelity to older meanings, more—perhaps the word is closer to the mark here—emulation. Coronations, the installation of high religious authorities, and the granting of knighthoods did not spread throughout society; but sugar did. Hence intensification meant the attachment of sugar uses to ceremonial occasions harking back to older usage but freed of much of the social and political content they formerly carried. Wedding cakes with their elaborate icings and figures, the use of spices and sweets with meat and fowl at holidays, the use of sweet foods at rituals of separation and departure (including funerals), and a lexicon in which the imagery of sweetness figures importantly all suggest such continuity.

The preservative powers of sucrose were recognized at a very early time, as the ninth-century record documenting the manufacture and export of fruit syrups, candied capers, and similar preserves from Persia demonstrates. The usefulness of sugar as a preservative is shared to some extent by honey, but sucrose is more effective. Its capacity to draw off moisture and thus to deprive micro-organisms of a breeding environment makes it a relatively safe vehicle for the suspension of edible solids, even meat, for lengthy periods. Just as liquid sugar or syrups can be used as a medium in which to immerse other substances, so crystalline sugars can be used to coat or seal off edible materials.

In Europe these properties were written about by the thirteenth or fourteenth century, and were probably well known before then. In the *Compendium Aromatarorium* (1488), Saladin d'Asculo described how to prevent fermentation by using concentrated sucrose solutions, and how to preserve dairy products by applying a thick coating of powdered sugar. Paracelsus also recorded sugar uses to prevent spoilage.[109] Preserved fruit was a delicacy known to English royalty by the fifteenth century, and doubtless earlier. The "perys in syrippe" served at the wedding feast of Henry IV and Joan of Navarre in 1403 are noteworthy, since at that time "almost the only way of preserving fruit was to boil it in syrup and flavour it heavily with spices."[110] Nearly two centuries later, the household book of Lord Middleton, at Woollaton Hall, Nottinghamshire, documents the purchase of two pounds, one ounce of "marmelade" at the astronomical price of 5s. 3d.—which shows "what a luxury such imported preserved fruits were."[111] Though exact equivalencies cannot be established, the money for two pounds of preserved fruit at that time would have bought approximately one pound of pepper or ginger—equally exotic imports—or nearly fourteen pounds of butter, or almost twenty-nine pounds of cheese.

Delicacies of this sort continued to be food for royalty and the very wealthy for centuries more; but as with other sugar uses, those of lesser rank aspired to consume them, too. Candied fruit was imported to England from the Mediterranean at least as early as the fourteenth century. Socade, "a form of conserve which often covers what we now term marmalade," appears in sixteenth-century cargo lists.[112] And the Skinners' Company banquet of 1560 featured both "marmelade" and "sukett" among the sweetmeats served. Since law did not prohibit the use of sugar by inferior social strata, potential users were constrained only by its rarity and high price. It would of course be more likely to be used by a guild or corporate group than to appear on the family tables of the individual members, at least at first.

The principal use of sugar as a preservative had a different form before the nineteenth century, however, which diminished almost to the vanishing point when the fruit-preservative usage acquired an importance it would never again surrender, after about 1875. Henry IV's 1403 wedding feast features "sugar plums, sugar made up with roses, comfitures of fruit, sage, ginger, cardamom, fennel, anise, coriander, cinnamon, powdered saffron"[113]—but this list mixes different sorts of sweetmeat together. The spices, which could be candied or not, come first. Plain spices were passed about on costly gold and silver spice plates, filigreed and engraved with coats of arms and often jewel-incrusted—obvious display items of rank for male nobility. With them went the drageoirs, as richly decorated and costly as the spice plates, but filled with sugared confections. Drageoirs were a female display prerogative, paralleling the spice plates. Both the spice plates and the drageoirs or comfit boxes were forms of privileged consumption, associated with royalty and the specially wealthy, until the end of the seventeenth century.[114]

From the fourteenth century onward, the ceremonial feasts of the English kings included the serving of comfits and spices. Both were used to accompany second and subsequent servings of wine. The spices—cardamom, cinnamon, coriander—were "digestives" (a word that is more commonly used today with this meaning in other languages besides English, such as French and Italian), or medicines to aid digestion. The candied sweets served in drageoirs were called "dragées." The word "drageoir" is lost to modern English; but "dragée" survives with three dictionary meanings, all of them significant. The first is a sugar-coated nut; the second, a pearllike sweet used to decorate cakes; and the third, a sugar-coated medication. Here three of sugar's principal and earliest uses are summed up in a single word. The term "comfit" (cognate with French *confiture* and with English "confection") is still used generally to mean a confection with a firm (fruit, nut, seed) center, coated with sugar.

The archetypes of the comfits may have been candied sugars, *zucchero rosato* and *zucchero violato*, mentioned in the fourteenth-century accounts of Balducci Pegolotti, a Venetian trader, and in the royal exchange accounts from the fourteenth century on.[115] But these delicacies did not embody the flowers, only their colors and aromas. Authentic comfits—objects coated with hardened sugar—are readily traceable to Venice, and doubtless backward in time to North Africa and the Middle East. It is of incidental interest that, before *confetti* came to mean bits of colored paper, it meant bits of colored candy, and in some languages—such as Russian—it still does. The word is cognate, of course, with comfit, *confit*, and confection.

But it is unlikely that most English people first encountered sugar used as a preservative in the form of candied fruits, or fruits preserved in syrup. These remained luxuries even after working people had begun to drink heavily sweetened tea, and they did not diffuse downward at the same rate as tea. By the mid-eighteenth century, to be sure, comfits and similar treats were known to the middle classes, and may have begun to become familiar in one form or another to working people as well. Pomet, although his work deals primarily with medicines rather than foods or confections, gives a concise description of these goodies:

> There are infinite Variety of Flowers, Seeds, Berries, Kernels, Plums, and the like which are, by the Confectioners, cover'd with Sugar, and bear the Name of Sugar-Plums, which would be endless to set down, and are too frivolous for a Work of this Nature: The most common of the Shops are Carraway-Confects, Coriander, and Nonpareille, which is nothing but Orrice-Powder, cover'd with Sugar; and what is much in Vogue at *Paris* is green

Anise: Besides these, we have Almond-Confects, Chocolate, Coffee, Berberries, Pistachia Nuts, &c.[116]

This is the older preservative use, which, though it survives in many rather trivial forms to this day, was outstripped by a quite different method. As with the sugar used to sweeten beverages, preservative sugar gained a completely new place in the British economy and in daily life, but only as large-scale consumption of preserved fruit came to typify English diet. Once again it was the transformation of a rare substance into a common one, and a costly treat into a cheap food, that made dependent transformations possible. From the "perys in syrippe" of the fourteenth-century chefs of royalty would eventually come the jams and marmalades of Tiptree, Keiller, Crosse and Blackwell, Chivers, and other canners in the nineteenth.

Because of the old fear of fruit that typified commoner English attitudes, the manufacturers and merchants of jellies, jams, and marmalades had to overcome some resistance and distrust. Moreover, until a safe preservative medium that was cheap enough to result in an economical product was available, these sweets could not be mass-produced. But when the price of sugar fell sharply after the big victories of the free-trade movement of the mid-nineteenth century, jam consumption began to catch hold among working people. At the same time, consumption of sugar in other forms rose in response to a fall in sugar prices. These changes in sucrose consumption were entangled with other changes in diet and taste as well. Jam and the working class—a phrase I have borrowed from an important article by Angeliki Torode[117]—were conjoined only from about 1870 onward. Semiliquid and liquid sweeteners invaded the proletarian diet and taste somewhat earlier, in the form of treacle. Though very different from jams or jellies, treacle probably helped "sell" preserves to new users. From its early, more molasseslike form, it was progressively refined into a clear, gold-colored syrup that mimicked honey and, by the late nineteenth century, cost much less.

Edward Smith's records of the diets of the Lancashire operatives in 1864 show that they lived largely on bread, oatmeal, bacon, a very little butter, treacle, and tea and coffee. Cheap jams made their appearance on the market in the 'eighties and immediately became very popular. Most of them contained very little of the fruit they were alleged to be made from and were simply concoctions made from the cheapest fruit or vegetable pulp obtainable, coloured and flavoured as required. Their sweetness made them very popular with poor families; bread and jam became the chief food of poor children for two meals out of three.[118]

John Burnett writes of the mid-nineteenth century that "bread was the staple of life for the 80 or 90 percent of the population that made up the working classes."[119] Hence we have a population already eating sugar, especially in tea, but also confined to a heavily carbohydrate diet. What else were people eating? The various foods that composed working people's diets were interrelated, and cannot be considered one by one if we want to calculate where sugar fits in. Some data from Scotland are especially instructive in that they unite the bread-eating with jam, revealing how this combination could undercut an older pattern because yet other changes in Scottish society at the time were opening the way.

R. H. Campbell's short study of Scottish diet between the mid-eighteenth century and World War I—by which time regional differences in diet within Great Britain are believed to have become negligible—is useful here, exactly because it gives a good indication of how sugar progressively penetrated the food preferences of ordinary people over time. Permanent agricultural laborers (called "hinds") in Scotland of the nineteenth century received up to two-thirds of their income in kind, including food. These landless workers were better fed, however, than were casual agricultural laborers. As payments in kind declined, partly in reaction to public criticism of arrangements retaining so much power in the hands of the employer, the diet of the hinds also declined. "Freedom of choice," says Campbell, "led to a decline in the standard of diet"—not an unfamiliar consequence.[120] All the same, Scottish workers continued to eat substantial quantities of oatmeal in various forms, even when choosing their own ingredients, because it remained a cheap food during much of the nineteenth century. Since oatmeal provided important nutrients not otherwise available at so low a cost, its cheapness actually underwrote a better diet than was available to English workers at the same salary level.

When Campbell provides comparative data for the industrial cities of Scotland (Edinburgh, Glasgow, and Dundee) at the end of the century, a different picture emerges. Diets here were judged to be deficient in protein, especially in animal protein, and the reasons were clear enough: "excessive use of bread, butter, and tea, instead of the porridge and milk of the rural diets."[121] Campbell asks the same questions as the Edinburgh investigators—"Why did people fail to retain the more satisfactory yet cheap diet of the rural areas? When a choice of diet became available, why was it exercised unwisely?" But he came up with an answer different from theirs.

The investigators had concluded that "when ... it comes to a question of using the ready cooked bread or the uncooked oatmeal, laziness decides which, and the family suffers."[122] "But the investigation in Dundee," Campbell writes,

> revealed conditions that more adequately explain the paradox of a decline in nutritional standards when cash income was rising. The organization of the jute industry provided opportunities for female labour, so that many housewives went out to work in Dundee. Nutritional standards declined still further and sharply when the wife went out to work. "When the mother is at work there is not time to prepare porridge or broth in the 'diet hour' ... usually breakfast and dinner become bread and butter meals. As the school interval for dinner is not the same as the mill 'diet hour' the children have to unlock the house and get 'pieces' for themselves...."
>
> Pressure on the housewife's time was in itself a sufficient explanation of the choice of an inferior diet. The need to save time rather than the need to economize or to maintain nutritional standards determined the choice.... Most notable was the increased consumption of bread. In one case in Dundee 6s 5d of a total expenditure of 12s 11d went on bread; one family of a father, mother and five children consumed 56lbs a week.... The cooking of vegetable broth was neglected in the cities. So long as vegetable broth was used extensively the Scottish custom of eating few vegetables in any other form was unimportant. Where the housewife had to go out to work, the preparation of broth was practically impossible. In Dundee the investigators found

that the broth pot was "an almost invariable feature" only of houses where the mother was at home.[123]

John Burnett's argument fits well not only with Campbell's assertions but also with the argument I am making about sugar.

White bread and tea passed, in the course of a hundred years, from the luxuries of the rich to become the hall-marks of a poverty-line diet. Social imitation was one reason, though not the most important.... Whereas they were mere adjuncts to the tables of the wealthy, they became all too often the total diet of the poor, the irreducible minimum beyond which lay only starvation. Paradoxically, they had become almost the cheapest foods on which life could be supported. White bread, though it was better with meat, butter or cheese, needs none of these; a cup of tea converted a cold meal into something like a hot one, and gave comfort and cheer besides. At 6s or 8s a pound in the middle of the nineteenth century tea was still a luxury, though the average consumption of a working-class household—2ozs a week, often eked out with pieces of burnt toast to colour the water—was scarcely extravagant. And in the circumstances of early industrialism this type of diet had an additional advantage that it could always be produced close at hand and required little or no preparation.[124]

But the clincher is what happened with jam. After the 1870s,

jam became an important food, especially for the working class. Free trade made possible the rise and prosperity of jam factories in this period. The abolition of the sugar duties made sugar cheap and plentiful; jam contains 50 to 65 per cent of its weight in sugar.... Most of the produce of the jam and preserves factories was for domestic consumption.... Urban working classes... consumed much of their fruit in the form of jam. Since the 1840s, people whose main staple was bread indulged in sugar or, when times were worse, in treacle, spreading it on bread as a substitute for butter, or using it in their tea instead of sugar. A pudding or a currant cake appears often in the budgets of working class families in the 1860s. Even the poor families interviewed by Seebohm Rowntree in his study of the rural labourer either purchased or made jam—usually out of windfalls or even stolen fruit. Only in the worst cases would a mother hesitate to open her jam-jar, because her children ate more bread if there was jam on it. In any case, the jam manufacturers, with the

exception of Blackwell and Chivers who made expensive preserves as well, agreed in 1905 that their most extensive and lu-
crative market lay in the working class to whom jam, once a
luxury, had now become a necessity, and a substitute for the
more expensive butter.[125]

Several points emerge from these observations. First, it seems clear
that, at least in Great Britain of the nineteenth century, food choices
were reckoned partly in terms of available time, and not solely in
terms of relative cost. Second, it is clear that fuel was an important
part of food costs, so that food that circumvented this outlay would
be more attractive. Third, the division of labor within the family
shaped the evolution of British food preferences; a wife's leaving
the house to earn a wage had a restrictive effect on the family diet,
even though her work might increase the family income. Though
not as conspicious in the above argument but at least equally important for the story of sugar, there is good evidence that the nutritional value of foods was not equally distributed within family
units; indeed, we shall examine evidence that wives and children
were systematically undernourished because of a culturally conventionalized stress upon adequate food for the "breadwinner."

There seems no doubt that sugar and its by-products were provided unusual access to working-class tastes by the factory system,
with its emphasis on the saving of time, and the poorly paid but
exhausting jobs it offered women and children. The decline of bread
baking at home was representative of the shift from a traditional
cooking system, costly in fuels and in time, toward what we would
now proclaim as "convenience eating." Sweetened preserves, which
could be left standing indefinitely without spoiling and without
refrigeration, which were cheap and appealing to children, and which
tasted better than more costly butter with store-purchased bread,
outstripped or replaced porridge, much as tea had replaced milk
and home-brewed beer. In practice, the convenience foods freed the
wage-earning wife from one or even two meal preparations per day,
meanwhile providing large numbers of calories to all her family.
Hot tea often replaced hot meals for children off the job, as well
as for adults on the job. These changes were an integral part of the

modernization of English society. The sociological changes that they accompanied would continue to mark the modernization of the rest of the world.

The nonmedicinal consumption of sucrose in England before 1700 took three principal forms besides decorative sugar and preserves: spices and dragées, sweet and sweetened alcoholic drinks, and baked sweet dishes. It was this last, most of all, that would eventually become the "sweet" (dessert) eaten at home by millions of English working people, so that the standardization of such dishes is a feature of the history both of English diet and of sugar itself.

Baked sweet dishes do not appear conspicuously in English recipes before the fifteenth century, but thereafter such recipes are common. In his selections, based on two fifteenth-century works, Austin has published a section entitled "Dyverse baked metis," which provides recipes employing egg yolks, cream, various spices including saffron, and sugar (in some cases honey), the resulting mixture to be baked into a custard in pastry cups, shells, or barquettes.[126] In succeeding centuries, such dishes become more and more common, but their place within the meal was not firm until late in the history of sugar usage. I believe the link between a particular course and the specific taste of sweetness could be forged only when sweet substances were cheap and plentiful enough to enable people to think in such terms, meal after meal. There is nothing natural or inevitable about eating sweet food at every meal or about expecting a sweet course. It appears to have become a common feature of western European eating only in the last couple of centuries, and to have settled into position as a final course even more recently. Yet it is by now so commonplace that we may have difficulty in imagining some completely different pattern. Since the connection between one taste (sweetness) and one course (dessert) is the firmest of all such links in the western food order, it is worth trying to see how it emerged.

Perhaps only in the late seventeenth century, and at the topmost level of society, did a sequence of dishes consigning sweet courses to the end of the meal finally became stabilized. In medieval banquets, Mead writes, "the place assigned to the dessert, insofar as it existed, appears to have been a matter of indifference."[127] The order of courses, even once the display (and, sometimes, the consumption) of subtleties had become patterned, was random with respect to sweet dishes. Henry IV's coronation feast, for instance, had "doucettys" as the third course among many, and there are no sweets at the end of the menu. Preserved fruits might be served at any point in the sequence; "quincys in comfyte" turn up near the beginning of the third course. Similarly, at Henry's wedding feast, though each of the three courses was climaxed with a subtlety, the only other candidates for a dessert course, cream of almonds and pears in syrup, turn up at the start of the third course. Mead believes the appetite for sweets was as keen in the fifteenth century as it is today but that medieval diners were simply not concerned about the order of their dishes.[128]

French royalty began to eat what looked like a dessert course in the fifteenth century. A feast given by two noblemen for the king of France and his court consisted of seven courses. Desserts began with the fifth: tarts, custards, plates of cream, oranges, and "*citrons comfits.*" The sixth course was made up of wafers and red hippocras, and the seventh of subtleties, each piece carrying the arms and device of the king. Mead is inclined to attribute the emergence of the dessert in English practice to imitation of the French model. Because so much of English royal custom came from the French courts, this seems probable.

It would be easy to suppose that the English working classes learned to eat dessert because such was the habit of their rulers, but here the explanation may be too facile. The first sugar habit learned by the English poor was part of the tea habit, and the tea habit spread downward from the rulers and outward from the cities at a rapid rate. But the public consumption of tea and the other drug beverages was not at first as part of a meal. Both tea and sugar were first consumed outside the traditional home diet, were only later assimilated into it; indeed, were probably at first associated more with work than with the home.

It is plausible that the earliest foreign or exotic "interval foods" were stimulants such as caffeine and a calorie-heavy sugar, combined in an easily prepared hot liquid form. Once learned, this combination of substances would then be taken into the home diet; cheaper sugar would facilitate the use of treacle and, soon enough, puddings, especially when store-baked bread became widely available. This chronology of successive additions is speculative, but it is reasonably accurate. It implies that a dessert course was the third, rather than the first, important sugar use for the poor.

The stabilization of the dessert—usually "pudding"—became firm in the nineteenth century, especially toward the end, when sugar use rose even more sharply. But this did not occur independently of other changes in diet and the structure of English meals. One fundamental such change was the decline in the consumption of bread and flour, as other foods became more available and less expensive, among them sugars. This decline continued into the twentieth century, in the United States as well as in the United Kingdom. It appears to be complementary to the rising curve for sugars, and to increasing meat (or at least fat) consumption. But whether changes of this kind represented—or eventuated in—an improvement in the diet of working people is moot.[129]

The part played by sugars in increasing the average total caloric intake makes it likely that sugars both complemented the complex carbohydrates and partly supplanted them. The pastries, hasty puddings, jam-smeared breads, treacle puddings, biscuits, tarts, buns, and candy that turned up more and more in the English diet after 1750, and in a deluge after 1850, offered almost unlimited ways in which the sugars could be locked onto complex carbohydrates in flour form. Added sugar was customary with hot beverages, and the eating of sweetened baked foods often accompanied these drinks. The drinking of tea, coffee, or chocolate (but most commonly tea) with meals, in moments of repose snatched from work, at rising, and at bedtime spread widely. The combination of such beverages with baked goods became common as well, though not an invariable practice.

While the dessert became a course in the sit-down lunches and dinners of most classes, sugar use itself spread far more widely. It became, in one form or another, the near-universal accompaniment of wheat products and hot beverages. Its caloric contribution rose from an estimated 2 percent of total intake at the start of the nineteenth century to a more probable 14 percent a century later. Even this somewhat startling latter figure may be an underestimate, since it is a national average and omits the differential effects of such factors as age, sex, and class on sugar consumption. That the appeal of sugar to the poor was greater—that it could satisfy hunger in the place of other, more nutritious foods—may have looked like a virtue.

The many new uses for sucrose that developed between the twelfth and eighteenth centuries eventuated in a modern multi-functional mass consumption. Such deepening differentiation—more uses, more frequency, more intensive use—typified the second half of the nineteenth century in the United Kingdom and, soon after, in other industrial and industrializing countries. An analogous sequence occurred in poorer, nonindustrial countries during our century. What had begun as a spice and a medicine was eventually transformed into a basic foodstuff, but a foodstuff of a special kind.

The uses of sugar overlapped because of the unusual versatility of sucrose. Food and medicine have been linked in thought and in act ever since human beings began viewing ingestion and fasting as instruments of health and purity; and sugars have been a bridge between "food" and "medicine" for millennia.[130] But sugar was not limited to medicinal uses, as we have seen. By the fifteenth century, sugar confections, often in a profusion distressing to the modern reader, had become an invariable accompaniment to nearly every courtly activity in England. English royalty manifested an affection for sweets that apparently exceeded even that of the kings and queens of the Continent. A German traveler of the sixteenth century, who met Elizabeth at court, wrote, "The Queen, in the 65th year of her age (as we were told), very majestic; her face oblong, fair but wrinkled; her eyes small, yet black and pleasant; her nose a little hooked, her lips narrow, and her teeth black (a defect the English seem subject to, from their too great use of sugar)."[131] He went on to say that the poor in England looked healthier than the rich, because they could not afford to indulge their penchant for sugar. In subsequent centuries, of course, this changed radically.

"This fondness of our countrymen and countrywomen for sweets," writes British historian William B. Rye,

> astonished the Spaniards who came with the Embassy of the Count Villamediana in 1603. At Canterbury the English ladies are described as peeping through the latticed windows... at the hidalgos, who presented the "curious impertinent fair ones" with the bonbons, comfits, and sweet meats that were upon the table, "which they enjoyed mightily; for (it is remarked) they eat nothing but what is sweetened with sugar, drinking it commonly with their wine and mixing it with their meat."[132]

Spain had been familiar with sucrose in various forms for centuries, and had been exporting it to England for more than a hundred years when this incident was recorded. That Spanish diplomats should have been so struck by the English sweet tooth in 1603, nearly half a century before England began importing sugar from her first "sugar colony," is worth noting. We can be sure, moreover, that these "curious impertinent fair ones" were neither servants nor dairy maids.

All the same, it would be difficult to contend that the history of sucrose consumption in England merely documents an innate liking. The American historian John Nef argued that the north European craving for sucrose originated in geographical factors. The "growth of economic civilization in the north," to use his phrase, meant using fruits and vegetables "with less natural succulence than those growing in Mediterranean soil."[133] To make them palatable, he claimed, it was necessary to sweeten them. But this is not convincing. Fruits such as the apple, the pear, and the cherry are arguably no less succulent than fruits from subtropical climes, nor is it easy to see why northern peoples would have a stronger craving for sweetness than peoples in the south, even if the highest rates of processed-sucrose consumption in the modern world are to be found principally among northern populations. People in subtropical regions, from south China through India, Persia, and North Africa, had been sugar eaters long before the Europeans knew much about sucrose, and the Venetians were fascinated by sugar when they first became acquainted with it, no later than the tenth century.[134]

Possibly more relevant to the peculiar English sweet tooth is a cultural datum concerning alcohol. Ale prepared from malted grain was England's chief alcoholic drink for perhaps a millennium, to be challenged by beer only around the middle of the fifteenth century. Ale has a sweetish, rather than bitter, taste, as long as the malt sugar in it is not completely fermented. When hops began to be added, around 1425, they contributed to the preservability of the drink—now properly described as beer—but also made it bitter-tasting. The bitterness apparently did not discourage consumption by those accustomed to the sweet taste of ale—but ale continued to be drunk thereafter.[135] A new bitter beverage was now available, in addition to a more familiar sweet one. Hence a familiarity with a sweet taste other than those of fruit and honey was maintained.

Beyond this, other sweet or sweetened drinks besides ale were long popular in England. Alcoholic beverages made from or with honey—mead, metheglin, hydromel, rhodomel, omphacomel, oe-nomel—constituted one such category. Honey was distilled after fermentation to make mead, or to be mixed with wine, grape juice, rose water, etc., to create these somewhat exotic intoxicants. But honey was relatively expensive and not very plentiful even before the sixteenth century, when the abolition of the monasteries dealt a near-fatal blow to honey production, destroying the only substantial market for (beeswax) candles, contributing to a rise in the price of honey, and cutting into the production of honey-based drinks.[136]

The other category consisted of beverages combining sugar and alcohol, especially wine. Sugar and sack—Falstaff's favorite—was one. But most popular was hippocras, a candied wine commonly flavored with spices as well as sugar, which displaced the older honeyed wines and fermented honey drinks as the importation of both wines and sugar rose. The English habit of adding sugar to wine was much remarked. The English "put a great deal of sugar in their drink," Hentzner wrote in 1598,[137] and when Fynes Moryson discussed English drinking habits in 1617, he commented: "Clownes and vulger men only use large drinking of *Beere* or *Ale* ...but Gentlemen *garrawse* onely in Wine, with whiche many mixe sugar—which I never observed in any other place or kingdom to be used for that purpose. And because the taste of the English is thus delighted with sweetness, the wines in tavernes (for I speak not of Merchants or Gentlemens cellars) are commonly mixed at the filling thereof, to make them pleasant."[138]

These observations suggest not so much a special English predilection for sweetness—though there may indeed have been such—as a long-standing familiarity with sweetened beverages. It is conceivable that the sweetening of the drug drinks—coffee, chocolate, and tea—became customary not only because they were bitter as well as unfamiliar, but also because the habit of adding sugar to beverages was an old one. When tea was touted as the beverage that "cheers without inebriating," its sweetness surely emerged as a favorable feature for a people whose sweet tooth had long been cultivated by sweet or sweetened alcoholic beverages. In their turn, of course, tea, coffee, and chocolate helped to encourage the sharp upward curve of sucrose consumption. It seems improbable that they were essential to it, but there is no doubt that they accelerated it.

Tea, coffee, and chocolate never displaced alcoholic drinks—they only vied with them. The rivalry was lengthy, and of course it has never ended. In British social history, the issue of temperance figured critically in that rivalry. Temperance itself was espoused for moral reasons: the protection of the family, virtues like thrift, reliability, honesty, and piety. But temperance was also a national economic issue: an effective, factory-based industrial capitalism could not be consolidated by an absentee-ridden, drunken labor force. Hence the issue of alcoholic versus nonalcoholic beverages was neither a moral nor an economic-political question alone; certainly it was not simply a matter of "taste" or of "good manners."

During the late seventeenth and eighteenth centuries, alcoholic-drink consumption rose nationally in Great Britain, but the consumption of tea and other "temperance" beverages grew even faster. Gin began to be imported from Holland in the seventeenth century, and by 1700 imports reached 500,000 gallons in some years.[139] An act of 1690, directed against the French, legalized the manufacture of a local *eau de vie* from grains. Called "British brandy," this curious offshoot of national rivalries continued to be produced until well into the eighteenth century.[140] Whereas ale and beer could be sold only at licensed houses from the mid-sixteenth century on—cider was added to the list in 1700—"spirits" could be sold without a license and with only a derisory tax. The consumption of gin had risen to an estimated five million gallons—that is, an increase of 1,000 percent—by 1735.

The rising price of grains with which to make hard liquor led to a renewed popularity for beer, which competed with tea in the mid-eighteenth century. And to these must be added rum; in 1698, only 207 gallons of rum were imported to England; in the period 1771–75, the annual average importation was well over two million gallons yearly.[141] Indeed, this understates the totals, partly because rum was distilled from the molasses that was a by-product of sugar making in Britain, partly because a great deal more was smuggled in. Tea, coffee, and chocolate, in other words, had many rivals; sugar was needed in the production and consumption of nearly all of these beverages.

Tea triumphed over the other bitter caffeine carriers because it could be used more economically without losing its taste entirely, because its price fell with fair steadiness in the eighteenth and nineteenth centuries (particularly after the East India Company's monopoly was broken in the 1830s), and because—a related consideration—its production was localized in British colonies. It turned out, moreover, to be a magnificent source of government revenues through taxation; by the 1840s, bohea, the cheapest China tea, was being taxed at 350 percent.

But tea was far more than an import directly profitable to the government. Some of the largest and most important retailing concerns in world history, such as Lipton (and some of its earliest competitors, such as Twining), were built on tea.[142] Touted as a temperance beverage, tea stimulated while carrying large quantities of calories. By the middle of the nineteenth century, the temperance movement had helped to convert Hanway's hated tea into a great blessing, as suggested by such effusions as the following:

> *With you I see, in ages yet unborn,*
> *Thy votaries the British Isles adorn,*
> *With joy I see enamour'd youths despise*

The goblet's luster for the false one's eyes;
Till rosy Bacchus shall his wreaths resign,
And love and tea triumph o'er the vine.[143]

Alcoholism did not disappear, nor did working-class families turn into teetotalers overnight, however. Alcohol consumption remained high among working people, and some laboring families were spending a third or even a half of all their income on drink throughout the eighteenth and nineteenth centuries. Still, the temperance movement definitely reduced drunkenness, particularly among the slightly better-off, more skilled workers.[144] In this gradual elimination or reduction of alcoholism, tea played a critical part. Here again, it is not clear how much influence the model of upper-class behavior may have had. The temperance movement was a product of middle- and upper-class thinking and morality—but this hardly means that alcoholism was a working-class monopoly.

I have stressed sugar's usefulness as a mark of rank—to validate one's social position, to elevate others, or to define them as inferior. Whether as a medicine, a spice, or a preservative, and particularly in the public display epitomized by the subtleties, sugar uses were molded into declarative, hierarchical functions. Certain scholars, emphasizing the function of luxuries in modernization, have seen this complex of customs somewhat differently. Werner Sombart, for example, argued that sugar (among many other substances) affected the rise of capitalism because the female love of luxury led to its increasing production and importation to European centers.

> On one point, however, we already seem to have arrived at complete agreement: the connection between the consumption of sweets and feminine dominance....
> This connection between feminism (old style) and sugar has been of the greatest importance for the history of economic development. Because of the predominant role of women during early capitalism, sugar rapidly became a favorite food; and only because of the widespread use of sugar were such stimulants as cocoa, coffee, and tea adopted so readily all over Europe. Trade in these four commodities and the production of cocoa, tea, coffee and sugar in the overseas colonies as well as the processing of

cocoa and the refining of raw sugar in Europe are outstanding factors in the development of capitalism.[145]

Probably only the final sentence in this passage can be accepted unreservedly. The "predominant role of women during early capitalism" is an enigmatic—one might almost say mysterious—assertion. The alleged importance of women in transforming sugar into a favorite food is similarly puzzling. Even the causation implicit in the sentence that follows—that sugar's availability underwrote the drug-beverage habit—is unacceptable as it stands. Yet Sombart was not wrong to look for some connection between women and sugar use, for he was driving at a serious analysis of the circumstances under which consumption occurs. In the case of sugar and the foods eaten with it, such an analysis means looking at work, and at time, as well as at the divisions between the sexes and among classes—in short, at the total sociology of consumption during the rise of a new economic order in western Europe.

Sugars began as luxuries, and as such embodied the social position of the wealthy and powerful. The distinction between spice plates and drageoirs, as noted earlier, may have reflected a male-female difference of a kind, but one between persons of the same stratum or rank. When these luxuries began to be employed by wealthy commoners, they multiplied and redifferentiated their uses. And as sugars came to be viewed as everyday necessities for larger and larger segments of the national population, they were progressively incorporated into innovative contexts, ritualized by their new consumers. Just as the spice plates and drageoirs of the nobility of an earlier era validated and proclaimed rank and status with reference to others—to spouses, to equals, and (by exclusion) to inferiors—so these new sugar uses served analogous social and psychological functions for ever-larger, less aristocratic groups.

Some of these new patterns were essentially transfers of the uses and meanings of those of higher position to lower ranks—an intensification of older forms. Yet others, and more commonly, involved the use of old materials in new contexts and, necessarily, with new or modified meanings—an extensification of previous usages. The development of tea as a social event serves to illustrate such processes.

Though tea turns up first in the tea- and coffeehouses of mid-seventeenth-century London and other cities and on the tables of the nobility and the aristocracy of the day as a sort of novelty, eighteenth-century writers make it clear that for the poor, and especially for rural workers, it accompanied more than leisure. Tea with sugar was the first substance to become part of a work break. The picture is quite otherwise for "the tea," a social event that could either interrupt work or constitute a form of play. "The tea" swiftly became an occasion for eating as well as drinking. Since the eighteenth-century custom among the middle classes was to eat a light lunch, people were hungry in the afternoon:

> Hence the need for tea was bound to arise, even had its existence not preceded the want of it. Tea was originally the prerogative of women, for the sexes were accustomed to separate at that epoch of an early dinner when the men began to take their wine seriously. Five o'clock tea implies tea served at the hour when dinner was finished—much as we now serve black coffee after lunch in imitation of the French—as which it preluded ombre, cribbage, backgammon and whist. This purely feminine development of a dish of tea into a "light refection" may be considered as an imitation of the old French "goûter," at which sweet wines...biscuits and petits-fours were served to both sexes.[146]

P. Morton Shand, a commentator on the English social scene, suggests that "the tea" can be traced to Continental custom and noble habits, but we can see that more than imitation was at work in the case of the laboring poor, for whom the beverage tea became important long before "the tea" was a social occasion. Still, the way Shand links substance to event is persuasive, even if somewhat impressionistic:

> When the sexes began to lead less segregated social lives in England, tea was served to the ladies in the drawing-room at the same time as port, madeira and sherry for the gentlemen....As women became less languorous and men less bearish manners

softened toward a greater sociability of intercourse which an enhanced sobriety in alcohol had initiated. Woman triumphed over her tea-cups and the decanters were gradually banished from her now indisputed sphere. Young men of the dawning romantic age were glad to be able to frequent the society of the ladies, and preferred their company to that of the irascible "three-bottle" stalwarts in the smoking-room. The year in which afternoon tea was first served in the august London clubs, those last remaining sanctuaries of male prerogatives, was a most important date in our social history....

Afternoon tea soon became an excuse for the indulgence of a woman's naturally sweet tooth [sic].... Tea must not be regarded as another meal, a second breakfast. The bread and butter was camouflage, the little cakes were the real lure, the *pièce d'aban-don*. It was not long before man completely capitulated to woman, accepting and sharing the supernumerary snack on her own terms, so that today there are few Englishmen who will consent to be deprived of their tea, whether at work or play, at home or abroad. Tea is an excuse for eating something, rather than an avowed meal. It is a break, a challenge to the crawling hours, it "makes a hole in the day." ... Another advantage is the extreme elasticity of its hour, so that one can order it at any time from 4 p.m., till half-past six.[147]

Shand's conjecture that tea and alcohol tended to be sex-divided beverages until the salon lured men to afternoon tea may be accurate for the middle classes after the 1660s, but it fails to explain what happened among working people. "Once tea became an established custom among the well-to-do," he adds, "the lower middle classes naturally began to imitate it, but in a form peculiarly their own (to which the heavy six o'clock tea of public schools offers the only parallel that I know of)."[148] In Shand's interpretation, the introduction of teatime altered the entire meal pattern. "Supper was brought forward by an hour or two, with the new refinement, tea, and the hybrid, really a repetition of breakfast, was baptised high tea ... more often described circuitously by the phrase 'I take an egg (or fish) with ... my tea.'"[149] It is clear that tea, the tea custom, and "teatime" took on different contextual significance—served differ-ent nutritive and ceremonial purposes, actualized different mean-ings—in different class settings.

A century later, the place of tea and sugar in working-class diet, together with treacle, tobacco, and many other imported foods, was completely secure. These were the new necessities. The figures for tea and sugar consumption after the 1850s mount steadily—in the case of sugar, to just below ninety pounds per person per year by the 1890s. As early as 1856, sugar consumption was forty times higher than it had been only 150 years earlier, though population had not much more than trebled during that period.[150] In the 1800s, the national consumption was about 300 million pounds per year; once the duties began to be equalized and the price to drop, consumption rose, to a billion pounds in 1852, and still higher in succeeding years. Without the price drops, consumption could not have risen so fast. But the place for sugar within the laboring diet was highly expandable, and new uses multiplied as the price fell. Between 1832 and 1854, the per-capita *increase* has been estimated at five pounds. "The allowance to servants," one scholar writes, "is from ¾ lb. to 1 lb. per week" in 1854, from which it could be deduced, "that 50 lbs, per year, at least, is not too much for grown persons."[151] Indeed not—it was higher than that by 1873, and in 1901 the per-capita figure for the first time rose above ninety pounds.

Even these startling figures blur and conceal the sociology of sugar consumption, because per-capita statistics are merely national averages. There is no doubt that the sucrose consumption of the poorer classes in the United Kingdom came to exceed that of the wealthier classes after 1850, once the sugar duties were equalized. Not only did sucrose-heavy foods—treacle, jams, raw sugar for tea and baking, puddings, and baked goods—come to form a bigger portion of the caloric input of the working-class diet (though probably not absorbing a larger proportion of the money spent on food), but sucrose was also an ingredient in more and more items in the daily meals. Children learned the sugar habit at a very tender age; sweetened tea was a part of every meal; jam, marmalade, or treacle figured in most. In the late nineteenth century dessert solidified into a course, sweetened condensed milk eventually became the "cream" that accompanied tea and cooked fruit, store-purchased sweet biscuits became a feature of the tea, and tea became a mark of hospitality for all classes.[152] It was also toward the end of the century that bread began to be supplanted by other food items, in a process that has since been repeated in many other countries.

Scholars have suggested that the decline in bread consumption was a sign of a rising standard of living, but "the falling curve representing bread and flour is complementary to the rising curve for sugar and sweetmeats."[153] Yet sugar-consumption figures are adequate for neither short-term nor long-term inference as an index of the standard of living.[154] Since the price of sugar fell by 30 percent between 1840 and 1850, and by a further 25 percent in the next two decades, consumption increases reflect a decline in the price of sugar relative to other commodities, and not necessarily an improved life standard. In any event, per-capita sucrose consumption (and, as is argued here, the sucrose consumption of laboring people in particular) rose rapidly during the second half of the nineteenth century.

Drummond and Wilbraham believe that the decline in bread and flour consumption was accompanied by an increase in both meat and sucrose consumption, but another researcher, using figures based on supply estimates, was able to find no increase in meat consumption. Throughout the quarter-century 1889–1913, weekly per-capita meat availability—the average amount available in the market nationally in the United Kingdom—was 2.2 pounds. But to make that figure relevant to this analysis, one must make allowances for class differentials in meat consumption as well as for differentials within families. On this latter point, Derek Oddy, another historian of nutrition, is clear. "Animal food in particular," he writes, "was largely consumed by him [the father] for his dinner or as 'relishes' for his supper."[155] He cites Dr. Edward Smith, who noted in 1863 that meat "for the family" was consumed exclusively by the father, and that the mother thought of this as morally right: "The important practical fact is however well established, that the labourer eats meat and bacon almost daily, whilst his wife and children may eat it but once a week, and that both himself and his household believe that course to be necessary, to enable him to perform his labour."[156] Mrs. Pember Reeves, a careful observer of the diet of laboring families, writes: "Meat is bought for men, and the chief expenditure is made in preparation for Sunday's dinner, when the man is at home. It is eaten cold by him the next day."[157]

These observations throw light upon the apparent increases in meat and sucrose consumption in the nineteenth-century working-class diet: "Bread is the staple food of poverty and people eat much less of it when they can afford to buy meat and indulge in the type of dish with which sugar is eaten."[158] There is an implicit hypothesis in this way of stating things, but no general rule. Even if a greater absolute sum is spent on food—indeed, even if a greater percentage of a higher income is spent on food—this is not sufficient evidence, of itself, that the diet has improved. Moreover, the high probability of culturally patterned differential consumption within the family—everybody eats more sugar, but women and children eat relatively more than adult men; everybody gets some meat, but adult men get disproportionately more than women and children— suggests a very different truth.

There are reasons to believe that the late-nineteenth-century diet was in fact unhealthy and uneconomical. Bread and, to a lesser extent, potatoes were the main foods, but the disproportionately high expenditure on meat provided little for the money. Small amounts of "tea, dripping [fat], butter, jam, sugar, and greens," remarked Mrs. Reeves, "may be regarded rather in the light of condiments than of food."[159] Such additions were essential, says Oddy, "to make the semblance of a meal in diets with high starch content."[160] But while the laboring husband got the meat, the wife and children got the sucrose: "We *see* that many a labourer, who has a wife and three or four children, is healthy and a good worker, although he earns only a pound a week. What we *do not see* is that in order to give him enough food, mother and children habitually go short, for the mother knows that all depends upon the wages of her husband."[161] Mrs. Reeves labeled potatoes "an invariable item" for the midday meal, but not necessarily for all of the family: "Trea-cle, or—as the shop round the corner calls it—'golden syrup,' will probably be eaten with the suet pudding, and the two together will form a midday meal for the mother and children in a working man's family."[162] "This clearly illustrates the complementary nature of certain foods," Oddy writes. "Some form of fat or sugar was an essential component of a meal to accompany the main, and largely starchy, food. In the absence of animal food sugar acted as a substitute and this in turn determined the type of starchy food eaten."[163]

We see here a return to the core-carbohydrate-and-fringe principle. In many western countries, however—of which the United Kingdom was the first—the "fringe" (of which processed fats and sugars are more representative than vegetables, fruit, or meat) began, as a corollary of modernity, to overtake the "core."

Insufficiently palatable food could result in general undernourishment:

> The limited consumption of animal foods indicated their use in the working-class diet as a vehicle for consuming larger amounts of carbohydrate foods and it is probable, therefore, that when the animal food content of the diet was reduced by economic factors, the consumption of starchy foods was restricted in turn.... The conclusion seems inescapable that families in this period with an income of less than, say, 30 shillings per week and with a family of growing children might well obtain only 2000–2200 calories and 50–60 grams protein per head per day. Given that the distribution of food within the family followed the general pattern suggested in which the father got a disproportionately large fraction of the total protein, it is impossible to envisage how the diverse physiological needs of a manual worker, his wife, and growing children could be met adequately. The inference which can be drawn from... first-hand observers of the working-class home in the second half of the nineteenth century is that under these conditions women and children were under-nourished.[164]

Increased sugar use had both positive and negative effects upon working-class life. On the one hand, given that the working-class diet was calorie-short, sugar doubtless provided at least some of the needed calories. It meant sweeter tea (which it came to accompany almost as a matter of course), more biscuits, and more desserts, hence affording variety as well as more calories. As we have seen, Lord Boyd-Orr singled out the increase in sucrose consumption as the most important change in British diet in a century.[165] Yet, at the same time, the caloric increase provided by sugar was had at the cost of alternative nutrition of a better kind. Though the spread of sugar into the cuisine probably brought about an aggregate decline in eating and preparation time, it is doubtful whether this was accompanied by nutritive gains from what was eaten. As the argument shifts from considerations of real income to matters of what is now called "life style," the answers seem less authoritative.

The increased number of sugar uses and the rise in sugar consumption coincided with vital changes in the modernization of eating habits and diet. One such was the rise of prepared and conserved foods, particularly but of course by no means only those conserved in sugar: foods in cans, bottles, and packages of various sorts, and substances both hard and soft, solid and liquid. The sugar medium varied from the jams, jellies, and marmalades, made from fruits or conserving them, through the liquid sugars, from treacle and "golden syrup" to the confectioners' simple syrup poured on or mixed with other foods and added to condensed milk (from which a favorite working-class "custard" was made),[166] to the biscuits (American "cookies") and cakes for which Britain is famous, and, eventually, to candies, both with chocolate ("soft") and without ("hard").

It was only a short step from the multiplication of these uses and products to the industrial work break, instituted in the last years of the nineteenth century, and hastened by the industrial canteens pioneered by producers of foods made from tropical commodities, where tea, coffee, cocoa, biscuits, and candy could be had inexpensively.[167] Prepared foods, in other words, accompany the increasing frequency of meals taken outside the home and outside the familial context. Permitting as they do the freedom to choose one's foods, these trends free the consumer from the order of courses, from the social discourse of the family dinner table, and from the patterning of meal and time. By the opening of the twentieth century, sugar epitomized the times: it supposedly provided "quick energy." And since then its blessings have been spread to other lands, where many features of the changes in life in British society before 1900 have been repeated.

The history of sucrose use in the United Kingdom reveals two basic changes, the first marking the popularization of sweetened tea and treacle, from about 1750 onward; and the second, the opening up of mass consumption, from about 1850 onward. During the period 1750–1850 every English person, no matter how isolated or how poor, and without regard to age or sex, learned about sugar. Most learned to like it enough to want more than they could afford. After 1850, as the price of sugar dropped sharply, that preference became realized in consumption. A rarity in 1650, a luxury in 1750, sugar had been transformed into a virtual necessity by 1850.

Furthermore, it seems certain that the biggest sucrose consumers, especially after 1850, came to be the poor, whereas before 1750 they had been the rich. This reversal marks the final transformation of sugar from a preciosity into a daily commodity and into one of the first consumables fulfilling the capitalistic view of the relation between labor productivity and consumption. The place of·sugar in the expanding capitalist economy at home was qualitatively different in 1850 from what it had been by 1750. This difference had to do both with the ongoing development of an industrial economy and with the changing relationships between that economy and the overseas colonies.

It was once thought that plantations producing goods such as raw sugar could benefit the homeland economy in two ways: through direct capital transfers of profits to homeland banks for reinvestment; and as markets for such metropolitan products as machinery, cloth, instruments of torture, and other industrial commodities. Disputes among scholars continue concerning these potential sources of gain to metropolitan capital, but there is yet a third potential contribution: the provision of low-cost food substitutes, such as tobacco, tea, and sugar, for the metropolitan laboring classes. By positively affecting the worker's energy output and productivity, such substitutes figured importantly in balancing the accounts of capitalism, particularly as it developed over time through the integration of the colonial sector.

The differences between the periods 1750–1850 and 1850–1950 help to make this clearer. During the first, sugar—particularly in combination with tea—did not make a significant caloric contribution to English working-class diet, though it did sweeten the tea while adding a small number of easily assimilated calories. More important, sweetened tea probably increased the worker's readiness to consume quantities of otherwise unadorned complex carbohydrates, particularly breads, while saving time for working wives and expenditures on cooking fuels. Tea and sugar played a fringe role to the core carbohydrates. During the second period, the caloric contribution of sugar rose, for it now appeared not only in tea and cereal but in many other foods as well and in ever-larger quantities. At the same time, we see the partial abandonment of the colonies' interests—or, better, perhaps, the rearrangement of priorities as far as the colonies were concerned. Cheap sugar, the single most important addition to the British working-class diet during the nineteenth century, now became paramount, even calorically. By 1900, it was contributing on average nearly one-sixth of per-capita caloric intake; if that figure could be revised to account for class, age, and intrafamily differentials, the percentage for working-class women and children would be astounding. In this second period, the core-fringe distinction begins to disappear.

The history of sugar consumption in the United Kingdom has been repeated, albeit with important differences, in many other countries. All over the world sugar has helped to fill the calorie gap for the laboring poor, and has become one of the first foods of the industrial work break. There is, moreover, at least some evidence that the culturally conventionalized pattern of intrafamily consumption—with the costly protein foods being largely monopolized by the adult male, and the sucrose being eaten in larger proportion by the wife and children—has wide applicability. Maldistribution of food within poor families may constitute a kind of culturally legitimized population control, since it systematically deprives the children of protein. "There are cogent but not publicly articulated arguments against devoting scarce resources to infant and child nutrition. In oversimplified terms, death of preschool children due to malnutrition is *de facto* the most widely used method of population control."[168] It is painfully easy to see how sucrose could be used in such a system of "population control." The Reagan administration's attempt to define sucrose-rich catsup as a "vegetable" in federally supported school lunch programs is a recent demonstration.

These materials also throw some light on the relationship between gender and sugar consumption. One (male) observer after another displays the curious expectation that women will like sweet things more than men; that they will employ sweet foods to achieve otherwise unattainable objectives; and that sweet things are, in both literal and figurative senses, more the domain of women than of men. Of course these frequent references are interesting in their own right: that there may be links between women and sweet tastes is a research problem in itself; but it will take far more careful and impartial investigation to solve it.

The history of sugar in the United Kingdom has been marked by many "accidental" events, such as the introduction of bitter stimulant beverages in the mid-seventeenth century. But sugar consumption's rise thereafter was not accidental; it was the direct consequence of underlying forces in British society and of the exercise of power. It is to the nature of that power, and the circumstances of its exercise, that I can now turn.

4 · Power

Over the course of less than two centuries, a nation most of whose citizens formerly subsisted almost exclusively on foods produced within its borders had become a prodigious consumer of imported goods. Usually these foods were new to those who consumed them, supplanting more familiar items, or they were novelties, gradually transformed from exotic treats into ordinary, everyday consumables. As these changes took place, the foods acquired new meanings, but those meanings—what the foods meant to people, and what people signaled by consuming them—were associated with social differences of all sorts, including those of age, gender, class, and occupation. They were also related to the will and intent of the nation's rulers, and to the economic, social, and political destiny of the nation itself.

There are plainly two different senses of the term "meaning" here. One refers to what might be called "inside" kinds of meaning—inside the rituals and schedules of the group, inside the meal or eating event, inside the social group itself—the meanings people indicate when they are demonstrating they know what things are supposed to mean. Thus, for example, hospitality "means" self-respect; self-respect "means" knowing one's place in the class system; and knowing one's place can "mean" offering appropriate forms of hospitality—greeting, inviting in, serving tea and sugar and treacle tarts, or whatever. At births and weddings, funerals and feast days, moments of repose from the day's work following the calendar of hours, days, weeks, months, and the lifetime itself, new forms of consumption might be grafted to older forms with similar or analogous meanings.

I have already suggested the two processes by which inside meanings are acquired and conventionalized. In "intensification," consumption replicates that practiced by others, usually of a higher social status—also imitates, even emulates. The wedding cake and its sculptured decorations, complete with dragées, congratulatory script, hardened sugar figures, was more than just a new "food"; consumption was firmly attached to a special event and ceremonialized as part of it. As the custom of having a wedding cake percolated down through society, one would expect the usages to change, because of great differences in means and circumstances, but since the emulative features of the custom were undoubtedly also important, this process was "intensification" nonetheless.

Much consumption behavior toward sugar and its accompaniments seems to have arisen among the British working classes without any imitation, especially when the contexts were different from those of the more privileged classes. Since sugar products became even more important to the poor than they once had been for the wealthy—as sources of calories even more than of status—and since the occasions for eating them multiplied, new uses and meanings arose at a great remove from the practices of the privileged. To these kinds of innovation the term "extensification" has been applied.

In both instances, new users appropriate the behavior and inside meanings they perceive as their own, and new uses and meanings sometimes appear that are not merely imitative. In "intensification," those in power are responsible both for the presence of the new products and, to a degree, for their meanings; with "extensification," those in power may take charge of the availability of the new products, but the new users inform them with meaning. In the wider historical process that concerns us—the diffusion of sugar to entire national populations—those who controlled the society held a commanding position not only in regard to the availability of sugar, but also in regard to at least some of the meanings that sugar products acquired.

The other sort of meaning can be grasped when one considers

what consumption, and its proliferated meanings for the participants, can signify for a society as a whole, and especially for those
who rule it; how those who govern or control the society perpetuate their status and profit from the intensified diffusion of inside
meanings, and of the consumption which the validations of these
meanings entail. One can see here that the kind or level of consumption of social groups is not a God-given constant; and certain
beliefs about human character and potentiality are open to amend-
ment. Conversely, the spread of internal meanings can be stimulated
and manipulated; the simultaneous control of both the foods themselves and the meanings they are made to connote can be a means
to pacific domination.

The substances and acts to which meanings attach—inside kinds
of meaning—serve to validate social events. Social learning and practice relate them to one another, and to what they stand for. Rice and
rings have meanings in weddings much as lilies and lighted candles
do in funerals. These are historically acquired—they arise, grow,
change, and die—and they are culture-specific as well as arbitrary,
for all are symbols. They have no universal meaning; they "mean"
because they occur in specific cultural and historical contexts, where
their relevant meanings are already known to the participants. No
symbol has a life of its own, and though it lacks any intrinsic connection with any other symbol, it may travel together with other symbols through time, each reinforcing the other by the "signals" its
presence creates. Just as the symbols may be traced back to a past
when they were not associated (the way tea and sugar were once not
associated, for instance), so may there come a time when their sub-
stantive associations are dissolved or invalidated by some change or
other (the way tea and its meanings dropped out of colonial American
drinking habits, and were replaced by coffee).

As for substances like tea, then, events like meals, or ideas and
meanings like hospitality and equality, human intelligence puts them
together into patterns in the course of social acts in specific times
and places, employing certain availabilities and under specific constraints. Birth and death are universal in the sense that they happen
to all human beings; our capacity to symbolize, to endow anything
with meaning and then to act in terms of that meaning, is similarly

universal and intrinsic to our nature—like learning to walk or to speak (or being born, or dying). But which materials we link to events and endow with meaning are unpredictably subject to cultural and historical forces. We make biological events like birth and death into social events because we are human; each human group does it in its own way. Large, complex societies, composed of many overlapping subgroups, usually lack any single assemblage of social practices by which life is endowed with meaning; their members differ widely in the way they can live, and in their historically influenced access to the acts, objects, and persons through which they validate their knowledge of life's meaning.

Seventeenth-century England, like its Continental neighbors, was deeply divided by considerations of birth, wealth, breeding, gender, occupation, and so on. The practices of consumption in such a society were deeply differentiated, and reinforced by rules. Hence the ways that new consumption practices were taken up and by whom, and the ways they spread to members of other groups, with or without their associated meanings, suggest how British society itself was organized, and mark the distribution of power within it.

Before the end of the seventeenth century, while sugar was still a precious and rare substance, it had little meaning for most English people, though if they ever got to taste sugar, they doubtless thought it desirable. The rich and powerful, however, derived an intense pleasure from their access to sugar—the purchase, display, consumption, and waste of sucrose in various forms—which involved social validation, affiliation, and distinction. The blending of sugar with other rare and precious spices in the preparation of food; the use of sugar as a fruit preservative; the combination of sugar with crushed pearls or fine gold in the manufacture of medical "remedies"; the magnificent subtleties giving concrete expression to temporal and spiritual power—all confirm what sugar meant, and how sugar use informed meanings, among the privileged.

This multiplicity of meanings was also revealed in language and in literature, and linguistic imagery suggested not only the association of sweet substances with certain sentiments, desires, and moods, but also the historical replacement, in large measure, of honey by sugar. Honey imagery was ancient in British, as in classical Greek and Latin, literature. Both substances were associated with happiness and well-being, with elevation of mood, and often with sexuality. The quality of sweetness, so important in the structure of human taste and preference, was applied to personality, to generous acts, to music, to poetry. The Indo-European root *swād* is the ultimate source of both "sweet" and "persuade"; in contemporary English, "sugared" or "honeyed" speech has been supplemented by "syrupy tones" and "sweet-talking."

Chaucer's references to sugar are scant; they mainly stress its rarity and preciousness. By Shakespeare's time, the references have multiplied, and though they remain concentrated upon rare substances, the imagery flowing from them is highly diversified. "White-handed mistress, one sweet word with thee," says Berowne in *Love's Labour's Lost*; "Honey, and milk, and sugar; there is three," the Princess puns in response. Or Touchstone, the clown, teasing Audrey in *As You Like It*, tells her that "honesty coupled to beauty is to have honey a sauce to sugar." Northumberland to Bolingbroke, in the wolds of Gloucestershire: "Your fair discourse hath been as sugar,/ Making the hard way sweet and delectable." Or, finally, Brabantio, before Othello and the Duke of Venice: "These sentences, to sugar, or to gall,/ Being strong on both sides, are equivocal." From the seventeenth century onward—and it may be worth noting that Shakespeare died nearly half a century *before* sugar from Barbados, the first English "sugar island," began to reach England—sugar imagery became ever commoner in English literature. Written usage of this sort mattered most to the literate, of course, but sugar imagery became an important part of everyday talk as well, competing with or supplanting honey imagery among the terms of endearment and affection. This imagery bridges the two very different "meanings" we have discussed: the inside meanings as sugar became commoner, and its employment in social settings by even the least privileged and poorest of Britain's citizens; and the significance of sugar for the empire, for the king, and for the classes whose wealth would be made and secured by the growing productivity of British labor at home and British enterprise abroad.

This second meaning is embodied in the writings of political economists like Josiah Child or Dalby Thomas, or physicians like

Frederick Slare, whose enthusiasms kept pace with the steady expansion of those portions of the empire within which sugar cane and other plantation crops could be grown. Their encomia were not limited to the medical, preservative, nutritive, and other proclaimed virtues of sugar. In fact, they mostly treated the beneficial character of sugar as self-evident. How trade would follow the flag; why plantation production befitted the nation, the crown, and—of course—the enslaved and coerced workers; the general importance of commerce as a stimulus to manufacturing; the civilizing benefits to the heathen of the British presence—all these themes were pressed into sugar's service. And though sugar was obviously not always and everywhere a moneymaker within the empire—many an investor, as well as many a planter, ended up a bankrupt (and sometimes a jailbird) because of it—its cumulative value to crown and capital alike was enormous.

As far as the British West Indies were concerned, the zenith of sugar's imperial role probably came in the late eighteenth century, during the rule of George III. Lowell Ragatz, historian of the British West Indian planter class, recounts the story, probably apocryphal, of George III's visit to Weymouth in the company of his prime minister. Irritated by the sight of a West Indian planter's opulent equipage, complete with outrider and livery as fine as his own, the king is reported to have exclaimed: "Sugar, sugar, eh?—all *that* sugar! How are the duties, eh, Pitt, how are the duties?"[1]

The meaning that sugar attained in the imperial economy was a wholly different matter from what it eventually meant in the lives of the English people, but the availability and price of sugar were the direct consequences of imperial policies that took shape partly in terms of what the market was, and more and more in terms of what it might become. As the home market was made to grow, the proportion of sugar that was re-exported dropped sharply, and production itself was levered more securely into the imperial orbit. And as control over production was consolidated, consumption at home continued to rise. Much later, when protectionist policy based on differential duties lost out in Parliament and the West Indian planters lost their protectionist advocates, sugar went on being consumed in ever-increasing quantities, even as African and Asian colonies entered into cane cultivation and sugar making, and even as beet-sugar production began to overtake cane-sugar production in the world economy at large. By that time—which is to say, by the mid-nineteenth century—the two sorts of meaning suggested here had become united to a certain extent.

The English people came to view sugar as essential; supplying them with it became as much a political as an economic obligation. At the same time, the owners of the immense fortunes created by the labor of millions of slaves stolen from Africa, on millions of acres of the New World stolen from the Indians—wealth in the form of commodities like sugar, molasses, and rum to be sold to Africans, Indians, colonials, and the British working class alike— had become even more solidly attached to the centers of power in English society at large. Many individual merchants, planters, and entrepreneurs lost out, but the long-term economic successes of the new commodity markets at home were never in doubt after the mid-seventeenth century. What sugar meant, from this vantage point, was what all such colonial production, trade, and metropolitan consumption came to mean: the growing strength and solidity of the empire and of the classes that dictated its policies.

But what most anthropologists have in mind when they think about meaning is entirely different. To paraphrase Clifford Geertz, human beings are caught up in webs of signification they themselves have spun. We are able to perceive and interpret the world only in terms of pre-existing, culture-specific systems for endowing reality with meaning. This perspective puts the cognitive order between us and the world itself—we must *think* the world to be able to *see* (classify) it, rather than the other way round—and it should be persuasive for anyone who considers culture as the prime defining feature of human uniqueness.

But if humanity gives meaning to the objective world, with different sets of meaning for different human groups, one must still ask how this is done and by whom in any given historical instance. Where does the locus of meaning reside? For most human beings most of the time, the meanings believed to inhere in things and in the relationships among things and acts are not given but, rather, are learned. Most of us, most of the time, act within plays the lines of which were written long ago, the images of which require recognition, not invention. To say this is not to deny individuality or the human capacity to add, transform, and reject meanings, but it is to insist that the webs of signification that we as individuals spin are exceedingly small and fine (and mostly trivial); for the most part they reside within other webs of immense scale, surpassing single lives in time and space.

It is not at all clear that such webs are single-stranded, or that the same webs exist for each of us. In complex modern societies such webs of signification can be imagined more easily than they can be demonstrated to exist. Our ability to explain their meanings is limited, because each generality we offer requires that we believe people in a complex society agree, at least *grosso modo*, that what something means is unmistakable. This is sometimes true, but not always. People's agreeing on what something *is* is not the same as their agreeing on what it *means*. Even on a quite simple level, this difficulty can be real. We need to learn that rice "means" fertility, and though that association may seem commonsensical or "natural" once we learn it, actually it is neither. If there is any explanation, it is historical. When we pass on to our children the meanings of what we do, our explanations consist largely of instructions to do what we learned to do before them. In societies arranged in groups or divisions or layers, the learned meanings will differ from one group to another—just as the learned dialect, say, may differ. The supposed webs of signification ought to be interpretable in terms of such differences, particularly if some meanings diffuse from one group to another. Otherwise, the assumption of a homogeneous web may mask, instead of reveal, how meanings are generated and transmitted. This is perhaps the point where meaning and power touch most clearly.

The profound changes in dietary and consumption patterns in eighteenth- and nineteenth-century Europe were not random or fortuitous, but the direct consequences of the same momentum that created a world economy, shaping the asymmetrical relationships between the metropolitan centers and their colonies and satellites, and the tremendous productive and distributive apparatuses, both technical and human, of modern capitalism. But this is not to say that these changes were intended, or that their ancillary consequences were well understood. The ways in which the English became the biggest sugar consumers in the world; the relationships between the colonial loci of sugar production and the metropolitan locus of its refining and consumption; the connections between sugar and slavery and the slave trade; the relation of sugar to bitter liquid stimulants; the role of the West Indian interest in protecting the plantation economy and winning special state support for sugar; the unexpected suitability of sugar for the crown's desire to impose duties—these and many other aspects of sugar's history must not be thrown together and labeled "causes" or "consequences" as if, once enumerated, they explained anything by themselves. But it is possible to point to certain long-term trends the general consequences of which are readily discerned. The steady and cumulative decline in the relative price of sugars is clear enough, in spite of occasional short-term increases. Generally speaking, the demand for sugar, even in thirteenth- and fourteenth-century England, was substantial, though the price put it beyond the means of most people. The earliest prices mentioned, for 1264, range from one to two shillings per pound, which would be the equivalent of at least several pounds sterling today. As the Atlantic islands came into sugar production at the end of the fifteenth century, the price in England fell to as low as three or four pence per pound. Prices rose again at the mid-sixteenth century, probably because of Henry VIII's debasement of currency and the influx of New World silver. But sugar prices did not climb at a rate as high as those for other "eastern" commodities, even after the fall of Egypt to the Turks (1518); possibly the Atlantic islands were already supplying much—or most—of England's sugar.[2] Even in those early centuries, the relative price of sugar was higher than it had been in the first decade of the century—while consumption continued to rise. In the view of Ellen Ellis, the economic crisis engendered by the currency debasement did not force England's "merchants and the landholders who were raising sheep, and selling the wool at a greatly enchanced price, [who] had been the chief consumers of sugar before," to "give up their consumption of the good things in life."[3]

In the course of the seventeenth century, the prices of sugar con-

tinued to fall. In 1600, the highest price for fine sugar was two
shillings; in 1685, the price stood at eight pence the pound. The
growing cheapness of sugar is suggested as well by the scale of units
in which it was purchased:

> In the earlier times rich people bought it by the pound, or at most
> by the loaf, a loaf of sugar being a favorite present to a distin-
> guished personage. Even such an opulent person as Lord Spencer
> buys stocks of sugar by the loaf, though on two occasions, 1613,
> 1614, the weight of twenty loaves bought is given. In 1664, it is
> first bought (and without the designation of loaves), by the hun-
> dredweight at eighty-four shillings. It is again purchased in the
> same manner in 1679.[4]

The increase in sugar production in the mid-seventeenth century
was so headlong that prices of sugar fell—between 1645 and 1680,
by 70 percent—with temporarily adverse effects upon Caribbean
producers.[5] The consequence of this decline for consumers was
equally important: the number of new users may have risen quite
sharply. Sheridan's estimates, cited earlier, suggest a fourfold increase in consumption during 1660–1700, followed by a trebling
between 1700 and 1740. Indeed, overproduction of sugar affected
the whole Atlantic economy for several decades. In Amsterdam, the
price of raw sugar fell by one-third between 1677 and 1687,[6] and
in England in 1686, muscovado sugar fell to a price so low it would
not be reached again for nearly two centuries:

> The growth of consumption during the seventeenth century may
> be partly explained by the cheapening of sugar, first by Brazilian
> and then by West Indian supplies; but the demand continued to
> grow long after the trend of prices took an upward turn in the
> 1730s. More than once a brief collapse of sugar prices seemed
> to indicate that production was outrunning demand: at the end
> of the fifteenth century, when Madeira, the Canaries and São
> Thomé were offering supplies to Europe on a new scale; in the
> 1680s when the massive growth of West Indian supply gave a
> check to the prosperity of the Brazilian plantations; and in the
> 1720s when Jamaica and St. Domingue emerged out of the trib-
> ulations of war to enlarge the scale of Caribbean production. But
> time and again rising demand came to the rescue, even absorbing
> without difficulty the sensational rise of production when Cuba

came on to the market in the 1770s; and at the end of the eighteenth century the prospects were bright enough to cause the
opening of production beyond the Americas, in Mauritius, Java
and the Philippines.[7]

The developments "beyond the Americas" represented the maturation of world trade in sucrose. Britain, acknowledging the transformation of sugar into a daily necessity, gradually replaced the
protectionism offered the West Indian planters with a "free market,"
thereby assuring practically unlimited quantities of sucrose—except
in times of war—to her own people. This triumph for "free trade"
was bought at some political cost; just as there were those who
profited from the end of the differential duties, there were others
who had benefited from them for centuries. The advocates of more
sugar for more people at cheaper prices won out.

The nature and scale of sucrose consumption in the United Kingdom had changed completely by 1850: the popularization of sucrose, barely begun in 1650, brought some of it into the hands of
even the very poor within a century; then, between 1750 and 1850,
it ceased to be a luxury and became a necessity. The gradual erosion
of the discriminatory duties thereafter, doubtless hastened by the
competitive effects of better beet-sugar manufacture upon the tropical cane-producing areas, tended to equalize competition among
producers, at least within the empire, meanwhile encouraging foreign producers to vie for the enormous British market.

It is impossible to say what percentage of the English populace
consumed what percentage of sucrose imported in a given year, or
to indicate in what degree and in what regards consumption increased and proliferated. But there is no doubt that the quantities
imported and retained during that two-century period when sucrose
changed from rarity to daily ingestible rose steadily; that the increase
was comparatively larger than the population increase; and that by
the mid-nineteenth century the British were eating more sugar than
ever before, and were as sugar-hungry as ever. These were the facts
upon which free-trade advocates based their successful campaigns;
they rightly believed they could count on an elasticity of demand
created during the preceding century of increasing sugar use, even
among the very poor. Per-capita consumption continued to climb

upward well into the twentieth century, leveling off at around 105 pounds per person per year only in the past decade.

Many (though not all) sucrose-eating populations in the West ate more and more sugar during the past century (a few reaching averages of 105–15 pounds yearly, or about one-third of a pound per person per day). In the case of the United Kingdom, the downward movement of prices after 1857 was accompanied by steady increases in consumption. But though price greatly affected the ability of the English—particularly the poorer classes—to buy as much sucrose as they wished, it does not explain why they ate so much of it even when it was relatively costly. The movement to bring down prices by opening trade pitted two different segments of the British capitalist classes against each other. Unsurprisingly, the segment allied with factory capitalism won out.

The political power needed to change the relative positions of competing sucrose sellers in the imperial market seems—and is—notably different from the more informal "power" that, at earlier points in British history, influenced the consumption choices of the emerging proletariat. One's choice of what one wants or needs to eat makes sense only in terms of one's preferences and aspirations—in terms, that is, of the social context of consumption. The consumption of products such as tobacco, tea, and sugar may have been one of the very rare ways in which British workers of the mid-nineteenth century achieved the fulfillment of the promises implicit in the political philosophy of a century earlier. Particularly for the working poor, eating more and more food with substantial amounts of sucrose in it was an appropriate response to what British society had become.

The theory of mercantilism—to the extent that one can reify a point of view that only occasionally coalesced into firm and unified policy—held that "demand" was a constant for any people or country. Markets did not grow; they reached an equilibrium. The political economist Charles Davenant put it this way: "For there is a limited stock of our own product to carry out, beyond which there is no passing: as for example, there is such a quantity of woollen manufactures, lead, tin, etc, which over and above our own consumption, we can export abroad, and our soil as it is now peopled, will not yield much more; and there is likewise a limited quantity of these goods which foreign consumption will not exceed."[8]

The received wisdom was that lowered prices could only mean lowered profits, without any compensation in the form of increased sales. So firmly did people believe in static markets that "the adoption by common people of dress and consumption habits previously confined to the rich, was received as a symptom of moral economic disorder. Such consumer behavior would drain the state of its treasure at the same time that it undermined God-ordained status distinctions. Sumptuary laws—invariably futile—continued to be enacted to obstruct the downward diffusion of upper-class fashions."[9] But in spite of the common view that the poor neither would nor should consume objects and substances preferred by the rich even if they could afford them, there were those who wanted to increase such consumption. Men like Thomas and Slare and Benjamin Moseley and George Porter, writing at different times and from quite different perspectives, argued both that demand should be expanded—indeed, created—by insisting that sugar was good for everyone; and that none should be deprived of the widespread benefits that would result from its consumption. From Dalby Thomas on, there were voices in Great Britain that spoke for the deliberate augmentation of demand, rather than for its leveling off to fit prior, status-determined differences.

The Dutch economic historian Jan DeVries argues that two features of economic life—often attributed to so-called precapitalist or primitive economies—had to be radically modified to enlarge demand. First, more families (or wage-earning individuals) had to become involved with the market, both as producers for sale and as buyers of consumption goods. Second, the disposition to satisfy only pre-existing levels of consumption and to work no more than these required—the so-called backward-sloping supply curve of labor—had to change. Many seventeenth- and even eighteenth-century theorists thought such a conservative disposition was natural, inherent to the laborer, and not subject to modification by outside forces. DeVries cites Sir William Petty, who, in his *Political Arithmetic*, written in the 1670s, argued: "It is observed by Clothiers and others, who employ great numbers of poor people, that when corn [grain] is extremely plentiful, that the labour of the poor is proportionately dear: and scarce to be had at all (so licentious are they who labour only to eat, or rather to drink)."[10] This view persisted in the eighteenth century: "Scarcity, to a certain degree... promotes industry.... The manufacturer [i.e., the worker] who can subsist on three days' work will be idle and drunken the rest of the week.... The poor in the manufacturing counties will never work any more time than is necessary just to live and support their weekly debauches."[11]

On the one hand, then, political economists supposed that "ordinary people" would work only enough to stay alive and not a minute longer; on the other, they thought that "ordinary people" would indulge themselves foolishly, seeking to consume substances that, for moral or medical or other reasons, were simply not good for them or for society. There was a diversity of opinions, some of which led to support for the expanding consumption of goods (such as sugar), usually on the grounds of its being good for the consumers and for the nation; and some to opposition to such expansion, usually on the grounds of its being physically or morally bad for the consumers and economically and politically bad for the nation. Over time, the struggle to increase consumption of any good on the grounds of the consumer's rights to his/her own buying power kept pace with the desire of more "progressive" capitalists to expand the market or their share of it. In a few cases this was not quite true—alcoholic beverages, for instance, could interfere with the efficiency of labor—but it certainly held in the case of tea, sugar, and like stimulants.

Though DeVries says, "We would credit seventeenth-century merchants and manufacturers with more imagination and radicalism than they possessed by saying that they acted to create a social order compatible with expanding demand,"[12] that social order did in fact emerge. Its effects upon the sugar market were truly sensational, and the reverse effects, though less important, were no less real.

The period 1600–1750 was one of rapidly increasing urban populations in northern Europe. The raising of livestock and the production of fodder displaced much vegetable farming; landless populations were employed more and more as agrarian wage-earning laborers moved into the growing cities. The cumulative effect was a greater dependence on the market on the part of more and more people, even for items of daily consumption such as bread and beer, and, soon enough, tobacco and sugar and tea. The concomitant growth of government taxation—taxation of a regressive sort, falling disproportionately upon those least able to pay—may have somewhat constrained consumer demand. But it also tended to force up domestic production for the market, to provide the wherewithal for payment—that is, local producers tried to produce more, so as to maintain their own buying power. One change, essential to my argument, was that proletarian work schedules were transformed by structural changes in the national economy, and created for the laboring classes new tasting opportunities and new occasions for eating and drinking.

This did not happen overnight. Nor, for that matter, did majority opinion encourage a mass market for sugar. Even after royalty and the planters' friends in Parliament had discovered that plantation products were eminently taxable, as well as edible, the better part of another century would pass before sugar protagonists based their argument firmly on the possibilities for enlarging consumption among the working poor. It was then that they became, in effect, the political enemies of the West Indian planters, by putting cheap sugar ahead of colonial preference.

The eminent British historian Eric Hobsbawm points out: "Neither economic theory nor the economic practice of the early Industrial Revolution relied on the purchasing power of the labouring population, whose wages, it was generally assumed, would not be far removed from the subsistence level."

> When by any chance some section of them earned enough to spend their money on the same sorts of goods as their "betters" (as happened from time to time during economic booms), middle-class opinion deplored or ridiculed such presumptuous lack of thrift. The economic advantages of high wages, whether as incentives to higher productivity or as additions to purchasing-

power, were not discovered until after the middle of the [nine-teenth] century, and then only by a minority of advanced and enlightened employers.[13]

All the same, the political fights that eventuated in the end of the preferential duties for West Indian sugars were an important step in unleashing proletarian buying power. Cheaper sugar came at a time when its increased consumption was guaranteed not by the sugar habit itself, but by the factory world and machine rhythms which were the background for its use. It was not just that labor worked harder in order to get more; those who paid its wages profited both from labor's higher productivity and from its height-ened use of store-purchased commodities.[14]

Few concepts in the social sciences have caused as many dis-agreements as the concept of power, and no satisfactory consensus on its definition has emerged. But there is no way to avoid the term—or one like it—when the objective is to clarify under what conditions the population of a entire country changes its behavior radically without the compulsion of open force and violence. Of course it is possible to interpret such a change as no more than the expression of will, of free choice—in the case of sugar, in obtaining a desired good previously not available. But this requires us to assume that each and every Briton, day by day and year by year, chose individually to seek and consume sucrose and other new and expensive products with which it was associated, until the United Kingdom was somehow transformed into a nation of sucrose eaters. To omit the concept of power is to treat as indifferent the social, economic, and political forces that benefited from the steady spread of demand for sugar. It asks an unjustified ingenuousness of us.

The history of sugar suggests strongly that the availability, and also the circumstances of availability, of sucrose—which became one of the most desired of all edible commodities in the empire—were determined by forces outside the reach of the English masses themselves. There had been a time, after all, when no one in England knew of sugar, followed by a period, centuries long, when it was a costly rarity. Only after around 1650 did sugar become important to England's ruling strata, so that more and more of it was imported:

mounting economic—and, soon enough, political—forces supported the seizure of colonies where cane could be grown and raw sugar manufactured, as well as the slave trade that supplied the needed labor. The proportion of imported sugar consumed in Britain increased and the price fell. Even though the buying power of those who came to like sucrose was limited, consumption rose steadily; more and more people consumed more and more sugar. The uses to which it was put and its place in the diet changed and proliferated; it grew more important in people's consciousness, in family budgets, and in the economic, social, and political life of the nation.

These changes have to do with "outside" meaning—the place of sucrose in the history of colonies, commerce, political intrigue, the making of policy and law—but they have to do with "inside" meaning as well, because the meanings people gave to sugar arose under conditions prescribed or determined not so much by the consumers as by those who made the product available. Before the rich and powerful who first ate sugar in England could give it new meanings, they had to have it. Then its uses changed as it became more common and familiar. We can assume that some meanings, conveyed by the forms of use, were freshly invented, others synthesized with what was learned from elsewhere.

After 1650 sugar prices decline and quantities increase; many more people get to taste it, mostly in conjunction with tea (or one of the other new beverages). The downward spread is slow and halting but continuous; some time before 1700, the pace quickens. For the new users, as we have seen, sugar comes to play a very different part in diet. On many sides there is ample evidence of a real push to seize more colonies, establish more plantations, import more slaves to them, build more ships, import more sucrose and other plantation products. And as these substances come within reach of the poor, the possibility of a steadily expanding domestic (national) market, as opposed to an export market, becomes clearer.

That genuine attempts were made to increase sugar consumption is hardly in doubt, even though many railed against these strange new products. Of course consumers must have wanted to consume sugar, and demonstrated as much by forgoing other consumption opportunities in order to have it. But one must go on to note the emergence of different groups within British society that came to benefit from the production—and consumption—of this new product.

When it was first produced in the West Indies, sugar easily won the attention and interest of Englishmen. Not only was it already prized as a luxury good by the nobility and the wealthy, but it soon appeared to be a promising (if risky) form of investment. The slave trade, shipping, the plantations themselves, the provision of credit against which plantations and stocks of slaves and sugar could be collateral, and, soon enough, opportunities for retailing and refining—all seemed to offer rewards to the rich and daring. But not only to the rich. The brilliant Trinidadian historian Eric Williams, in his pathbreaking study of the slave trade and sugar, points out that though the Liverpool trade oligopoly rested in the hands of only ten or so firms, many slavers were financed by a highly democratic pooling of the modest resources of "attorneys, drapers, grocers, barbers and tailors. The shares in the ventures were subdivided, one having one-eighth, another one-fifteenth, a third one thirty-second part of a share and so on."[15] "The little fellows" had no comparable opportunity to invest in plantations, however: whereas investment shares at home could be aggregated into slaving ships and banks, plantations were almost always run as individually owned enterprises, and most planters came from families of at least some means back at home.

But some men of limited means did end up rich planters. Richard Pares's magnificent *A West-India Fortune* (1950), which details the career of the sugar-cane-planting Pinneys of Nevis, reveals that Azariah Pinney, the founder of the family fortune, was sent dry goods by his father and siblings, from the sale of which he was able eventually to acquire a small plantation, around which the Pinney riches subsequently grew. Pares, who probably knew as much about the evolution of the British West Indian planter classes as anyone ever has, shows us no rags-to-riches ambience in the sugar islands, but stresses instead the importance of familial support at home for younger sons striking out overseas, and of the value of special skills like bookkeeping, practicing law, and retailing in enabling even those persons without the wherewithal eventually to become planters themselves.[16] Perhaps the principal point is that the plantation colonies afforded pioneering opportunities, as did the slave trade and the derivative trading and commercial activities the plantation system made possible in the colonies and at home.

The creditors, both great and petty, who had invested in various aspects of the sugar economy naturally had a stake in its success. To these can be added the planters, many of whom came from already rich families, but who often added to their wealth by their plantation operations. Their style of life during the maturity of the plantation era is as famous as was, during certain periods, their political influence at home. Even as sober and dispassionate a historian as Pares can write:

> Many colonies made no laws at all about the feeding of slaves before the humanitarians forced them into it at the end of the eighteenth century; and even where there were laws, the standards which they enforced were pitiably low. The French *code noir* stipulated for a supply of protein which would amount to little more than a kipper a day; and this *code* was not at all well observed. Some planters normally gave their slaves no food at all, but fobbed them off with payments of rum wherewith to buy food, or with Saturdays and Sundays to till their own provision grounds and feed themselves. The rum was drunk, the Saturdays or Sundays encroached upon or wasted, and the slaves starved. Their masters almost wholly disregarded their needs for protein, and could not see why they went on hunger-strike, or lost their sleep catching land crabs, or died. When I think of the colossal banquets of the Barbados planters, as Ligon describes them, of the money which the West Indians at home poured out upon the Yorkshire electorate and Harriette Wilson, of the younger William Beckford's private orchestra and escapades in Lisbon, of Fonthill Abbey or even of the Codrington Library, and remember that the money was got by working African slaves twelve hours a day on such a diet, I can only feel anger and shame.[17]

Williams tells us a good deal about these planters in the colonies, and of their ability to sway Parliament, of which many were members.

> Allied with the other great monopolists of the eighteenth century,

the landed aristocracy and the commercial bourgeoisie of the
seaport towns, this powerful West India interest exerted in the
unreformed Parliament an influence sufficient to make every
statesman pause, and represented a solid phalanx "of whose support in emergency every administration in turn has experienced
the value." They put up a determined resistance to abolition,
emancipation, and the abrogation of their monopoly. They were
always on the warpath to oppose any increase of the duties on
sugar.[18]

The planters, bankers, slavers, shippers, refiners, grocers, and
people in government whose interests lay along such lines or who
accurately foretold the unfolding fiscal possibilities sugar offered
were among those groups whose power counted in this story. All
of these people exercised power of one sort or another in increasing
the disposition of the crown and Parliament to support and to
favor the extension of the rights of the planters, the maintenance
of slavery, the availability of sugar and its by-products (molasses
and rum) to the people at large. It is to their efforts that England
owed the institutionalization of a rum ration in the navy (begun
"unofficially" after the capture of Jamaica in 1655): half a pint
per day from 1731 on. In the late eighteenth century it was
increased to a pint a day for adult sailors—much-needed creeping
socialism for an infant industry. The official allocations of sugar
and treacle to the poorhouses in the late eighteenth century were
similar support measures.

When the protection of the West Indian interests became too
expensive for their erstwhile supporters, who were sensitive to the
immense potentialities of the untapped sugar consumer market at
home only awaiting lower prices, power was applied in different
ways. The same had been true when the abolitionists—opposing
first the slave trade, and later slavery itself—many of them with
economic interests radically different from those of the planters,
took stands that the planters saw as destructive of the plantations.
Different interest groups might align themselves together at one
time, but shifting economic fortunes often pitted such powerful allies
against one another. (Citing an observer who reported in 1764 that
fifty or sixty West Indian voters could turn the balance in the House

of Commons any direction they wished, Eric Williams adds that there was a new combination in the Reformed Parliament that was just as strong: "It was the Lancashire cotton interest, and its slogan was not monopoly but laissez faire."[19])

The various blocs, then, were ready to change sides—and often did. But their seeming fickleness in no way reduced the power they were able to exercise in critical situations. The political and economic influence of the governing strata set the terms by which increasing quantities of sugar and like commodities became available throughout English society. This influence took the form of specific legislative initiatives affecting duties and tariffs, or the purchase of supplies of sugar, molasses, and rum for dispensing through government agencies, like the navy and the almshouses; or regulations affecting matters of purity, standards of quality, etc. But it also involved the informal exercise of power: a combination of official prerogatives with the use of pressures made possible through cliques, family connections, university and public-school contacts, covert coercion, friendship, club membership, the strategic application of wealth, job promises, cajolery, and much else—most of it familiar to any serious reader of today's newspapers.

Such power and its application have to do with "outside" meaning—with the setting of the terms within which the various forms of sucrose were made available. But power was also exercised in the shaping of "inside" meaning.

In 1685, when the young Edmund Verney went up to Oxford, his father's letter to him, detailing the contents of his student trunk, included mention of oranges, lemons, raisins, and nutmegs—as well as "three pounds of Brown Sugar, one pound of white poudered sugar made up in quarters, one pound of Brown sugar candy, one-quarter of a pound of white sugar candy."[20] Not every young man went to Oxford, and few parents were so rich and solicitous, yet the "everyday treat" quality of this list, only thirty years after the conquest of Jamaica, is telling.

Among countless Britons poorer than the Verneys, the fall in sugar prices toward the end of that century encouraged the eating of puddings, among other treats, but also encouraged additional uses of sugar, transmitted from the boards and kitchens of the wealthy. The suet puddings Arthur Young describes on the menus at the almshouse at Nacton, for example, were innovations, institutionalized in the eighteenth century, fed to the desperately poor. It was of these people that Young wrote with some impatience:

> Pease porridge used to be dinner on the two last days [Friday and Saturday], but they petitioned for bread and butter instead of it, which [they] found their favourite dinner, because they have tea to it. I expressed surprize at this being allowed; but they said they were permitted to spend 2d. in the shilling of what they earned, as they please; and they laid it all out in tea and sugar to drink with their bread and butter dinners.
>
> Indulgence renders it necessary to let them do as they please with it, but it would be better expended in something else.[21]

The various uses of sugar eventually acquired many local, particular, and distinctive meanings, and only exacting regional research will substantiate this diversification on local and regional levels—funeral cakes and Christmas pies, puddings and candies, custards and all the rest. But two kinds of use are involved. Counterposed to the downward and outward "intensification" of upper-class usages (and some of their meanings), there was the largely independent invention of new uses; in the conjuncture of these two lines of development the relationship of power to "inside meaning" is revealed.

In the course of everyday life, social groups transmute acts, substances, and the relationships among them into units of different meaning. Rituals involving eating, for instance, may be marked by unusual foods (items otherwise tabooed or those prepared in a traditional or archaic manner), or by ordinary foods taking on a wholly different significance because of the ritual context. Examples are plentiful of both: the Passover *seder*, the Eucharist, Thanksgiving turkey, and so on. The custom of marking the end of a time unit ("week"), or a day of rest, by distinctive food consumption is also widespread.

In seventeenth- and eighteenth-century England, new and modified sucrose uses were wedged into ritual and ceremonial contexts at court and among the rich and powerful. Most such practices were

originally French or Italian and had come to England by way of
royal visits, the settlement of confectioners and sugar sculptors in
England, and the international social reciprocities of the dominant
classes. As these uses of sugar were diffused downward, they were
probably simplified, not only for reasons of economy—the differentials in wealth were of course staggering—but also because for
the vast mass of people they could not involve comparable validations of status. The unusual combinations of spices and sweets
accompanying holiday meats and fowl; the wide variety of sugared
treats for religious holidays; the gifts of sweet foods to express
thanks or to wish well to the ill; the use of sweet drinks and baked
goods at rituals of separation and departure (including funerals)—
these and other such usages provide examples of both extensification
and intensification.

Ceremonies and rituals that underlined or dramatized the exercise
of temporal or secular power and authority drifted down the social
ladder without the force that underlay them and that they had once
served to symbolize. It was the *economic ability* to consume in that
fashion, rather than the *status right*, that came to matter. Over time,
sugar proved to be a superb vehicle for just such transformations.
By the time the laboring poor were using sucrose for ceremonial
purposes, the relationships of their consumption behavior to their
self-identification was consistent with the rest of what was hap-
pening in English society. It was possible even for the relatively poor
to consume sugar conspicuously in providing hospitality, meeting
ceremonial obligations, and validating social links, for it was now
an inexpensive good that continued to seem like a luxury, imparting
an aura of privilege to those who served it and to whom it was
served.

The practices that turned sugar into something extraordinary,
ceremonial, and especially meaningful ("intensification"), and the
more common transformation of sugar into something ordinary,
everyday, and essential ("extensification"), were surely not perceived as qualitatively different, or even as separate, processes by
any social class. But distinguishing between them has some utility
here, for it can throw light upon the controlling groups in English
society. Because sugar was new for most people, it acquired its

meanings within English life during a downward spread from the dominant classes, whose norms provided certain models.

Substances like tea, sugar, rum, and tobacco were used by working people in accord with the tempos of working-class life. Those centuries when England was transformed, albeit irregularly and unevenly, from a predominantly rural, agrarian, and precapitalist society were centuries of novelty in consumption. Sugar was taken up just as work schedules were quickening, as the movement from countryside to city was accelerating, and as the factory system was taking shape and spreading. Such changes more and more affected the patterning of eating habits. We have already seen how hot liquid stimulants sweetened with calorie-laden sugar, and tobacco, among other novelties, transformed meals and even the definition of the meal, while economic changes transformed the schedules of eating.

It is at this point that the ideas of meaning and power touch. Surely none of the sugar touts of the seventeenth century foresaw the nation of sucrose eaters their England was soon to become, yet they, and the classes they endorsed, ensured the steady growth of a society ever richer in sugar, and enriched by the slave trade, the plantation system, slavery itself, and, soon enough, the spread of factory industry in the metropolis. As the exemplar of luxuries turned into affordable proletarian goodies by dint of individual effort, sucrose was one of the people's opiates, and its consumption was a symbolic demonstration that the system that produced it was successful.

In the mid-nineteenth century one of the most able protagonists of the equalization of duties—a fight waged to get cheaper sugar onto the British market—was George R. Porter, himself a broker in sugar and a shrewd observer of English eating habits. "Without being one of the absolute necessities of life," he wrote in 1851, "long habit has in this country led almost every class to the daily use of it, so that there is no people in Europe by whom it is consumed to anything like the same extent."[22] Porter argued against sugar duties by asserting that the people of Great Britain were ready to eat much more of it if they could only afford it, and that the duties were a disproportionate and unjust burden upon the poor. For the rich, he said, sugar was so minor an item in the family budget in the 1840s that they would buy the same quantity whether it cost sixpence or a shilling; it was otherwise for the less fortunate. In order to make his case more persuasive, Porter hazarded some clever guesses about differential consumption, first establishing that overall consumption had fallen during those years in the period 1830–49 when the price of sugar rose: "With one exception only, that of the year 1835, every rise in price has been accompanied by diminished consumption, while every fall in the market has produced an increased demand." He then assumed (on the basis of "inquiries carefully made") that rich and middle-rank families, whom he estimated to be perhaps one-fifth of the national population of Britain, consumed in the 1830s about forty pounds of sugar per year per person, for all purposes.[23] Porter concluded that the annual per-capita consumption of the *other* four-fifths of the British population would have been fifteen pounds in 1831, nine pounds in 1840 (when duties were higher), and twenty pounds in 1849. Against such calculations he put the interesting observation that every person serving on one of Her Majesty's ships was allowed one and one-half ounces per day (or thirty-four pounds per year) by official issue; while the allowance to aged paupers in government almshouses at that time was nearly twenty-three pounds per year.

To put it somewhat differently, before the preferential duties (designed to ease the lot of the West Indian planters and—ostensibly—of the newly freed West Indian people) were removed and the price of sugar began to seek its world level, Britain taxed the poor regressively for their sugar, and hence kept sugar consumption substantially lower among the poorer classes than it was even among the sailors and paupers who were its official charges. The West Indian plantations had been profitable from the first because of the desire for sugar (and like products) in Europe; as we have seen, English internal demand eventually overshadowed almost completely the re-export trade. Sugar, then, was a cornerstone of British West Indian slavery and the slave trade, and the enslaved Africans who produced the sugar were linked in clear economic relationships to the British laboring people who were learning to eat it.

Emancipation was a defeat for the planter classes, but a victory for those at home who believed in expanded commerce and heightened consumption. The indemnities paid to the planters (and ostensibly intended to "protect" the newly freed, as well) were paid by the British government; but they were more than amply compensated for by the sugar duties, paid out of all proportion by the poor. When the legislation supporting those duties began to crumble in 1852 under the attacks of the free-trade advocates, the disingenuous assertion arose that the duties protected the West Indian freedmen, but in fact the preferential duties did not help the freedmen one whit. The duties certainly did protect the West Indian planters, however, made mechanization of the sugar industry a less attractive alternative, and kept the price of sugar in Great Britain elevated.

Throughout the British West Indies, the planters' "sufferings" after freedom were resolved, with the connivance of the Foreign Office, by the importation of contracted laborers from India, China, and elsewhere, and special legislation to keep freedmen from voting and from acquiring land. The overall aim was to prevent the newly freed from either securing a livelihood independent of the sugar industry, or from using collective bargaining and strikes to negotiate wages and working conditions, as the proletarians in the metropolis were doing. These strategies worked; even though the West Indies never again produced so high a proportion of the sucrose consumed by the United Kingdom, they remained "sugar islands," their people doomed to straddle two economic adaptations—as reconstituted peasants and as rural proletarians—neither of which could become economically secure. During the two centuries when enslaved Africans had produced Britain's sugar in her Caribbean colonies, they were tied intimately to the emerging factory populations of the English cities by economic reciprocity and the circumstances of their emergence. Now free but almost entirely ignored by the metropolis, the West Indian people became invisible, until their migration to the center of empire brought them back into uneasy view more than a century later.

None of this would have been of concern to men like Porter. He was interested in increasing sugar consumption at home, not in whether the West Indian planters (and certainly not in whether the

West Indian freedmen) could make a living. He found fault with those who, "without much consideration, have chosen to identify a high price of sugar with the happiness of the lately-emancipated slave population of our West India colonies," and argued that being free was reward enough for the ex-slaves.[24] It was Porter, and other "free-trade" advocates, who carried the day. Within two decades, the special protections for West Indian sugar had all been removed.

As prices fell, new sucrose uses were added on—the development of marmalades and preserves, condensed milk, chocolate, and sherbet. The desire of the British working classes for sugar, in the half-century after the first cracks appeared in the preferential duty system, seemed insatiable. This certainly involved prior experiences with sugar and the balance of their diet:

> Sugar for a great part of our population is a stimulant, a source of immediate energy if not inspiration, whether it is turned into alcohol or whether it is consumed raw. As a matter of fact, the very high consumption of sugar in some poor families is very closely correlated with the poverty of their diet in what one might call secondary satisfactions of diet and in its immediate stimulating faculties. This is a very important point in sugar consumption, especially when this includes sweets and "spreads" (on breads) for children. Then there is this question—what is food or expenditure on food and how far is it a necessity? The question put in that way perhaps does not mean much, but I remember a statement—I think it is Bernard Shaw's "Essay on Rent"—that you feed your work horses with hay and your hunters with oats. This is how we treat our human population: we feed our decorative professions on foods that yield them a great deal of stimulation, a great many secondary satisfactions, and we feed our lower population with a very unstimulating and a very poor diet. ...From the economic point of view, conventions determine what particular foodstuffs are going to be bought by any given amount of available income and a great many of these are pure class conventions.[25]

Ashby touches here on an aspect of the transformation of English diet that reverts to the early diffusion of sucrose and stimulant beverages. Once one has read the encomia to tea and sugar by Slare and Moseley, together with the Reverend Davies's indignant remonstrance that the poor would drink milk or small beer instead of tea if they could afford it, it would be simplistic to conclude that people ate more sugar after 1850 just because its price declined. Meaning and power touch this time at the point when a sugar-hungry population had access to well-nigh-unlimited supplies of sugar—once they were habituated to its use. That is why production must be linked to consumption, and so-called inside meanings to the larger, "outside" meanings.

> It is a pretty general observation, that those things which give us most delight, by the free use of them, become hurtful; this cannot be said of sugar; for as no ill property belongs to it, so nothing pernicious can possibly attend its use.... It might be hop'd that those who have complain'd of the cholic from the use of Tea, might, by being less profuse in that, and more so in the free use of the finest Sugar, by its soft and balsamick quality, prevent that disorder.[26]

So wrote an anonymous saccharophile of the mid-eighteenth century whose enthusiasms were boundless. Mothers' milk, he tells us, is improved by the addition of sugar. Molasses is more nutritious than butter or cheese, especially on bread, and ale and beer are served better when brewed with it. Rum is healthier than brandy. Even unripe fruit can be made palatable with sugar.

Intemperate praise of this sort was common at the time, and the reader should make no mistake: whatever else the message, these paeans were also political tracts, read by parliamentarians, judges, physicians, military officers, businessmen, squires—and these "progressive" ideas had a cumulative effect upon legislative attitudes toward sugar and other imported foodstuffs. Yet the creation of a radically new diet for the people of the United Kingdom—some features of which were shared by all classes, and others differentially distributed—cannot possibly be explained by reference to simple legislation or some single, narrowly defined "cause." Our primate liking for sweetness, our capacity to endow the material world with symbolic meaning, and our complication of the biology of ingestion with our social structures all played a part in the rise of sucrose consumption in England. But these neither explain why consumption varied over time or from one class to another, nor get at why social groups can affect the behavior of other groups, at different points in time or in different ways.

The heightened productivity of the laboring classes, the radically altered conditions of their lives, including their prior diet, their readiness to emulate their rulers, the evolving world economy, and the spread of the capitalist spirit—these factors cannot be measured or weighted against one another. But they can be distinguished from factors such as our primate nature, our symbolic faculty, and our disposition to organize our biological satisfactions in social terms, for these latter are constants, givens, the operation of which can be described, but not explained in terms of their origins or differential effects.

Before analyzing how sucrose or any other food or taste fits into the meal systems of the component groups or classes of a complex society, we ought to be able to explain how it got there in the first place (particularly in the case of a recent import such as sucrose), what forces influenced its increasing use, and what made its consumption important—changing it (in this instance) from rarity, novelty, or bauble into absolute necessity. That anthropologists engaged in the study of food in modern societies should apparently be so unconcerned with where the foods come from and who produces them is odd, since such disinterest diverges so radically from the traditional concerns of anthropologists of food. When food enters into the description of a preliterate society such as the Trobriand Islanders, the Tikopia, or the Bemba, the nature and circumstances of its production, sources, and availability are essential features of sociological analysis.[27] But such features are not analyzed when the food systems of modern societies are studied, probably because the production of the foods and the circumstances of their consumption seem so remote from each other. It is of course true that few of us now produce our own food and that we usually buy all that we eat— or the largest proportion of it—from other nonproducers. A far cry from the small, largely self-supporting "primitive" societies anthropologists supposedly study, complex modern societies appear to have divorced food production from food consumption; but why what quantities of food were made available when they were, and how such availabilities shaped choices, are questions deserving answers all the same. There is still a connection between production and consumption, and in the case of sugar, the facts suggest that early on production was actually undertaken with specific groups of consumers in mind—the national population of the United Kingdom, in fact.

If a study of the ritualization of foods in British life were undertaken without reference either to time or to class divisions, the search for meaning would be limited to what was presumably shared by all English people at one point in time. So resolutely unhistorical a position would make the system of meaning coterminous with the present—and thus obscure, rather than clarify, the uses and meanings of food. Divorcing the process from time, like divorcing the consumption of sugar from its production, confines the discussion to a single point; explaining why things are as they are is confined to existing relationships among the parts of a social system. But looking backward enables us to see how the relationships among the parts of such a system took on their characteristic form over time.

As the first exotic luxury transformed into a proletarian necessity, sugar was among the first imports to take on a new and different political and military importance to the broadening capitalist classes in the metropolis—different, that is, from gold, ivory, silk, and other durable luxuries. Whereas the plantations were long viewed as sources of profit through direct capital transfers for reinvestment *at* home, or through the absorption of finished goods *from* home,[28] the hypothesis offered here is that sugar and other drug foods, by provisioning, sating—and, indeed, drugging—farm and factory workers, sharply reduced the overall cost of creating and reproducing the metropolitan proletariat.

How did the British laboring classes become sugar eaters, after all? The readiness of working people to work harder in order to be able to earn—and thus consume—more was a crucial feature of the evolution of modern patterns of eating. A new commercial spirit had to recognize this readiness, perceiving it as a virtue to be encouraged and exploited. Unleashing that spirit accompanied great changes in the economic and political order, which transformed English agrarian life, "freed" the rural population, led to the con-

POWER   •181

quest and harnessing of the tropical colonies, and resulted in the
introduction of new comestibles into the motherland. My argument
is that the heightened consumption of goods like sucrose was the
direct consequence of deep alterations in the lives of working people,
which made new forms of foods and eating conceivable and "natural," like new schedules of work, new sorts of labor, and new
conditions of daily life.

But this does not mean that British working people were merely
the passive witnesses of change. An eighteenth-century writer observed:

> In England the several ranks of men slide into each other almost
> imperceptibly; and a spirit of equality runs through every part
> of the constitution. Hence arises a strong emulation in all the
> several stations and conditions to vie with each other; and a
> perpetual restless ambition in each of the inferior ranks to raise
> themselves to the level of those immediately above them. In such
> a state as this fashion must have an uncontrolled sway. And a
> fashionable luxury must spread through it like a contagion.[29]

Though this commentator surely exaggerated "the spirit of equality" of his time, other writers have commented on the role of the
laboring classes themselves in taking on the habits and customs of
their "betters."[30]

Different attitudes among the controllers of society toward working people, and the disposition of working people to experiment
with novel foods eaten by wealthier people—such tendencies no
doubt worked together in the late eighteenth century. In the next
century, other nations followed the United Kingdom; becoming
more urban and industrialized, changing eating schedules to meet
work schedules, teaching laborers to eat away from home, to eat
prepared food more frequently, and to consume more sugar along
the way. Managers of such societies recognized the potentiality of
workers to increase their own productivity if sufficiently stimulated,
and to open themselves to new, learnable needs.

The determinate "cause" of such changes is a context, or a set
of situations, created by broad economic forces; within that context
new food "choices" are made—indeed, are given shape before they
are even perceived as choices. The choice between a "Danish" pastry

and a "French" doughnut during a ten-minute coffee break is a choice, but the circumstances under which this choice is made may not be freely chosen. Like the choice between a McDonald's hamburger and a Gino's chicken leg during a thirty-minute lunch hour, the choice itself is far less important than the constraints under which the choice is being made.

In much the same way, imitation (or emulation) does not take place in some unhistorical but symbolically meaningful vacuum. What working people actually imitate in the behavior of those with power over them, and what they mean (intend and communicate) with such behavior, is not always clear. The history of the tea habit is a case in point. What laboring Englishmen did by way of imitation in this regard was to drink tea with sugar and milk (usually inferior tea, sometimes twice-used tea, or even hot water poured over bread crusts, sweetened with treacle), as did others more privileged than they. Taking to the custom with a vengeance, they increased their consumption of heavily sweetened tea steadily, until World War I briefly interrupted the upward climb. But does it explain very much to call this upswing the outcome of working people's imitation of their social betters? That the sweetened tea was hot, stimulating, and calorie-rich; that hard work for wages under difficult conditions typified the circumstances under which tea came to be drunk; that tea had the power to make a cold meal seem like a hot one—these seem equally important points. Still another factor was the intimate relationship between where these foods were produced, on whose initiative, by what sorts of workers, and under whose control, and where they were consumed. The empire, after all, had an internal structure that had seen the creation of the categories of plantation slave and (eventually) factory proletarian within a single political system, and had profited immensely from their provisioning one another under the imperial thumb.

Where does this leave us, though? Why did the English people become such enthusiastic sugar consumers? Not because of the innate primate liking for sweetness; not because our species is symbolically communicative and builds meaning into all it does, including eating; not because socially inferior groups imitate their "superiors"; not even because people in cold, wet climes supposedly like sugar more than other people. Certain homelier facts seem more persuasive. The diet of the British worker was both calorically and nutritively inadequate and monotonous. Often working people could not get hot food, especially for their breakfasts and midday meals. New schedules of work and rest, changing conditions of employment, the end of the dependent relationship of agricultural laborer to squire, the development of a putting-out system, then a factory system—these were among the contextual conditions for changes in food habits. It is in their light that the vaunted disposition of people to imitate their betters can be made to rest on a broader interpretive basis. When we read the encomia to sugar and remember that this was a society swiftly adopting a more urban, time-conscious, and industrial character, it is not surprising that Slare sounded nearer the truth of things than Hanway.

Still, sugar, tea, and like products represented the growing freedom of ordinary folks, their opportunity to participate in the elevation of their own standards of living. But to assert this is to raise some questions. The proclaimed freedom to choose meant freedom only within a range of possibilities laid down by forces over which those who were, supposedly, freely choosing exercised no control at all. That substances like sugar could be changed from curiosities or adornments in English life into essential ingredients of decent self-respecting hospitality required that people weave them into the fabric of their daily lives, endowing them with meaning and teaching each other to enjoy their consumption.

It was not by processes of symbol making and meaning investment that sugar was made available to the English people, but because of political, economic, and military undertakings the organization of which would have been unimaginable to the ordinary citizen. The immense quantities of coerced labor required to produce sucrose and bitter stimulant beverages also had to be arranged for, or the substances in the quantities desired would not have been forthcoming. Only with these arrangements secured could the wonderful and uniquely human capacity to find and bestow meaning be exercised. In short, the creation of a commodity that would permit taste and the symbolic faculty to be exercised was far beyond the reach of both the enslaved Africans who produced the sugar, on the one hand, and of the proletarianized English people who consumed it, on the other. Slave and proletarian together powered the imperial economic system that kept the one supplied with manacles and the other with sugar and rum; but neither had more than minimal influence over it. The growing freedom of the consumer to choose was one kind of freedom, but not another.

Porter's argument that lowered sugar prices were always followed by higher consumption was amply borne out in the second half of the nineteenth century, a period during which taxes and duties on sugars dropped as well. A comparable abolition of government levies was a long time coming, but by 1872 they were cut in half. Tax historian S. Dowell's reflections on this illuminate nicely the preceding two centuries for us:

> Here undoubtedly, in the opinion of many careful and provident persons who bore in mind our fiscal system in the whole, and, regarding advance in prosperity by leaps and bounds as a temporary and not the normal condition of the progress of the nation, fixed their attention on the eventualities of the future, we should have stayed the process of reduction, which, if carried further, threatened the annihilation of the tax. This tax, with those on tea and coffee, held, in their opinion, a position of peculiar importance: to be kept, in time of peace, at low rates at which, so evenly do these taxes lie over the whole surface of the nation, the pressure was not felt by anyone, they were powerful engines available when the nation should be called upon for a general effort in time of war. To abolish these taxes would be to remove the mainstays of our system of taxation.[31]

The part such taxes played in the creation of state extraction systems, sustained by skimming from the costs of personal consumption, is significant. Of sugar and other exotic products—particularly the bitter, habit-forming stimulants which English people combined it with—sugar was the most aptly taxable, partly because it was poorly suited to smuggling (unlike tea, for instance). As its yield of wealth to the exchequer grew, so its value as a taxable item was enshrined: there arose a powerful vested interest in its continued and expanded consumption. Like tea or tobacco, it could be counted upon to yield revenues even when scarce supplies drove up its price.

Contemporary renderings, in sugar paste, of miniature figures in nineteenth-century costume. (Above: *Laurent Sully Jaulmes/Musée des Arts Décoratifs/Centre de Documentation du Sucre*. Below: *Philippe Rousselet/Centre de Documentation du Sucre*)

All Saints' Day, *Día de los Muertos*, is celebrated in Mexico with candy skulls, tombs, and wreaths, and an astounding display of artistic/culinary ingenuity. The artistic and ritual association between sugar and death is not a Mexican monopoly; in much of Europe, candied funeral treats are popular. The link between Easter and sugar is neatly contrastive. *(C. Gibier/Centre de Documentation du Sucre)*

This sugar mold, which
includes a bust of George V,
was prepared for the
king's silver jubilee (1935).
It harks back to the work
of royal sugar bakers of
earlier centuries.
*(C. Gibier/Musée des Arts
Décoratifs/Centre de
Documentation du Sucre)*

A scale model (1:80) by sugar baker Mary Ford and her husband of the British
royal state coach, fashioned for the silver jubilee of Queen Elizabeth II (1977).
(C. Gibier/Centre de Documentation du Sucre)

The Cathedral of Notre Dame at Amiens, in scale (1:80), created in 1977 by sugar baker Hubert Lahm. Twenty thousand sugar cubes and 176 pounds of glaze were used in the construction of this work, which stands 59 inches high, 70 inches long, and 36 inches wide. *(Centre de Documentation du Sucre)*

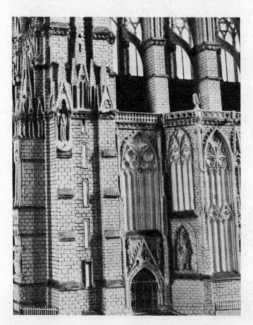

Detail.

A model sailing ship on an elaborate base, entirely fashioned from sugar paste by baker Hiroomi Tatematsu. *(Centre de Documentation du Sucre)*

This model medieval castle was constructed by English chefs at a West Sussex restaurant (1977). It probably typifies the work of royal sugar bakers of an earlier era. *(Centre de Documentation du Sucre)*

This sculpture, *Caesar's Thumb*, suggests how art and appetite intersect in the history of sugar. Though carried to levels of extreme delicacy in some works, sugar paste can also be employed as if it were clay or stone. *(C. Gibier/Centre de Documentation du Sucre)*

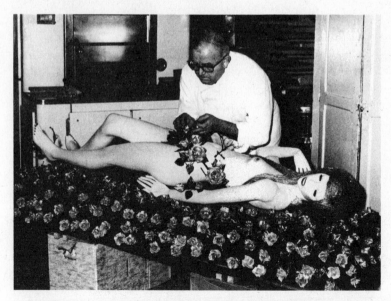

Etienne Tholoniat, a great French sugar baker, puts the finishing touches on a life-size chocolate nude with spun-sugar hair. She is lying on a bed of six hundred sugar roses. *(Centre de Documentation du Sucre)*

And, as Dowell says, because its consumption was so widespread, "the pressure was not felt by anyone." Thus was the new freedom to afford sugar a key to governance itself.

With the change in place of such commodities in the English diet, and the growing recognition of the ultimate consequences of mass consumption, the world market gradually set the price of sugar. But even this overstates the case, for probably no single food commodity on the world market has been subjected to so much politicking as sugar. If it earlier was too important to be left to West Indian planters, it later became too important to be left entirely exposed to market forces. Sucrose was a source of bureaucratic, as well as mercantile and industrial, wealth. Once the magnitude of its market and potential market was grasped, maintaining control over it became important. Sugar led all else in dramatizing the tremendous power concealed in mass consumption. Control over it, and responsibility for the eventual outcome, led to a sweeping revision of the philosophy that determined the connections between metropolis and colony. It might not be too much to say that the fate of the British West Indies was sealed, once it became cheaper for the British masses to have their sugar from elsewhere, and more profitable for the British bourgeoisie to sell more sugar at lower prices.

To the extent that we can define things for others under circumstances that make it difficult for them to test the meanings we attribute to those things, we are exercising control over whether those others use these things, consume them or fail to consume them, prize them or disdain them. We affect their self-definition by motivating their consumption, thereby entering intimately into the organization of their very personalities: who and what they think they are. Tobacco, sugar, and tea were the first objects within capitalism that conveyed with their use the complex idea that one could *become* different by *consuming* differently. This idea has little to do with nutrition or primates or sweet tooths, and less than it appears to have with symbols. But it is closely connected to England's fundamental transformation from a hierarchical, status-based, medieval society to a social-democratic, capitalist, and industrial society.

The argument advanced here, that big background alterations in the tempo and nature of work and daily life influenced changes in diet, is difficult or impossible to prove. The further assumption is that the nature of the new foods was important in their eventual acceptance. The substances transformed by British capitalism from upper-class luxuries into working-class necessities are of a certain type. Like alcohol or tobacco, they provide respite from reality, and deaden hunger pangs. Like coffee or chocolate or tea, they provide stimulus to greater effort without providing nutrition. Like sugar they provide calories, while increasing the attractiveness of these other substances when combined with them. There was no conspiracy at work to wreck the nutrition of the British working class, to turn them into addicts, or to ruin their teeth. But the ever-rising consumption of sugar was an artifact of intraclass struggles for profit—struggles that eventuated in a world-market solution for drug foods, as industrial capitalism cut its protectionist losses and expanded a mass market to satisfy proletarian consumers once regarded as sinful or indolent.

In this perspective, sugar was an ideal substance. It served to make a busy life seem less so; in the pause that refreshes, it eased, or seemed to ease, the changes back and forth from work to rest; it provided swifter sensations of fullness or satisfaction than complex carbohydrates did; it combined easily with many other foods, in some of which it was also used (tea and biscuit, coffee and bun, chocolate and jam-smeared bread). And as we have seen, it was symbolically powerful, for its use could be endowed with many subsidiary meanings. No wonder the rich and powerful liked it so much, and no wonder the poor learned to love it.

5 · Eating and Being

By 1900, sugar in the form of processed sucrose had become an essential ingredient in the British national diet. Combined with bitter beverages, it was consumed daily by almost every living Briton. It was added to foods in the kitchen and at table, and could be found in prepared delicacies such as jams, biscuits, and pastries, which were consumed at tea and frequently with meals. Sugar had also become a common feature of festive and ceremonial foods from season to season and from birth to death. Bread and salt had been the basis of western man's daily fare and daily imagery for millennia; now sugar had joined them. Bread and salt—and sugar. A loaf of bread, a jug of wine—and sugar. The diet of a whole species was gradually being remade.

The vastly expanded use and increasing individual consumption of processed sucrose from 1650 to 1900 was made possible by many achievements, among them the ever-greater technical mastery of sugar chemistry, and a fuller scientific comprehension of sugar's remarkable versatility. It was the result of the application of new chemical knowledge to a versatility long-esteemed, but never before so imaginatively and completely exploited. By the time of World War I, the enforced rationing of sugar was regarded as among the most painful and immediate of the petty hardships caused by war—and of course the more acutely felt by poorer and less privileged Britons.[1] For the poor, the tastes for sweetened tea, treacle pudding, condensed-milk custard, biscuits, jam-smeared bread, candy, and chocolate were acquired early and depressingly well. The more comfortable classes' sweet tooth—just as noteworthy in terms of what is called "national character"—was tempered because they had so many other luxuries within reach.

The experience of the English in having sugar pumped into every crevice of their diet was, as I have said, repeated in other lands, at times more swiftly, after 1900—but with some significant differences. Take, first, the United States, which had battened upon molasses and its yield, rum, even before the thirteen colonies revolted.[2] By 1880–84, the United States was consuming thirty-eight pounds of sucrose per person per year—already well ahead of all other major world consumers except the United Kingdom. In three short years consumption had risen to 60.9 pounds.[3] Within another decade, United States consumption rose still higher. And after 1898–99—not a date picked out of a hat—it rose higher yet. Whatever British capitalists had learned about sugar as a source of profit after 1650, North American capitalists learned far more quickly; those interested in the rise of North American imperialism could do worse than looking carefully at the history of U.S. sugar consumption.

It is not entirely clear to what extent the perceived need of the United States to introject tropical sugar-producing areas, by transforming them into various sorts of colonies, was homologous with the imperial objectives of other powers a century or so earlier. But the mercantilist elements in this aspect of American foreign policy, especially clear in the expansion of American military power in the Caribbean sugar bowl, appear very late. Instead of Barbados the United States had Puerto Rico; instead of Jamaica, Cuba; for the Pacific areas, there were Hawaii and the Philippines. Not surprisingly, from the time when the consumer market in the United States became substantial—beginning around the end of the Civil War—until the present, U.S. sugar policy has been a major political football, and a source of stupendous (and often illicit) gain.[4]

The experience of France offers a startling contrast to that of the Americans and the British. Like England and unlike the United States, France early developed "sugar colonies," exported sugar and its related products in enormous quantities in the eighteenth century, and developed a sweet tooth of its own. During much of the seventeenth century, French interests dominated the European sugar trade, not yielding to the British until afterward. French capital benefited from the slave trade and the sugar trade, much as did British capital. Bordeaux and Nantes played roles structurally similar to those of Liverpool and Bristol. And there were many parallels in the colonial experience: the early conquests of Martinique and Guadeloupe, like Barbados, and the beginnings of a sugar industry there using *engagés* as indentured servants were used in Barbados; shifting to a larger colony, Saint Domingue, as Britain took Jamaica under Cromwell; and so on. (True, England moved faster and farther; and in the Haitian Revolution France was defeated and ejected by the slave revolutionaries.)

But the French sugar interests, no matter how zealous, were unable to push French consumption to the point where it would deeply affect the nature of French cuisine or the forms of French meal taking. To this day the average French person consumes less sucrose than the average Englishman (though the gap is closing). Only slowly has France begun to approach the United Kingdom, Ireland, the Netherlands, Switzerland, Denmark, Iceland, the United States, and Australia—the world's leading sucrose consumers. In 1775, gross British sugar consumption was two and one-half times that of the French—when the French population may have been four times that of England and Wales. This would have meant French per-capita consumption at that time was but one-tenth that of Britain. Richard Sheridan, an American historian of the British Caribbean, accepts the view that eighteenth-century French consumption reflected far lower standards of living; but as he suggests, one should also consider the drinking habits of these two nations.[5] While the English people moved from beer and ale through gin and rum and partially back to beer and ale again, meanwhile acquiring a profound liking for heavily sweetened tea, the French remained primarily wine drinkers throughout. The acquisition of a coffee habit in the seventeenth century, though certainly important—Michelet believed the French Revolution was in part traceable to its effects!—did not reduce wine drinking. The wine habit may have negatively influenced the disposition to consume sweet substances, even while providing abundant calories.

Beyond this, there is the matter of cuisine itself. Brillat-Savarin referred to sugar as the universal condiment; but, as P. Morton Shand, commenting on English tastes, wrote, "he was using the word in its wider general sense of a flavoring, and not with the particular and specialized meaning it has since acquired."[6] Sweetness does not seem ever to have been enshrined as a taste to be contrasted with all others in the French taste spectrum—bitter, sour, salt, hot—as it has in England and America. Though dessert has a firm place in French meals, the position of cheese is even sturdier. Sweetness occurs in French food in sometimes surprising fashion— often as if it were a spice. This is rather like the Chinese usage, where sweetness also occurs somewhat unexpectedly, and also not always as the climax to a meal. The less conspicuous role of sugar in French and Chinese cuisines may have something to do with their excellence.[7] It is not necessarily a mischievous question to ask whether sugar damaged English cooking, or whether English cooking in the seventeenth century had more *need* of sugar than French.

When we turn to the so-called less developed countries, yet another perspective is afforded us. Sucrose, contributing as it does something like one-seventh of the average caloric intake of populations in many developed countries (which means, of course, more than that for certain economic sectors and age groups), is so powerful a symbol of the good life that some eminent authorities suggest its caloric contribution could safely become even greater.[8] Linked with the general welfare centuries ago, sucrose is still viewed as beneficial by many observers. To examine the reasons why, it may be useful to say a little more about sugar itself—that is, sucrose from sugar cane—even at this late point.

In the modern world, where the efficient use of energy counts more and more each day, the efficiency of sugar-cane production is a potent factor in sugar's success. G. B. Hagelberg, one of the keenest students of the world sucrose industry alive, writes, "As a rule, sugar cane (and sugar beet) produce larger quantities of utilizable calories per land unit in a given time than any other cultivated plant in their respective climatic zones."[9] Per hectare (2.47 acres), sugar cane yields, under optimum conditions, about twenty tons of dry material, some half of which is in the form of sugar usable as food or feed; the other ten tons of cane "trash," or bagasse, is usable as fuel and for the manufacture of paper products, building materials, and furfuraldehyde (a liquid aldehyde used in manufacturing nylon and resins, and as a solvent). Assuming certain raw material and processing parameters, the fifty tons of millable cane stalks obtainable from one hectare under Caribbean conditions will yield:

1. *5.6 tons of high grade raw sugar.* On the basis of an annual per capita consumption of 40 kilograms [88 lbs.], this quantity is sufficient for 140 persons, providing the equivalent of 420 kilocalories a day to each or about one-seventh [14 percent] of the total daily caloric intake.

2. *13.3 tons of wet bagasse (49 percent moisture, 2 percent soluble solids).* As fuel, this has a value equivalent to 2.4 tons of fuel oil. Alternatively, depithed and bone dry, this quantity of bagasse can yield somewhat over two tons of bleached paper pulp. Assuming that 500 kilograms of steam are required to process one ton of cane and that 2.3 tons of steam are generated per ton of wet bagasse, use of the bagasse as fuel to process the 50 tons of cane for sugar should actually leave a surplus of roughly 2.4 tons of wet bagasse or about 5 tons of steam for other purposes.

3. *1.35 tons of final or blackstrap molasses.* Roughly a third of the weight of final cane molasses is sucrose that cannot be commercially recovered as centrifugal sugar and about a fifth is composed of reducing sugars.... This quantity of molasses [with some additions] is almost sufficient to fatten one bull from 200 to 400 kilograms live weight.[10]

To these remarkable calculations we must add something concerning sugar's relative efficiency as a calorie supplier. As agricultural yields have risen with better modern scientific methods, sugar cane's long-standing superiority to other crops has grown proportionately. An acre of good subtropical land will now produce more than eight million calories in sugar, beyond the other products it yields. Comparisons with temperate-zone crops are somewhat biased in sugar's favor, but they are striking, all the same. It is estimated that to produce eight million calories with potatoes would require more than four acres; with wheat, between nine and twelve acres. (It is senseless to add beef to this comparison: to produce eight million calories of beef requires over 135 acres![11]) Such calculations seem stark enough in a world that confronts profound energy problems, but they must be projected backward as well (even allowing that sugar-extraction methods centuries ago were nowhere near so efficient as they are now). Such statistics throw light upon the past, while raising vital questions about the future.

Where the need for calories, let alone other food values, is a serious problem, sucrose may not be a good nutritional answer (in large quantities, I think it is a terrible one); but circumstances early made it, and have kept it, what looks like a good economic answer. When one adds to this the remarkable energy-transforming nature of plants like sugar cane and maize—even at high levels of human input in the form of fertilizers, cultivation, etc., the solar-energy input is approximately 90 percent of the total energy consumed in producing a usable food—the appeal of sucrose as a solution to food problems becomes almost irresistible.

If we take into account the underlying hominid predisposition toward sweetness, and add to it the astounding caloric yield of sucrose and the efficiency of production that yield betokens, together with the steady decline in the cost of sugar over the centuries, we have some reason for sugar's success in gaining new consumers. Of course none of this is to overlook the concerted effort to create demand, nor does it help us understand why some consumer markets have been much better than others over the centuries. But even the most sophisticated contemporary antisaccharites are compelled to recognize sugar's appeal on grounds of taste, energy economy, relative cost, and calories—an appeal sugar manufacturers clearly recognize, and which their political, professorial, and professional supporters push vigorously.

If we pick up once more the argument that the human diet since the invention of agriculture has centered upon a core complex carbohydrate "fringed" with contrasting tastes and textures to stimulate appetite (and usually improving nutrition also), then the exact role of sucrose in dietary change is difficult to establish. One might be prepared to group sweet with sour, salt, and bitter as a taste that afforded a contrast to the principal complex carbohydrates. But if the sweet fringe expands so that the proportion of the complex-carbohydrate core is reduced—to where it provides perhaps only half of the caloric intake instead of 75 or 90 percent—then the whole architecture of the meal itself has changed. There is nothing mysterious about this. During the history of western cuisine, among the wealthy and powerful, protein-rich foods like meat, fish, and poultry were probably the first major items to supplant copious starch consumption, and such foods undoubtedly grew more important even for the laboring classes between the seventeenth and twentieth centuries, but not in comparable proportions. Instead, the introduction of foods like sucrose made it possible to raise the caloric content of the proletarian diet without increasing proportionately the quantities of meat, fish, poultry, and dairy products.

Refined sugar thus became a symbol of the modern and industrial. It early came to be viewed in this way, penetrating one cuisine after another, accompanying or following on "westernization" or "modernization" or "development." Sucrose turns up as a pioneering and popular sign of "progress" among Native North Americans, Eskimos, Africans, and Pacific islanders. Commonly, people learn about it in one of two ways: either they exchange their labor or products or wages for it (along with other desired western goods); or else it is given to them as part of the charity provided by the West—charity usually donated after the westerners recognize the economic disorganization arising from their protracted contact with "less developed" traditional cultures.

These are roughly the same processes that, at an earlier time, marked the spread of European power and the economy of western capitalism, from region to region and from continent to continent. Even in the case of societies that have been sucrose consumers for centuries, one of the corollaries of "development" is that older, traditional kinds of sugar are being gradually replaced with the white, refined product, which the manufacturers like to call "pure." In countries like Mexico, Jamaica, and Colombia, for example, all very old sugar producers and consumers, the use of white sugar and of products fabricated with simple syrup has spread downward from the Europeanized elites to the urban working classes, then outward to the countryside, serving as a convenient marker of social position or, at least, aspiration; the older sugars are meanwhile eliminated because they are "old-fashioned" or "unsanitary" or "less convenient." Not all of these pejorative labels are wrong: noncentrifugal sugars are not so usable in processed foods and beverages, and the enterprises that produce them are usually less efficient than modern factories. But notions of modernity enter in strongly as more processed sugars diffuse to wider circles of consumers. Eventually, the traditional sugars survive as heirlooms of a sort—expensive relics of the past—whereupon they may reappear as stylish "natural" or conspicuous items on the tables of the rich, whose consumption habits helped to make them rare and expensive in the first place, now produced in modern ways that make money for people quite different from those who formerly produced them.[12]

The forces that impel consumers to spend more on "traditional" consumption at one point, and on "modern" consumption at another, are complicated and many-sided. One reason we do not understand them better in the case of sugar is that sucrose vendors have always been interested in patterns of consumption only in order to be able to change them; it is the openness of the patterns to change that concerns them. Vendors also understand that the patterns will not yield unless the conditions under which consumption occurs are changed—not just what is worn, but where and when, and with whom; not just what is eaten, but where and when, and with whom.

A radical change in the perceived situation—for example, learning to feel continuously hurried—can serve to motivate people to try different things. For sucrose sellers, the aim is to increase the role of the market in consumption. This may involve making consumers insecure about their consumption; motivating them to try to identify themselves differently by what they consume; or convincing them they can change the view others have of them by what they consume. The precise ways in which people change from the traditional to the new or modern are not fully understood. We see how people move from old-fashioned brown-sugar loaves or "heads" to paper boxes or bags of refined white sugar, from local beverages to Coca-Cola, from homemade candy to store-bought candy; but we understand far too little of precisely what steps or changes this involves. What seems likely is that such changes repeat or re-enact earlier, similar sequences. As different stages of change succeed one another, we may see recapitulated in them the fairly regular or recurrent historical stages by which outside forces dominated consumption—and, antecedent to it, labor power—at earlier points in western history.

We have seen how the relationships between the metropolises and their sources of sucrose have changed radically over time, as the position of sucrose in social life shifted. At first, sugar was brought from afar, purchased from foreign producers. Later, each metropolis acquired its own tropical colonies for the production of sugar on a mercantilist basis, simultaneously enriching the state and its commercial and financial classes, stimulating the consumption of both its home manufactures and colonial products, and increasing the market involvement of its own hinterlands. With the perfection of temperate-zone beet-sugar processing, the move from protectionism to a "free market" received more encouragement. Though the colonies remained important sources of gain, the opening of trade and the mastery of beet-sugar processing—the first important seizure by temperate agriculture of what were previously the productive capacities of a tropical region[13]—helped to counterbalance the subsequent political challenges to the industrial capitalists at home made by the planter classes in the colonies.

The character and level of sucrose consumption reflect wider processes in yet another way: the differential allocation of sucrose to different uses is a coefficient of other features of development. It is possible to contrast household sucrose use, in candy making, jam making, baking, etc., with its nonhousehold industrial uses, as in factory-baked goods and the manufacture of other prepared and processed foods, both sweet and nonsweet (salad dressings, breadings, catsup, etc.). Statistics show clearly that the more developed the country, the higher the percentage of nonhousehold, industrial use, and recent history confirms as much. Two students of changes in the American use of refined sugar have demonstrated that direct consumer or household use (assumed to be synonymous with purchases of granulated sugar in packages of less than fifty pounds) declined from 52.1 pounds per year in 1909–13 to 24.7 pounds in 1971; while industrial use (food products and beverages) has risen during the same period from 19.3 pounds to 70.2 pounds.[14] This trend also shows up, though much less dramatically, in developing countries.

Industrial use takes two different forms, however, as far as the consumer is concerned: on the one hand, there is consumption outside the home (in restaurants, at snack bars, checkout counters, theaters, etc.), which has risen, *pari passu*, together with other developmental indices; on the other, there is the ever-increasing use of prepared foods in the home itself. These different forms of sucrose consumption in manufactured and processed foods are connected; both are responses to wider social forces, and they also show up in the developing countries. That societies increasing their per-capita sugar consumption apace may also be moving away from household toward nonhousehold consumption is a way of saying that their citizens are bound to eat more meals away from home, and to eat more prepared foods within the home.

Neither trend indicates specifically the social meanings of the changes themselves. The relationship between sucrose and these broad social changes is emblematic rather than essential—sugar is even more important for what it reveals than for what it does— and we can examine what it does to understand better what has made the doing possible. Because sucrose is, in both its production and its consumption, at the contact points of capitalist intent, it is worthwhile tracing the scale, content, and form of the changes in its consumption.

At the production end, sugar early became one of the leading motivations for making overseas agricultural experiments of a mixed sort—that is, with capitalist means and unfree labor. At the consumption end, it was, as we have seen, one of the first items transformed from luxury to necessity, and thereby from rarity to mass-produced good, a transformation embodying both the promise and the fulfillment of capitalism itself. Sucrose production during the last five centuries of western expansion shows an irregular but noticeable geographic movement: first, it was a rarity, a medicine, a spice, coming from afar, traded for but not produced (indeed, the production was somewhat mysterious); then it became an expensive commodity produced from cane in overseas tropical colonies of the very temperate power whose citizens consumed it, these citizens being proletarianized but not proletarian (which is to say, disfranchised but not yet exclusively wage-earning labor); third, it was a less costly commodity produced elsewhere (not necessarily in the colonies of the same power) by various forms of labor, including proletarians; and, lastly, it became an inexpensive everyday commodity, often produced from sugar beets within national boundaries of the same power, much of it by proletarians for proletarians, but most of it bought and sold worldwide in a "free" market.

"Development," as it is called, has meant among other things a relatively steady increase in sugar consumption since perhaps the mid-nineteenth century. Around 1800 the part of world sucrose production that reached the market amounted to some 250,000 tons.[15] By 1880 that figure had risen fifteenfold, to 3.8 million tons. From 1880 until the onset of World War I—the period when sugar production was technically modernized—the production of centrifugal ("modern") sugar rose to more than sixteen million tons. And though the period between world wars was one of economic depression and stagnation, it ended with world sugar production at over thirty million tons. In spite of sharp declines during the war, sucrose production resumed its remarkable climb after 1945. From 1900 to 1970, world production of centrifugal sugar increased by about 500 percent, according to one source; another estimates the increase as being more like 800 percent.[16] Since world population approximately doubled during those same seventy years, this means that the "available" sugar per person per day worldwide rose from twenty-one to fifty-one grams. By 1970, something like 9 percent of all available food calories in the world were in the form of sucrose, and that figure is probably higher now.

Many of the really big consuming countries today are European, but by no means all. Iceland was the biggest per-capita consumer as of 1972—about 150 grams per person per day; Ireland, the Netherlands, Denmark, and England were consuming more than 135 grams per person per day at that time. One hundred and fifty grams works out to slightly more than 120 pounds of sucrose per year, or about a third of a pound of sucrose per person per day. For countries that are already big consumers, like Ireland and England, sucrose may contribute 15–18 percent of total energy consumption per capita. Allocation of differential quantities by age and class, if we had the data, would reveal a remarkable, if not shocking, dependency of some age/class sectors upon sucrose.[17] It seems certain that less privileged groups (not necessarily the poorest in the less developed countries; more likely the poorest in the more developed countries) consume disproportionate quantities; and it seems likely that younger persons consume more than older or elderly persons. These are not much better than wild guesses; hunches about regional, urban-rural, racial, and sexual differences in sugar-consumption patterns worldwide would be even riskier.

With development comes a higher percentage of sucrose use in prepared foods. Indeed, the shift to indirect use, like sugar consumption itself, has become a development signal of a kind. Health researcher Arvid Wretlind estimated that the percentage of total sucrose consumed which was used by food industries a decade ago in the Netherlands was 60, and in England 47.[18] Other analysts have found that, in the United States, the proportion of total sucrose consumed which was used in food preparation came to an estimated 65.5 percent of the total in 1977.[19] So large a commitment to indirect use does not occur in quite the same way in the less developed world, even when sugar consumption is rising.

Increasing sugar consumption is only one of the ways "development" changes food habits and choices, of course. While caloric intake probably increases as sugar consumption rises, this increase is partly achieved by substitutions, one of the clearest being the replacement of complex carbohydrates (starches) with simple carbohydrates (sucrose). In England, grain consumption decreased from a high of nearly 250 pounds per person per year to less than 170 pounds between 1938 and 1969; sugar consumption during the same period increased from a low of about 70 pounds (1942) to about 115 pounds; and one authority set the per-capita figure at 125 pounds for 1975.[20] This whittling away of the complex carbohydrates is of interest quite aside from its nutritional implications, given the change it betokens in the ancient relationship between starch core and the flavor fringe.*

*A word of caution here. Most of this discussion is based on so-called disappearance data, which tell us how much sucrose, complex carbohydrate, fat, etc., disappeared in a given period. These data are supplied by the Economic Research Service of the United States Department of Agriculture, for instance. Obviously it would be better to know exactly how much sucrose and other foods are actually consumed; but such data, even for small numbers of people, are practically inaccessible. See Page and Friend 1974; Cantor 1975.

The disproportionate contribution of the fringe to caloric intake, as the core's contribution declines, is only one aspect of the change. Together with the sugar increases come remarkable increases in the consumption of fats. Two students of this change, using the years 1909–13 as their comparison base, have shown for the United States that the average daily per-capita consumption of sugars as a proportion of carbohydrates increased in sixty years from 31.5 percent to 52.6 percent; the total daily average per-capita consumption of complex carbohydrates fell from about 350 grams to about 180 grams; while the consumption of dietary fat increased by 25 percent to 155 grams.[21] In the past fifteen years there have been further sharp increases in fat consumption, from 126 pounds to 135 pounds per person by 1979. If these figures are accurate, they mean that the average per-capita annual consumption of food fats and processed sugars in the United States in 1979 reached 265 pounds.[22] This works out to almost exactly three-quarters of a pound of fat and sugar per person per day.

The apparent connection between fats and sugars—and their effect on the consumption of complex carbohydrates—has nutritional, psychological, and economic implications.[23] But what does this trend mean culturally?

First, it is associated with the increasing tendency to eat outside the home. The multiplication of syndicated food dispensaries, so-called fast-food systems, since World War II, and particularly in the last two decades, is highly significant. In the United States, the National Advertising Bureau tells us, the "typical American eater" visits a fast-food restaurant nine times a month. One-third of all food dollars are spent on meals away from home, according to the *Wall Street Journal*. (Of course we want to know at what rates these trends are revealing themselves, to what specific segments of the population they apply, and over how long a time—and we do not know.)

Second, there is the increased consumption of prepared foods within the home, along with a heightened differentiation of the foods themselves: we now are "free" to choose several different precooked and frozen veal dishes, for instance, packaged by the same manufacturer but different in "style" (*milanese, marinara, limonata, or-*

eganata, francese). The number of foods that require nothing but temperature changes before eating has risen in proportion to the total number of prepared and partially prepared foods, including those that may require more than heating to be done to them before they can be consumed. And the variety of heating and chilling media, usually running on high-energy output—woks, steamers, bakers, broilers, deep fryers, radiation and convection ovens—has also risen sharply, all vended on the basis of "speediness," "convenience," "economy," and "cleanliness."

These developments directly affect the role playing that has traditionally accompanied family meals. Anthropological students of food and eating have thought it valid to analogize from linguistics to describe what happens, both in any given meal and in the patterning of meals. Thus, Mary Douglas tells us that "the binary or other contrasts must be seen in their syntagmatic relations." By this, she explains, she means putting into analyzable order food units descending from daily menu to mouthful, and ascending from daily to weekly or yearly, and from everyday to special, festive, and ceremonial. Paradigmatic relations characterize the components within a meal, and syntagmatic relations characterize those among meals; or, to cite Douglas again, "On the two axes of syntagm and paradigm, chain and choice, sequence and set, call it what you will, [Halliday] has shown how food elements can be ranged until they are all accounted for either in grammatical terms or down to the last lexical item."[24]

But the whole momentum of modern life has been away from any such "lexicon" or "grammar," and the analogy is not a good one. Describing the foods in a meal in linguistic terminology hardly "accounts for" them, because the structural constraints on ingestion are not comparable to those on language; we can eat without meals, but we cannot speak without grammar. The function of grammar in language has to be agreed upon by the speakers—that is, held in common and understood by them—for communication to take place at all. Hence the relation of so-called grammar to eating is only a cute artifact of description. Eating will of course continue, even if the very idea of "meal" as we know it disappears.

Viewed from the perspective of the modern-food technologist, abolition of any such "grammar" is the best way of increasing consumption of mass-produced food products while maximizing what he might refer to as "freedom of individual choice." Increased consumption may not be the admitted intent; but it would be hard to conjecture what else it is. The "paradigm" of the meal, the "syntagm" of the meal schedule, and time restraints on eating may all be considered as obstructions to the exercise of individual preference.

In contrast, meals that must be eaten by everyone at the same time require advancement, postponement, or cancellation of competing events by the participants. Meals consisting of the same items for all eaters must be based on a least common denominator, rather than on each person's greatest preferences. Meals that are eaten in some fixed order may run counter to one or another participant's preference for soup last or dessert later. Ceremonial meals that involve some invariant item (lamb, turkey) may be unpleasant for an individual who dislikes that food. When one is serving oneself from a serving plate, the helpings must be adjusted to the desires of others who are eating. All of these constraints reveal that social eating is precisely that: *social*, involving communication, give and take, a search for consensus, some common sense about individual needs, compromise through attending to the needs of others. Social interaction leaves room for the operation of opinion and in-group influence. But some might call these constraints upon individual freedom.

The food technologist interested in selling products aims willy-nilly at the obliteration of such schedules and "grammars," and at a standardized, even if large, "lexicon"—making it possible for everyone to eat exactly what he or she wants to eat, in exactly the quantities and under exactly the circumstances (time, place, occasion) he or she prefers. Incidental to this is the elimination of the social significance of eating together. Ideally, in these terms, an obese daughter may now eat a series of yogurts, an enthusiastic television-watching father a TV dinner, a jogging mother large quantities of granola, and an alienated son no end of pizzas, Cokes, or ice creams.[25]

As food availability has been generalized across modern society, the structures of meals and the calendar of diet in daily life have tended to disappear. Coffee and Coca-Cola are now appropriate at any time and with any accompaniment. So, too, are breaded, deep-fried bits of complex carbohydrate and protein (potatoes, corn and wheat bread sticks, chicken, scallops, shrimp, pork, fish pieces). Synthetic juices that split the difference between the food faddists and the Pepsi Generation; fiber-rich cereals made calorie-heavy with raisins, figs, dates, honey, nuts, and nut substitutes; crackers, cheeses, dips, pretzels, and "munchies"—together these now provide a nu-tritive medium within which social events occur, rather than the other way round. The meal, which had a clear internal structure, dictated at least to some degree by the one-cook-to-one-family pat-tern and the consequences of socialization within such a pattern, as well as by "tradition," can now mean different items and different sequences for each consumer. The week's round of food, which once meant chicken or some equivalent on Sunday, or fish on Friday, is no longer so stable, nor viewed as so necessary by the participants. And the year's round of food, which brought bock beer, shad, fresh dill, and new potatoes, each in its turn, turkey twice a year, and fruit cake with hard sauce at New Year's, survives only on suffer-ance, finessed by turkey burgers, year-round bock beer, and other modern wonders.

These transformations have made ingestion more individualized and noninteractive; they have desocialized eating. Choices to be made about eating—when, where, what, how much, how quickly—are now made with less reference to fellow eaters, and within ranges predetermined, on the one hand, by food technology and, on the other, by what are perceived as time constraints.

The experience of time in modern society is often one of an insoluble shortage, and this perception may be essential to the smooth functioning of an economic system based on the principle of ever-expanded consumption.[26] Anthropologists and economists have struggled with the paradox implicit in modern society—that its vastly more productive technologies result in individuals having (or feeling they have) less time, rather than more. Because of time pres-sure, people try to condense their consumption pleasure by con-suming different things (such as movies and popcorn) simultaneously. This simultaneous (but often peculiarly unsatisfying) experience seems to the individual to be a "natural" one—just as does the proliferation of fruit stands, croissant carts, coffee machines, and the like on the corners and in the building basements, laundry rooms, and hallways of American cities, in gas stations, at checkout counters, in theater lobbies, and elsewhere. Maximum enjoyment in minimum time has come to mean both divided (simultaneous) consumption— one eats while walking or working, drinks while driving or watching entertainment—and higher frequency of occasions for consumption. Watching the Cowboys play the Steelers while eating Fritos and drinking Coca-Cola, while smoking a joint, while one's girl sits on one's lap, can be packing a great deal of experience into a short time and thereby maximizing enjoyment. Or it can be experienced quite differently, depending upon the values one holds. Most important, however, people who experience pleasures simultaneously in these ways are taught to think about the consumption itself— not about the circumstances that led them to consume in that fashion, other than to sense that there was "not enough time" to do otherwise.[27]

Since the only objective way to increase time is to alter percentages for the activities it encompasses, and since the workday has remained relatively the same length for a century, most adjustments in available time tend to be cosmetic, or to involve "time-saving." The development of prepared food to be eaten in the home, as well as eating out, are both regarded as time-saving practices. Of course, consuming prepared food means surrendering much of one's choice in what one eats. But, not surprisingly, the food industry touts it as increasing one's freedom of choice—especially when the industry omits reference to what the food itself contains. Thus is the dialectic between supposed individual freedom and social patterning perpetuated.

In discussing the penetration of sucrose into the rhythms of the British workday, I was able to give only summary treatment to such fundamental changes as the alterations in the workday, the change in the sexual division of labor, revised allocations of effort, and the inversions of eating time and preparation time. We know that the scheduling of events and rituals changed radically for the British working class when sugar became common, but the research done on this aspect is too broad (and hence too shallow) to permit documentation in any serious fashion. Alterations in the perception of time must have been at least as important as the actual objective remaking of the workday, and these rarely express the exercise of power directly. Indeed, it is just because such power is revealed only indirectly that it can remain mysterious—setting the terms of work as if the machines demanded it, or as if daylight made it necessary, or as if the others in the work force fixed the tempo, or as if eating had to fit within a unit of time, rather than its being the act of eating itself that determines how much time it should take.

One of the effects of changing the time formula is that it subtly recasts people's images of their lives and of themselves. How much time people actually have for different pursuits, how much time they believe they have, and the relationship between these are aspects of daily life shaped by externalities and, in particular in the modern world, by the reorganization of the workday.[28] What seem visible to the worker, however, are the changed conditions of work. These new conditions shape in turn what is left of his time; yet how much time one "has" may be only fleetingly perceived as dependent, ultimately, on the work regime. People live inside the time they think they have; they may experience subjective changes in their moods, conditioned by their ability to live up to (or, often, not to live up to) their own standards of performance; but only now and then do they conceive of their performance as affected by alterations that give and take away time, or their will to feel they are controlling the use of time.

The patterning of time is linked to the patterning of ingestion; material on the United States is sufficiently detailed to clarify the line of argument here. The rise in the use of prepared foods, the increase in meals eaten out, and the decline of the meal itself as a ritual (particularly for kin groups) have led in recent decades to different patterns of sucrose usage as well as to increases in the consumption of sugars overall.

Between 1955 and 1965, per-capita usage of certain sweets and sugars—candy, for example—actually dropped 10 percent. But during the same period, the per-capita consumption of frozen-milk "desserts" rose 31 percent; of baked goods 50 percent; and of soft drinks 78 percent.[29] From these figures, I think it is possible to infer an increasing intervention in meal schedules. "The daily three-meal pattern, although mentioned as a valid rule by almost all the subjects [of a recent study,] is no longer a reality," says the French anthropologist Claude Fischler. Though the research on which this assertion is based is too slight to be generalized, it indicates that 75 percent of American families do not take breakfast together. Dinners eaten together are down to three a week or less, and these meals usually last no more than twenty minutes. Yet among urban, middle-class families, the number of "contacts" between any family member and food might run as high as twenty daily.[30] Such figures hark back to the hunting-and-gathering existence of our species, when food was eaten as it became available, without much reference to situation or circumstance.

One fascinating expression of this modern American way of eating is found in what we know is consumed and what people recall they have consumed. Whereas the Department of Agriculture figures demonstrate that we dispose of about 3,200 calories per capita per day, the average white female adult, for example, can recall, when asked what she ate on the previous day, only 1,560 calories, a noticeably low average, and less than half the "disappearance" figure.[31] Since average weight has risen steadily in this country, these recall data are difficult to accept as accurate. They suggest a pattern of ragged and discontinuous but very frequent snacks that are surely forgotten by those who do the eating.

Sucrose fits snugly into the picture, as the facts concerning sweetened frozen-milk products, baked goods, and soft drinks demonstrate. The "desserts" or baked goods together with beverages (more commonly than not, soft drinks) constitute brief, meallike interventions during the day, which further erode the traditional three-meal pattern. Enlarged mid-morning and mid-afternoon snacks have the effect of making the meals on either side more snacklike.

In short, it would appear that the meal structure—the "paradigmatics" and "syntagmatics" of ingestion—is dissolving. To what extent this is true for any given social group in any given western country is, of course, unknown; but it is clear that the history of sugar consumption predates—and in certain ways prefigures—the spread of unscheduled eating as an aspect of modern life.

There is yet one other way in which sugar has affected the modernization of consumption. The high sucrose content of many prepared and processed foods that *do not taste sweet* (such as flour-dredged meats, poultry, and fish that are baked, broiled, or deep-fried) is an important source of the increase in sucrose consumption and substantiates the astonishing versatility of sucrose. When used in non-yeast-raised baked goods, we are told, "texture, grain and crumb became smoother, softer and whiter.... This tenderizing effect of sugars has long been recognized."[32] Sucrose also supplies "body" to soft drinks, because "a heavy liquid is more appealing to the mouth than water."[33] Sugar inhibits staleness in bread—"shelf life" is important in a society that wants its supermarkets open twenty-four hours a day for "convenience"—stabilizes the chemical content of salt, mitigates the acidity of catsup, serves as a medium for yeast. In all of these uses, its sweetness is largely irrelevant; indeed, many food manufacturers would dearly love a chemical having all of the qualities of sucrose *without* the calories and, in some cases, even without the sweetness.[34] That is how far we have come since the seventeenth century.

Yet in spite of these many virtues, the fate of sucrose is by no means entirely assured. In the last decade, yet another sugar, high-fructose corn syrup, has been making inroads into the sugar market, particularly among prepared-food manufacturers. The most crushing blow came when Coca-Cola partly replaced sucrose with HFCS; it seems probable that other defeats will follow.[35] At any rate, corn syrups are cutting into the consumption of other sugars and will probably do so more and more.

While per-capita sucrose use in the United States has hovered for some time now around the hundred-pounds-per-year level, the consumption of other sweeteners has risen steadily for at least seventy years. (This is one reason why the somewhat sanctimonious assertions that "sugar consumption" has not risen—here meaning *sucrose* consumption—usually trumpeted by either sugar-corporation representatives or well-sweetened professors of nutrition, must be viewed with reserve.) Thus the per-capita "disappearance" figure for all nondietary sugars (i.e., sugars not occurring naturally, as in fruits) is nearly 130 pounds per year. If disappearance is the same as consumption, then the daily per-capita total nondietary consumption of sugars is nearly six ounces per day.

The fact that the eater does not perceive much of this sugar as sweet has two aspects. First, the sucrose may be used in small enough proportions so that its taste is undiscernible—though doubtless there is much individual variation in taste sensitivity to sweetness. Second, it is probable that sweetness is perceived less when it is not expected, noticed less in foods that are not considered "sweet." If we include nonsucrose sweeteners like HFCS in this consumption picture, the situation gives rise to what one scholar has called "the interconvertibility factor,"[36] such that more and more edible substances are becoming more and more substitutable. The German experiments with deriving edible substances from naturally occurring petroleum during World War II were, then, only harbingers of the future. This same scholar suggests that the margarine/butter dyad is one of the oldest "analogue relationships,"[37] in which an unlikely food eventually becomes partly indistinguishable from the product it imitates; the sucrose/HFCS dyad gives rise to comparable questions. Whether worldwide, in national markets, or in class-divided consumption patterns, the rivalries between sucrose and other caloric and noncaloric sweeteners, like the rivalry between dairy and nondairy products, are by no means fully understood. At such nodal points of change, culture and technology, culture and economics, culture and politics are in confrontation. And some of the issues to which the recent success of HFCS has given rise—to note again only the most significant such example for the present argument—will not be fully settled in the lifetime of any of us.

From the very beginning of this book, my argument has been that sugar—sucrose—has to be viewed in its multiple functions, and as a culturally defined good. I have emphasized its unusual symbolic "carrying power," a symbolic weight that endured among the rich and powerful until sucrose became common, cheap, and desired, when it spread widely through the working classes of all western nations, carrying with it many of its older meanings but also acquiring new ones. The affective weight of sweetness, always considerable, was not so much diminished as qualitatively changed by its abundance. The good life, the rich life, the full life—was the sweet life.

The advent of margarine, invented by the French chemist Mège Mouriès but made into a world commodity by the Dutch, can be counterposed to the history of sucrose in symbolically interesting ways. As we have seen, the gradual erosion of complex-carbohydrate consumption has been from two sides—sugars on one, fats on the other. These foods occur together in such items as milk desserts; they are epitomized among liquids by condensed milk, among semisolids by ice cream, and among solids by chocolate candy. In the last half-century or so, sugar-fat combinations have taken two other important industrially processed forms: in salty-food/sweet-drink combinations (hamburgers with Coca-Cola, hot dogs with orange soda, pastrami with celery tonic), and in the combination of sweet, cold drinks with deep-fried items in which sugar figures in the exterior coating. These latter represent a special triumph of situationally conditioned taste over nutrition. The fat side is advertised with words like "juicy," "succulent," "hot," "luscious," "savory," "rich," "satisfying," and "finger-licking good." The sugar side is touted with words like "crisp," "fresh," "invigorating," "icy," "wholesome," "refreshing," and "vibrant." These sets of words are counterposed in the language of commercial attraction.[38]

The combination of sugars and fats, as food choice or preference, is a very important one.

> Richness in diet is frequently associated with fat and sugar in the diet and "eating out" with fast foods and snack foods. The latter also not only are identified with high fat and high sugar but reflect "fast" as part of the life style and, in some respects, reinforce fast living.... Fat and sugar are more than functional aids to shelf life; they are equally associated with the richness of food and, therefore, its acceptability.[39]

The food technologist's lexicon for the uses of sugar and fat pays special attention to sugar's way of making foods more palatable.

Baked products are judged by their quality of "go-away." Proper proportions of sugar and fat result in good "good go-away"—which means that the mouthful of food can be swallowed without leaving the inside of the mouth coated with fat particles. The help of sugar in achieving good go-away is vital. It is now permissible to add up to 10 percent sugar to manufactured peanut butters in the U.S. No other food, they say, has such poor go-away as peanut butter; sugar improves its go-away marvelously. Soft-drink manufacturers, substituting saccharin for sugar, struggle with a comparable problem. Gums of various sorts are introduced to make the soft drink taste heavier in the mouth, the way sugar would make it heavy, since the mouth—food technologists tell us—prefers liquids that are heavier than water. The term "mouth feel" is used to describe the felt "body" of liquids (like soft drinks), to which sugar supplies agreeable weight or balance. It can be seen that this terminology is not really concerned with taste: texture, perhaps, or "feel," but not taste.

These observations suggest that the lay person's awareness of the nature of his/her own perceptions of food is undeveloped. Much that is subsumed under "taste" in modern eating is not taste at all, but something else. The reaction to deep-fried foods covered with batter is probably a good illustration. The inclusion of sugar in the batter facilitates caramelization, sealing the food so that it can be cooked without losing its own fatty and liquid contents. Whatever sucrose or other sugars are used, their sweetness function is supplanted by one of sugar's other food uses; sweetness in the meal comes from the beverages with which such deep-fried foods are consumed. This is not the place to develop further some of the sociopsychological implications of the heightened uses of convenience and fast foods, with their combinations of cold, effervescent, usually stimulant sweet liquids with hot fatty proteins and complex carbohydrates, often "finished" with sucrose-rich batters. Perhaps people associate the "rich life" with such foods, and perhaps the oral stimuli they provide "have numerous pleasant associations that relate to early life experiences."[40]

I have tried to suggest some of the ways that modern eating habits have altered the place of sugar. While many of the world's peoples are still learning to eat sucrose in the ways and quantities that marked its spread through England and the West, others are moving into a wholly different period of eating history. Roland Barthes argued that the famous place of food in French life has been qualitatively changing, and his argument seems to hold for modern societies generally:

> Food serves as a sign not only for themes, but also for situations; and this, all told, means for a way of life that is emphasized, much more than expressed, by it. To eat is a behavior that develops beyond its own ends, replacing, summing up, and signalizing other behaviors, and it is precisely for these reasons that it is a sign. What are these other behaviors? Today, we might almost say that "polysemia" of food characterizes modernities; in the past, only festive occasions were signalized by food in any positive organized manner. But today, work also has its own kind of food (on the level of a sign, that is): energy-giving and light food is experienced as a very sign of, rather than only a help toward, participation in modern life.... We are witnessing an extraordinary expansion of the areas associated with food: food is becoming incorporated into an ever-lengthening list of situations. This adaptation is usually made in the name of hygiene and better living, but in reality, to stress this fact once more, food is also charged with signifying the situation in which it is used. It has a twofold value, being nutrition as well as protocol, and its value as protocol becomes increasingly more important as soon as the basic needs are satisfied, as they are in France. In other words, we might say that in contemporary French society, *food has a constant tendency to transform itself into situation*.[41]

The peculiar versatility of sugars has led to their remarkable permeation through so many foods and into nearly all cuisines. But the subsidiary or additional uses of some sugars, particularly sucrose, have become more important, not less, as prepared foods inside and outside the home grow more popular. The function of sweetness in the patterning of ingestion has changed, even while the nonsweetening uses of sucrose and corn sweeteners have expanded. That sugars not only have remained important in our new diets and eating habits but have become proportionately much more so is additional evidence of their versatility.

The track sugar has left in modern history is one involving masses of people and resources, thrown into productive combination by social, economic, and political forces that were actively remaking the entire world. The technical and human energies these forces released were unequaled in world history, and many of their consequences have been beneficial. But the place of sugars in the modern diet, the strangely imperceptible attrition of people's control over what they eat, with the eater becoming the consumer of a mass-produced food rather than the controller and cook of it, the manifold forces that work to hold consumption in channels predictable enough to maintain food-industry profits, the paradoxical narrowing of individual choice, and of opportunity to resist this trend, in the guise of increasing convenience, ease, and "freedom"—these factors suggest the extent to which we have surrendered our autonomy over our food.

Subtle encouragements to be modern, efficient, up to date, and individualistic have become steadily more sophisticated. We are what we eat; in the modern western world, we are *made* more and more into what we eat, whenever forces we have no control over persuade us that our consumption and our identity are linked.

> More and more of the so-called "creative" people who design products are not in the laboratories and, therefore, least open to technological and scientific constraints. Marketing executives have found that ideas generated by nontechnical people are more realistically associated with markets and are less inhibited by restraints which would concern technical people. As a consequence new product funds tend to be invested more in services associated with advertising than those of technical groups....
>
> The effect of such product development practices on consumption is important.... If we define what has been referred to as richness as a concomitant of flavor, then the repeated incorporation of "richness" into a new product would not only provide regular reinforcement for recognizing "richness," but, with all of its omnipresent associations promoted as good, result in increased consumption of fat and sugar.... There is supposedly a safety factor associated with fat consumption and probably also with sweetener consumption. But the statistics, at least on the average, support the conclusion that as preparation of food moves from kitchen to factory, the perception of richness and the continuing

emphasis on richness, certainly in snack foods, has contributed not only to reinforcement but also the resultant increased consumption....It would appear that such increases due to the relative inelasticity of demand for food could seriously unbalance nutrition....What is perhaps more disturbing is the degree to which the discretionary limits of consumers are being reduced by the system which designs food like any other consumer item....[42]

Lionel Tiger, an anthropologist proceeding from a somewhat different perspective, arrives at similarly critical conclusions. He points out that as belief systems in modern societies become more secularized, individuals change the way they view their own safety, and an "extermination model," as he calls it, results. That is, individuals attach to such environmental risks as exposure to radiation or chemicals, and perhaps especially to eating, a statistical reckoning of their life chances. To believe one has an X-percent chance of developing cancer after Y number of cigarettes is rather different, says Tiger, "from the relatively straightforward connection to a theological dominant in terms of whom the rules of right and wrong are plain and the results of particular actions relatively clearly identifiable."[43] But, perhaps more important, this change to a statistical, epidemiological approach to risk burdens the individual with inhibitions in regard to eating:

> The decision about personal destiny, as far as health is concerned, is stressed directly on the individual, despite the fact that everywhere in the community blandishments exist to increase individual risk of disease development: for example, the countless public feeding facilities such as the fast food outlets who rely unduly on foods that are not highly desirable from the disease prevention point of view. So while the individual is faced with an entirely personal decision to take, he or she must take it in a social context which is relatively provocative in a destructive sense, because of the community's indifference to or lack of information about suitable patterns of eating, or the vested interest of persons and groups committed to maintaining advantageous positions in the economy which depend upon less than medically desirable eating habits.[44]

Fischler, the French anthropologist, appalled by the way "snacking" has supplanted meal taking (it is clear that the very word offends him, and he declares proudly that there is no equivalent in French!), speaks of the replacement of gastronomy by "*gastro-anomie*," and raises questions about the trend toward desocialized, aperiodic eating. One senses today a quickening of such diffusion, a speeding up, even in large, ancient societies that were apparently once resistant to such processes, such as China and Japan. The changing nature of the industrial workday, the cheap calories (both in cost and in resource use) provided by sucrose, and the special-interest groups intent on pushing its consumption[45] make such cumulative pressure difficult to resist on an individual or a group educational basis.

Food may be no more than a sign of yet larger, more fundamental processes—or so it seems. Diet is remade because the entire productive character of societies is recast and, with it, the very nature of time, of work, and of leisure. If these occurrences raise questions for us and about us—if they seem to others, as they seem to me, to have escaped from human control even though they are very much the outcome of organized human intent—then we need to understand them far better than we do. We may aspire to change the world, rather than merely to observe it. But we need to understand how it works in order to change it in socially effective ways.

We anthropologists for too long have paradoxically denied the way the world has changed and continues changing, as well as our ability—responsibility, even—to contribute to a broad understanding of the changes. If we have been betrayed by our own romanticism, we have also lagged in recognizing and asserting our strengths. Those strengths continue to lie in fieldwork (there is little in this book, I confess), and in a full appreciation of humanity's historical nature as a species. Anthropological interest in how person, substance, and act are integrated meaningfully can be pursued in the modern world as well as in the primitive one. Studies of the everyday in modern life, of the changing character of mundane matters like food, viewed from the joined perspective of production and consumption, use and function, and concerned with the differential emergence and variation of meaning, may be one way to inspirit a discipline now dangerously close to losing its sense of purpose.

To move from so minor a matter as sugar to the state of the

world in general may seem like yet another chorus of the bone song—the hip bone's connected to the leg bone, etc. But we have already seen how sucrose, this "favored child of capitalism"—Fernando Ortiz's lapidary phrase[46]—epitomized the transition from one kind of society to another. The first sweetened cup of hot tea to be drunk by an English worker was a significant historical event, because it prefigured the transformation of an entire society, a total remaking of its economic and social basis. We must struggle to understand fully the consequences of that and kindred events, for upon them was erected an entirely different conception of the relationship between producers and consumers, of the meaning of work, of the definition of self, of the nature of things. What commodities are, and what commodities mean, would thereafter be forever different. And for that same reason, what persons are, and what being a person means, changed accordingly. In understanding the relationship between commodity and person, we unearth anew the history of ourselves.

Bibliography

Achebe, C. 1973. *Girls at war and other stories*. Garden City, N.Y.: Doubleday.

Adams, John. 1819. *Novanglus, or political essays published in...the years 1774 and 1775...* Boston: Hewe and Goss.

Adams, R. M. 1977. World picture, anthropological frame. *American Anthropologist* 79(2):265–79.

Anderson, E. 1952. *Plants, man and life*. Boston: Little, Brown.

Andrews, K. R. 1978. *The Spanish Caribbean*. New Haven: Yale University Press.

Anonymous. 1752. *An essay on sugar*. London: E. Comyns.

Anonymous. 1777. *An essay on tea, sugar, white bread...and other modern luxuries*. Salisbury, England: J. Hodson.

Appleby, A. 1978. *Famine in Tudor and Stuart England*. Stanford, Calif.: Stanford University Press.

Artschwager, E., and Brandes, E. W. 1958. *Sugar cane: origin, classification characteristics, and descriptions of representative clones*. U.S. Department of Agriculture Handbook No. 122. Washington, D.C.: Government Printing Office.

Austin, T., ed. 1888. *Two fifteenth-century cookery-books*. London: N. Trubner.

Aykroyd, W. R. 1967. *Sweet malefactor*. London: Heinemann.

Ayrton, E. 1974. *The cookery of England*. Harmondsworth: Penguin.

Balducci Pegolotti, F. di. 1936. *La practica della mercatura*, ed. A. Evans. Mediaeval Academy of America Publication No. 24. Cambridge, Mass.: The Mediaeval Academy of America.

Balikci, A. 1970. *The Netsilik Eskimo*. New York: Natural History Press.

Banaji, J. 1979. Modes of production in a materialist conception of history. *Capital and Class* 7:1–44.

Bannister, R. 1890. Sugar, coffee, tea and cocoa: their origin, preparation and uses. *Journal of the Society of Arts* 38:972–96, 997–1014, 1017–36, 1038–52.

Barnes, A. C. 1974. *The sugar cane*. New York: John Wiley.

Barthes, R. 1975 [1961]. Toward a psychosociology of contemporary food consumption. In *European diet from preindustrial to modern times*, ed. Elborg and Robert Forster, pp. 47–59. New York: Harper and Row.

Baxa, J., and Bruhns, G. 1967. *Zucker im Leben der Völker*. Berlin: Dr. Albert Bartens.

Beauchamp, G. K.; Maller, O.; and Rogers, J. G., Jr. 1977. Flavor preferences in cats (*Felis catus* and *Panthera* sp.). *Journal of Comparative and Physiological Psychology* 91(5):1118–27.

Beer, G. L. 1948 [1893]. *The commercial policy of England toward the American colonies*. Columbia University Studies in History, Economics and Public Laws. Vol. 3, No. 2. New York: Peter Smith.

Beidler, L. M. 1975. The biological and cultural role of sweeteners. In *Sweeteners: issues and uncertainties*. National Academy of Sciences Academy Forum, Fourth of a Series, pp. 11–18. Washington, D.C.: National Academy of Sciences.

Benveniste, M. 1970. *The crusaders in the Holy Land*. Jerusalem: Hebrew University Press.

Berthier, P. 1966. *Les anciennes sucreries du Maroc et leurs reseaux hydrauliques*. Rabat, Morocco: Imprimeries Françaises et Marocaines.

Bolens, L. 1972. L'eau et l'irrigation d'après les traités d'agronomie andalous au Moyen-Age (XIᶜ–XIIᶜ siècles). *Options Méditerranées* 16:65–77.

Botsford, J. B. 1924. *English society in the eighteenth century as influenced from overseas*. New York: Macmillan.

Bowden, W. 1967. Agricultural prices, farm profits, and rents. In *The agrarian history of England and Wales*. Vol. 4, *1500–1640*, ed. Joan Thirsk, pp. 593–695. Cambridge: Cambridge University Press.

Braudel, F. 1973. *Capitalism and material life, 1400–1800*. New York: Harper and Row.

Braverman, H. 1974. *Labor and monopoly capital*. New York: Monthly Review Press.

Brillat-Savarin, J.-A. 1970 [1825]. *The philosopher in the kitchen*. Harmondsworth: Penguin.

Burnett, J. 1966. *Plenty and want*. London: Thomas Nelson.

_____. 1969. *A history of the cost of living*. Harmondsworth: Penguin.

Campbell, D. 1926. *Arabian medicine and its influence on the Middle Ages*. Vol 1. London: Kegan Paul, Trench, Trubner and Co.

Campbell, R. H. 1966. Diet in Scotland, an example of regional variation. In *Our changing fare*, ed. T. C. Barker, J. C. McKenzie, and J. Yudkin, pp. 47–60. London: MacGibbon and Kee.

Cantor, S. 1969. Carbohydrates and their roles in foods: introduction to the symposium. In *Carbohydrates and their roles*, ed. H. W. Schultz, R. F. Cain, and R. W. Wrolstad, pp. 1–11. Westport, Conn.: Avi.

———. 1975. Patterns of use. In *Sweeteners: issues and uncertainties*. National Academy of Sciences Academy Forum, Fourth of a Series, pp. 19–35. Washington, D.C.: National Academy of Sciences.

———. 1978. Patterns of use of sweeteners. In *Sweeteners and dental caries*, ed. J. H. Shaw and G. G. Roussos. Special Supplement Feeding, Weight and Obesity Abstracts, pp. 111–28. Washington, D.C.: Information Retrieval Inc.

———. 1981. Sweeteners from cereals: the interconversion function. In *Cereals: a renewable resource*, ed. W. Pomerantz and L. Munck, pp. 291–305. St. Paul, Minn.: American Association of Cereal Chemists.

Cantor, S., and Cantor, M. 1977. Socioeconomic factors in fat and sugar consumption. In *The chemical senses and nutrition*, ed. M. Kare and O. Maller, pp. 429–46. New York: Academic Press.

Castro, A. Barros de. 1980. Brasil, 1610: mudanças técnicas e conflitos sociais. *Pesquisa e Planejamento Econômico* 10(3):679–712.

Cavendish, G. 1959 [1641]. *The life and death of Cardinal Wolsey*. Oxford: Oxford University Press.

Chamberlayn, J. 1685. *The manner of making coffee, tea and chocolate*. London.

Child, Sir J. 1694. *A new discourse of trade*. 2nd ed. London: Sam. Crouch.

Childe, V. G. 1936. *Man makes himself*. London: Watts.

Chrispeels, M. J., and Sadava, D. 1977. *Plants, food and people*. San Francisco: W. H. Freeman.

Cohen, M. N. 1977. *The food crisis in prehistory*. New Haven: Yale University Press.

Coleman, D. C. 1977. *The economy of England, 1450–1750*. London and New York: Oxford University Press.

Crane, E. 1975 and 1976. *Honey*. London: Heinemann.

Crane, F. 1762. Treacle. *Notes and Queries*, 3rd ser., 21–22 February 1762, pp. 145–46.

Curtin, P. 1969. *The Atlantic slave trade*. Madison, Wis.: University of Wisconsin Press.

Davies, D. 1795. *The case of labourers in husbandry*. London: G. G. and J. Robinson.

Davies, K. G. 1974. *The North Atlantic world in the seventeenth century*. Europe and the world in the age of expansion. Vol. 4, ed. B. C. Shafer. Minneapolis: University of Minnesota Press.

Davis, R. 1954. English foreign trade, 1660–1700. *Economic History Review* 7:150–66.

———. 1973. *The rise of the Atlantic economies*. Ithaca, N.Y.: Cornell University Press.

————. 1979. *The Industrial Revolution and British overseas trade*. Leicester, England: Leicester University Press.

Deerr, N. 1949. *The history of sugar*. Vol. 1. London: Chapman and Hall.

————. 1950. *The history of sugar*. Vol. 2. London: Chapman and Hall.

Delzell, L. E. 1980. The family that eats together...might prefer not to. *Ms.* 8:56–57.

DeSnoo, K. 1937. Das trinkende Kind im Uterus. *Monatschrift für Geburtshilfe and Gynäkologie* 105:88.

DeVries, J. 1976. *Economy of Europe in an age of crisis, 1600–1750*. Cambridge: Cambridge University Press.

Dodd, G. 1856. *The food of London*. London: Longman, Brown, Green, and Longmans.

Dorveaux, P. 1917. *Le sucre au moyen age*. Paris: Honoré Champion.

Douglas, M. 1972. Deciphering a meal. *Daedalus* 101:61–82.

Dowell, S. 1884. *A history of taxation and taxes in England*. London: Longmans, Green.

Drabble, M. 1977. *The ice age*. New York: Popular Library.

Drummond, J. C., and Wilbraham, A. 1958. *The Englishman's food: a history of five centuries of English diet*. London: Jonathan Cape.

Dunn, R. S. 1972. *Sugar and slaves*. Chapel Hill: University of North Carolina Press.

Edelen, G. 1968. Introduction. In *The description of England*, by William Harrison, ed. Georges Edelen. Ithaca, N.Y.: Cornell University Press.

Edelman, J. 1971. The role of sucrose in green plants. In *Sugar: chemical, biological and nutritional aspects of sucrose*, ed. J. Yudkin, J. Edelman, and L. Hough, pp. 95–102. London: Butterworth.

Eden, Sir F. M. 1797. *The state of the poor*. 3 vols. London: J. Davis, for B. and J. White.

Ellis, E. 1905. *An introduction to the history of sugar as a commodity*. Philadelphia: J. C. Winston.

Evans, A. 1936. See Balducci Pegolotti, F. di.

Everitt, A. 1967a. Farm labourers. In *The agrarian history of England and Wales*. Vol. 4. *1500–1640*, ed. Joan Thirsk, pp. 396–465. Cambridge: Cambridge University Press.

————1967b. The marketing of agricultural produce. In *The agrarian history of England and Wales*. Vol. 4, *1500–1640*, ed. Joan Thirsk, pp. 466–592. Cambridge: Cambridge University Press.

Falconer, W. 1796. Sketch of the history of sugar in the early times, and through the Middle Ages. *Memoirs of the Literary and Philosophical Society of Manchester* 4(2):291–301.

Fay, C. R. 1948. *English economic history mainly since 1700*. Cambridge: Cambridge University Press.

Fernández-Armesto, F. 1982. *The Canary Islands after the conquest*. Oxford: Clarendon.

Firth, R. 1937. *We the Tikopia*. London: George Allen and Unwin.

Fischler, C. 1979. Gastro-nomie et gastro-anomie. *Communications* 31:189–210.

_____. 1980. Food habits, social change and the nature/culture dilemma. *Social Science Information* 19(6):937–53.

Forbes, D. 1744. *Some considerations on the present state of Scotland*. Edinburgh: W. Sands, A. Murray, and J. Cochran.

Forbes, R. J. 1966. *Studies in ancient technology*. Vol. 5. Leiden: E. J. Brill.

Forster, T. 1767. *An enquiry into the causes of the present high prices of provisions*. London.

Galloway, J. H. 1977. The Mediterranean sugar industry. *Geographical Review* 67(2):177–92.

Gelder, L. van. 1982. Inventing food-free rituals. *Ms.* 11:25–26.

Genovese, E. D. 1965. *The political economy of slavery*. New York: Pantheon.

_____. 1974. *Roll, Jordan roll: the world the slaveholders made*. New York: Pantheon.

George, M. D. 1925. *London life in the eighteenth century*. London: Kegan Paul, Trench, and Trubner.

Gilboy, E. B. 1932. Demand as a factor in the Industrial Revolution. In *Facts and factors in economic history: articles by former students of Edwin Francis Gay*, pp. 620–39. New York: Russell and Russell.

Gillespie, J. E. 1920. *The influence of overseas expansion on England to 1700*. Columbia University Studies in History, Economics and Public Laws, Vol. 91. New York: Columbia University Press.

Glasse, H. 1747. *The art of cookery made plain and easy*. London.

_____. 1760. *The compleat confectioner: or, the whole art of confectionery*. Dublin: John Exshaw.

Greenfield, S. 1979. Plantations, sugar cane and slavery. In *Roots and branches*, ed. M. Craton. Toronto: Pergamon.

Hagelberg, G. B. 1974. *The Caribbean sugar industries: constraints and opportunities*. Antilles Research Program, Yale University. Occasional Papers 3. New Haven: Antilles Research Program.

_____. 1976. *Outline of the world sugar economy*. Forschungsbericht 3. Berlin: Institut für Zuckerindustrie.

Hanway, J. 1767. *Letters on the importance of the rising generation of the labouring part of our fellow-subjects*. 2 vols. London.

Harington, Sir J. n.d. [1607]. *The Englishmans doctor or the school of Salernum*. London: John Helme and John Press.

Harlow, V. T. 1926. *A history of Barbados, 1625–1685*. London: Clarendon.

Harris, D. R. 1969. Agricultural systems, ecosystems and the origins of agriculture. In *The domestication and exploitation of plants and animals*, ed. P. J. Ucko and G. W. Dimbleby, pp. 3–15. Chicago: Aldine.

Harrison, S. G. 1950. Manna and its sources. *Kew Royal Botanical Garden Bulletin* 3:407–17.

Harrison, W. 1968 [1587]. *The description of England*, ed. Georges Edelen. Ithaca, N.Y.: Cornell University Press.

Hart, J. 1633. *Klinike or the diet of the diseased*. London: John Beale.

Hazlitt, W. C. 1886. *Old English cookery books and ancient cuisine*. London: E. Stock.

Heeren, A. 1846 [1809]. *A manual of the history of the political system of Europe and its colonies*. London: Henry G. Bohn.

Henning, H. 1916. *Der Geruch*. Leipzig: Johann Ambrosius Barth.

Hentzner, P. 1757 [1598]. *A journey into England*. Strawberry Hill, England.

Heyd, W. von. 1959 [1879]. *Histoire du commerce du Levant*. 2 vols. Amsterdam: Adolf M. Hakkert.

Hobsbawm, E. 1968. *Industry and empire*. The Pelican Economic History of Europe. Vol. 4. Harmondsworth: Penguin.

Hugill, A. 1978. *Sugar and all that...a history of Tate & Lyle*. London: Gentry.

Hunt, S. R. 1963. Sugar and spice. *Pharmaceutical Journal* 191:632–35.

Huntingford, G. W. B. 1953. The Masai group. In *Ethnographic Survey of Africa, East Central Africa*. Part VIII, *The Southern Nilo-Hamites*, ed. D. Forde, pp. 102–26. London: International African Institute.

International Sugar Council. 1963. *The world sugar economy: structure and policies*. Vol. 2, *The world picture*. London: Brown, Wright and Truscott.

James, C. L. R. 1938. *The black Jacobins*. London: Secker and Warburg.

Jerome, N. W. 1977. Taste experience and the development of a dietary preference for sweet in humans: ethnic and cultural variations in early taste experience. In *Taste and development: the genesis of sweet preference*. Fogarty International Center Proceedings. No. 32, ed. J. M. Weiffenbach, pp. 235–48. Bethesda, Md.: U.S. Department of Health, Education, and Welfare.

Joinville, J. de. 1957 [1309]. Chronicle. In *Memoirs of the Crusades*, trans. F. T. Marzials. New York: E. P. Dutton.

Kare, M. 1975. Monellin. In *Sweeteners: issues and uncertainties*. National Academy of Sciences Academy Forum, Fourth of a Series, pp. 196–206. Washington, D.C.: National Academy of Sciences.

Klein, R. E.; Habicht, J. P.; and Yarborough, C. 1971. Effects of protein-calorie malnutrition on mental development. *Advances in Pediatrics* 18:75–87.

Kremers, E., and Urdang, G. 1963. *History of pharmacy*. Revised by Glenn Sonnedecker. Philadelphia: J. B. Lippincott.

Labarge, M. W. 1965. *A baronial household of the thirteenth century*. London: Eyre and Spottiswoode.

Le Grand d'Aussy, P. J. B. 1815 [1781]. *Histoire de la vie privée des Français*. 3 vols. Paris: Laurent-Beaupré.

Leverett, D. H. 1982. Fluorides and the changing prevalence of dental caries. *Science* 217:26–30.

Levey, M. 1973. *Early Arabic pharmacology*. Leiden: E. J. Brill.

Lewis, Sir W. A. 1978. *The evolution of the international economic order*. Princeton, N.J.: Princeton University Press.

Linder, S. 1970. *The harried leisure class*. New York: Columbia University Press.

Lippmann, E. von. 1970 [1929]. *Geschichte des Zuckers*. Niederwalluf bei Wiesbaden: Dr. Martin Sandig.

Lloyd, E. M. H. 1936. Food supplies and consumption at different economic levels. *Journal of the Proceedings of the Agricultural Society* 4(2):89–110 ff.

Lopez, R. S., and Raymond, I. 1955. *Medieval trade in the Mediterranean world*. New York: Columbia University Press.

Louis, J. C., and Yazijian, H. C. 1980. *The cola wars*. New York: Everest House.

McKendrick, N.; Brewer, J.; and Plumb, J. H. 1982. *The birth of a consumer society*. Bloomington, Ind.: Indiana University Press.

McKendry, M. 1973. *Seven centuries of English cooking*. London: Weidenfeld and Nicolson.

MacPherson, D. 1812. *The history of the European commerce with India*. London: Longman, Hurst, Rees, Orme & Brown.

Major, R. 1945. Thomas Willis. In *Classic descriptions of disease*, ed. R. Major, pp. 238–42. Springfield: Charles C Thomas.

Malinowski, B. 1950 [1922]. *Argonauts of the Western Pacific*. London: George Routledge and Son.

———. 1935. *Coral gardens and their magic*. 2 vols. London: Geo. Allen and Unwin.

Maller, O., and Desor, J. A. 1973. Effect of taste on ingestion by human newborns. In *Fourth symposium on oral sensation and perception*, ed. J. F. Bosma, pp. 279–91. Washington, D.C.: Government Printing Office.

Malowist, M. 1969. Les débuts du système de plantations dans la période des grandes découvertes. *Africana Bulletin* 10:9–30.

Marshall, L. 1961. Sharing, talking and giving: relief of social tensions among !Kung Bushmen. *Africa* 31:231–49.

Marx, K. 1939 [1867]. *Capital*. Vol. 1. New York: International Publishers.

———. 1965 [1858]. *Pre-capitalist economic formations*. New York: International Publishers.

_____. 1968 [1846]. Letter to P. V. Annenkov, Dec. 28, 1846. In *Karl Marx and Frederick Engels, Selected Works*. New York: International Publishers.

_____. 1969. [Ms.] *Theories of surplus-value* (Vol. 4 of *Capital*), Part 2. London: Lawrence and Wishart.

Masefield, G. B. 1967. Crops and livestock. In *Cambridge Economic History of Europe*. Vol. 4, ed. E. E. Rich and C. H. Wilson, pp. 275–80. Cambridge: Cambridge University Press.

Mathias, P. 1967. *Retailing revolution*. London: Longmans.

_____. 1979. *The transformation of England: essays in the economic and social history of England in the eighteenth century*. New York: Columbia University Press.

Mathieson, W. L. 1926. *British slavery and its abolition*. London: Longmans, Green.

Mauro, F. 1960. *Le Portugal et l'Atlantique au XVIIᵉ siècle*. Paris: Ecole Pratique des Hautes Etudes.

Mead, W. E. 1967 [1931]. *The English medieval feast*. London: George Allen and Unwin.

Mill, J. S. 1876 [1848]. *Principles of political economy*. New York: D. Appleton.

Mintz, S. W. 1959. The plantation as a sociocultural type. In *Plantation systems of the New World*. Social Science Monographs 7, pp. 42–50. Washington, D.C.: Pan American Union.

_____. 1977. The so-called world system: local initiative and local response. *Dialectical Anthropology* 2:253–70.

_____. 1979. Slavery and the rise of the peasantry. *Historical Reflections* 6(1):215–42.

Moseley, B. 1800. *A treatise on sugar with miscellaneous medical observations*. 2nd ed. London: John Nichols.

Moskowitz, H. 1974. The psychology of sweetness. In *Sugars in nutrition*, ed. H. L. Sipple and K. W. McNutt, pp. 37–64. New York: Academic Press.

Mount, J. L. 1975. *The food and health of western man*. New York: Wiley.

Murphy, B. 1973. *A history of the British economy, 1086–1970*. London: Longman.

Nef, J. U. 1950. *War and human progress*. Cambridge, Mass.: Harvard University Press.

Oberg, K. 1973. *The social economy of the Tlingit Indians*. American Ethnological Society Monograph 55. Seattle: University of Washington Press.

Oddy, D. 1976. A nutritional analysis of historical evidence: the working-class diet 1880–1914. In *The making of the modern British diet*, ed. D. Oddy and D. Miller, pp. 214–31. London: Croom and Helm.

Oldmixon, J. 1708. *The British Empire in America*. 2 vols. London.

Orr, J. B. (Lord). 1937. *Food, health and income*. London: Macmillan.

Ortiz, F. 1947. *Cuban counterpoint*. New York: Knopf.

Orwell, G. 1984 [1937]. *The road to Wigan Pier*. Penguin: Harmondsworth.

Our English home: its early history and progress. 3rd ed. 1876. Oxford and London: James Parker.

Page, L., and Friend, B. 1974. Level of use of sugars in the United States. In *Sugars in nutrition*, ed. H. L. Sipple and K. W. McNutt, pp. 93–107. New York: Academic Press.

Pares, R. 1950. *A West-India fortune*. London: Longmans, Green.

———. 1960. *Merchants and planters*. Economic History Review Supplements 4, Economic History Society. Cambridge: Cambridge University Press.

Partridge, R. 1584. *The treasure of commodious conceites, and hidden secrets, commonly called the good huswives closet of provision for the health of her houshold*. London.

Paton, D. N.; Dunlop, J. C.; and Inglis, E. M. 1902. *A study of the diet of the labouring classes in Edinburgh*. Edinburgh: Otto Schulze and Co.

Pegolotti, F. di Balducci. See Balducci Pegolotti, F. di.

Pellat, C. 1954. Ğāhiẓiana, I. Le *Kitāb al-Tabaṣṣur bi-l-Tiğāra* attribué à Ğāhiz. *Arabica. Revue d'Etudes Arabes* 1(2):153–65.

Pereira, M. Soares. See Soares Pereira, M.

Pfaffman, C.; Bartoshuk, L. M.; and McBurney, D. H. 1971. Taste psychophysics. In *Handbook of sensory physiology*. Vol. 4, *Chemical senses*, Part 2, ed. L. Beidler, pp. 82–102. Berlin: Springer.

Phillips, W. D., Jr. n.d. [1982?]. Sugar production and trade in the Mediterranean at the time of the Crusades. Manuscript (photocopy). 24 pp.

Pimentel, D.; Hurd, L. E.; Bellotti, A. C.; Forster, M. J.; Oka, I. N.; Sholes, O. D.; and Whitman, R. J. 1973. Food production and the energy crisis. *Science* 182 (4111):443–49.

Pittenger, P. S. 1947. *Sugars and sugar derivatives in pharmacy*. Scientific Report Series No. 5. New York: Sugar Research Foundation, Inc.

Platt, Sir H. 1596. *Delightes for ladies*. London.

———. 1675. *Delightes for ladies*. 11th ed. London.

Pollexfen, J. 1697. *A discourse of trade, coyn and paper credit*. To which is added the argument of a Learned Counsel [Sir Henry Pollexfen]. London.

Pomet, P. 1748. *A complete history of drugs*. 4th ed. London.

Popovic, A. 1965. Ali Ben Muhammad et la révolte des esclaves à Basra. Ph.D. diss., Université de Paris.

Porter, G. R. 1831. *The nature and properties of the sugar cane*. Philadelphia: Carey and Lea.

_____. 1851. *The progress of the nation*. London: John Murray.

Postan, M. M. 1939. The fifteenth century. *Economic History Review* 9:160–67.

Pyler, E. J. 1973. *Baking science and technology*. 2nd ed. Chicago: Siebel Publishing Co.

Ragatz, L. J. 1928. *The fall of the planter class in the British Caribbean, 1763–1833*. New York: Century.

Ratekin, M. 1954. The early sugar industry in Española. *Hispanic American Historical Review* 34:1–19.

Reed, W. 1866. *The history of sugar and sugar-yielding plants*. London: Longmans, Green.

Reeves, Mrs. M. S. P. 1913. *Round about a pound a week*. London: G. Bell.

Renner, H. D. 1944. *The origin of food habits*. London: Faber and Faber.

Richards, Audrey I. 1932. *Hunger and work in a savage tribe*. London: Geo. Routledge and Sons Ltd.

_____. 1939. *Land, labour and diet in Northern Rhodesia*. London: Oxford University Press.

Ritter, K. 1841. Über die geographische Verbreitung des Zuckerrohrs (*Saccharum officinarum*) in der altem Welt vor dessen Verpflanzung in die neue Welt. *Abhandlungen der Königlichen Akademie der Wissenschaften zu Berlin, aus dem Jahre 1839*, pp. 306–412.

Robertson Smith, W. 1889. *Lectures on the religion of the Semites*. New York: D. Appleton.

Rogers, J. E. T. 1963 [1866]. *History of agriculture and prices in England*. 4 vols. Oxford: Oxford University Press.

Roseberry, W. 1982. Balinese cockfights and the seduction of anthropology. *Social Research* 49(4):1013–28.

Rosengarten, F. 1973. *The book of spices*. New York: Pyramid.

Rowntree, B. S. 1922. *Poverty: a study of town life*. New ed. New York: Longmans, Green.

Rozin, E. 1973. *The flavor-principle workbook*. New York: Hawthorn.

Rozin, E., and Rozin, P. 1981. Culinary themes and variations. *Natural History* 90(2):6–14.

Rozin, P. 1976a. Psychobiological and cultural determinants of food-choice. In *Appetite and food intake*. Life Sciences Research Report 2. Dahlem Workshop on Appetite and Food Intake, ed. T. Silverstone, pp. 285–312. Berlin: Dahlem Conferenzen.

_____. 1976b. The use of characteristic flavorings in human culinary practice. In *Flavor: its chemical, behavioral and commercial aspects*, ed. C. M. Apt, pp. 101–27. Boulder, Col.: Westview.

Rye, W. B. 1865. *England as seen by foreigners*. London: John Russell.

Salmasius, C. 1977 [1633]. *Bericht von 1663 aus Paris: Über den Zucker*.

Manuskript-fragment aus dem Nachlass des Claudius Salmasius. Berlin: Institut für Zuckerindustrie.

Salmi-Bianchi, J.-M. 1969. Les anciennes sucreries du Maroc. *Annales: Economies, Sociétés, Civilisations* 24:1176–80.

Salzman, L. F. 1931. *English trade in the Middle Ages*. Oxford: Clarendon Press.

Sass, Lorna J. 1981. The preference for sweets, spices, and almond milk in late medieval English cuisine. In *Food in perspective*. Ed. Alexander Fenton and Trefor Owen, pp. 253–60. Edinburgh: John Donald Publishers.

Sauer, C. O. 1952. *Agricultural origins and dispersals*. New York: American Geographical Society.

———. 1966. *The early Spanish Main*. Berkeley and Los Angeles: University of California.

Schneider, J. 1977. Was there a precapitalist world system? *Peasant Studies* 6(1):20–29.

Shand, P. M. 1927. *A book of food*. London: Jonathan Cape.

Shapiro, N. 1957. Sugar and cane sugar in Hebrew literature. *Hebrew Medical Journal* 2:89–94, 128–30 (numbered in reverse; bilingual publication).

Sheridan, R. 1974. *Sugar and slavery*. Lodge Hill, Barbados: Caribbean Universities Press.

Simmonds, P. L. 1854. *The commercial products of the vegetable kingdom*. London: T. F. A. Day.

Slare, F. 1715. *Observations upon Bezoar-stones. With a vindication of sugars against the charge of Dr. Willis, other physicians, and common prejudices*. London: Tim Goodwin.

Smith, Adam. 1776. *An inquiry into the nature and causes of the wealth of nations*. Dublin: printed for Whitestone, Chamberlaine, W. Watson [etc.].

Smith, R. F. 1960. *The United States and Cuba: business and diplomacy, 1917–1960*. New Haven: College and University Press.

Smith, W. Robertson. See Robertson Smith, W.

Soares Pereira, M. 1955. *A origem dos cilindros na moagem da cana*. Rio de Janeiro: Instituto do Açúcar e do Álcool.

Sombart, W. 1967 [1919]. *Luxury and capitalism*. Ann Arbor: University of Michigan Press.

Stare, F. J. 1948. Fiasco in food. *Atlantic Monthly* 181:21–22.

———. 1975. Role of sugar in modern nutrition. *World Review of Nutrition and Dietetics* 22:239–47.

Steinhart, J. S., and Steinhart, C. E. 1974. Energy use in the U.S. food system. *Science* 184(4134):307–16.

Strickland, A. 1878. *Lives of the queens of England*. 6 vols. London: G. Bell & Sons.

Sugar Association, Inc. n.d. [1979?]. *Why sugar?* Washington, D.C.: The Sugar Association, Inc.

Symons, D. 1979. *The evolution of human sexuality.* New York: Oxford University Press.

Taylor, A. J. 1975. Introduction. In *The standard of living in Britain in the Industrial Revolution,* ed. A. J. Taylor, pp. xi–lv. London: Methuen.

Thomas, R. P. 1968. The sugar colonies of the old empire: profit or loss for Great Britain? *Economic History Review* 21(1):30–45.

Thomas, R. P., and McCloskey, D. 1981. Overseas trade and empire, 1700–1860. In *The economic history of Britain since 1700,* ed. R. Floud and D. McCloskey, pp. 87–102. Cambridge: Cambridge University Press.

Thompson, E. P. 1967. Time, work discipline and industrial capitalism. *Past and Present* 38:56–97.

Tiger, L. 1979. Anthropological concepts. *Preventive Medicine* 8:600–7.

Timoshenko, V. P., and Swerling, B. C. 1957. *The world's sugar: progress and policy.* Stanford, Calif.: Stanford University Press.

Torode, A. 1966. Trends in fruit consumption. In *Our changing fare,* ed. T. C. Barker, J. C. McKenzie, and J. Yudkin, pp. 115–34. London: MacGibbon and Kee.

Trevelyan, G. M. 1945. *English social history.* London: Longmans, Green.

Tryon, T. [Physiologus Philotheus]. 1700. *Friendly advice to gentlemen-planters of the East and West Indies.* London.

Turner, B. S. 1982. The discourse of diet. *Theory, Culture and Society* 1(1):23–32.

Ukers, W. H. 1935. *All about tea.* 2 vols. New York: The Tea and Coffee Trade Journal Co.

Van Gelder, L. See Gelder, L. van.

Vaughan, W. 1600. *Naturall and artificiall directions for health.* London.
———. 1633. *Directions for health.* 7th ed. London.

Venner, T. 1620. *Via recta ad vitam longam, or a plaine philosophical discourse.* London.

Wakefield, E. G. 1968 [1833]. England and America. In *The collected works of Edward Gibbon Wakefield,* ed. M. F. L. Prichard, pp. 317–430. Glasgow and London: Collins.

Wallerstein, I. 1974. *The modern world-system: capitalist agriculture and the origins of the world-economy in the sixteenth century.* New York: Academic Press.

———. 1980. *The modern world-system: mercantilism and the consolidation of the European world-economy, 1600–1750.* New York: Academic Press.

Warner, J. N. 1962. Sugar cane: an indigenous Papuan cultigen. *Ethnology* 1(4):405–11.

Warner, R. 1791. *Antiquitates culinariae; or curious tracts relating to the culinary affairs of the Old English*. London: Blamire.

Warton, T. 1824. *The history of English poetry from the close of the eleventh to the commencement of the eighteenth century*. Vol. 1. London: T. Tegg.

Watson, A. M. 1974. The Arab agricultural revolution and its diffusion, 700–1100. *Journal of Economic History* 34(1):8–35.

Watson, K. J. 1978. Sugar sculpture for grand ducal weddings from the Giambologna workshop. *Connoisseur* 199(799):20–26.

Williams, E. 1942. *The Negro in the Caribbean*. Bronze Booklet No. 8 Washington, D.C.: The Associates in Negro Folk Education.

———. 1944. *Capitalism and slavery*. Chapel Hill, N.C.: University of North Carolina Press.

Williamson, J. A. 1931. *A short history of British expansion*. 2nd ed. New York: Macmillan.

Wolf, E. R. 1982. *Europe and the people without history*. Berkeley, Calif.: University of California Press.

Wretlind, A. 1974. World sugar production and usage in Europe. In *Sugars in nutrition*, ed. H. L. Sipple and K. W. McNutt, pp. 81–92. New York: Academic Press.

Wright, I. A. 1916. *The early history of Cuba*. New York: Macmillan.

Young, A. 1771. *The farmer's tour through the east of England*. 4 vols. London: W. Strahan.

Notes

Introduction

1. Hagelberg (1974: 51–52; 1976: 5) points out that noncentrifugal sugars still figure importantly in consumption in a number of countries, and estimates (*in lit.*, July 30, 1983) that world output stands at around twelve million tonnes (one metric ton = 2,204.6 pounds), a significant figure.
2. Among the most interesting studies, I would note those by Claudius Salmasius, Frederick Slare, William Falconer, William Reed, Benjamin Moseley, Karl Ritter, Richard Bannister, Ellen Ellis, George R. Porter, Noel Deerr, Jacob Baxa and Guntwin Bruhns, and, above all, Edmund von Lippmann. Specific references to their works are provided in the bibliography.
3. Malinowski 1950 [1922]: 4–22. See also his self-criticism in Malinowski 1935: I, 479–81.
4. R. Adams 1977: 221.

1. Food, Sociality, and Sugar

1. Richards 1932: 1.
2. Robertson Smith 1889: 269.

3. *Ibid.*
4. Marshall 1961: 236.
5. Of course this assertion glosses over an immense quantity of research, both archaeological and ethnological, which I cannot deal with here. Most scholars believe that settled agricultural life, based on stable cereal (or root) cultivation, was a precondition for the emergence of complex political systems (states), as in post-Neolithic Egypt, Mesopotamia, Mexico, and so on. One authority (Cohen 1977) has suggested that, even earlier, the successes in domesticating plants and animals actually served to resolve a food crisis caused by the decline of big game. Once stable cultivation was established, the human population began to increase rapidly. Sauer 1952 and Anderson 1952 provide classic introductions to the saga of plant domestication. The archaeologist V. Gordon Childe likened its consequences to a revolution, and coined the term "Neolithic Revolution" to describe it (1936). Useful information on domestication is provided in Chrispeels and Sadava 1977, and in an article by David Harris (1969).
6. Richards 1939: 46–49.
7. E. Rozin 1973, P. Rozin 1976a, E. Rozin and P. Rozin 1981.
8. See, for instance, Pimentel *et al.* 1973, Steinhart and Steinhart 1974.
9. See, for instance, Balikci 1970 on the Eskimos, Oberg 1973 on the Tlingit, and Huntingford 1953 on the Masai.
10. Roseberry 1982: 1026.
11. Maller and Desor 1973: 279–91.
12. Jerome 1977: 243.
13. Beidler 1975, Kare 1975, P. Rozin 1976a, 1976b.
14. Symons 1979: 73.
15. Beauchamp, Maller, and Rogers 1977.
16. DeSnoo 1937: 88.
17. Jerome 1977: 236.
18. The improvement of sucrose extraction from the sugar beet, building on studies that were pioneered by Marggraff (1709–1782), was accomplished by his pupil Franz Achard (1753–1821). But it was Benjamin Delessert who manufactured loaves of white sugar in 1812, to Napoleon's delight. The French beet sugar industry received favored treatment until its product was fully competitive with cane sugar coming from French tropical colonies, such as Martinique and Guadeloupe.
19. Henning 1916. A useful recent discussion can be found in Pfaffman, Bartoshuk, and McBurney 1971. Henning sought to represent the relations among the tastes of bitterness, saltiness, sourness, and sweetness by a diagram having four faces. The four primary tastes are at the apices, binary tastes along the edges, and tertiary tastes on the surfaces, thus:

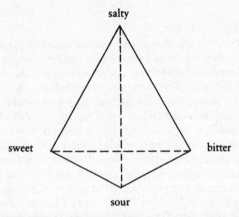

Taste tetrahedron (Henning 1916) as reproduced in Pfaffman et al. 1971: 97.

Pfaffman *et al.* believe that the diagram works, at least for representing successive taste sensations. The implications of a taste system consisting of four scientifically verifiable primary tastes are very substantial, but most authorities treat this position circumspectly.

The use of the term "sweet" to describe water (and not just fresh water as opposed to saltwater or to brackish water, but also to describe the taste of water drunk after something salty, bitter, or sour has been ingested) and to describe certain foods, such as scallops and crabmeat, dramatizes the very wide range of the experience of sweetness as opposed to the relatively narrow range of sugars and of a lexicon of taste. The differences are sufficiently bewildering to lead one of the best students of sweetness to write: "As psychologists explore sweetness, and indeed the chemical senses, they are constantly required to emulate Janus—looking one way toward the behavior of model systems in the search for regularities and laws, but also to actual foods, where consumption occurs and where regularities give way to irregularities and laws of behavior to abundant exceptions" (Moskowitz 1974: 62).

2. Production

1. Edelman 1971. The family of naturally occurring substances called carbohydrates, formed from carbon, hydrogen, and oxygen, includes the sugars, of which sucrose is most important to this account. It can be found in all grasses, in some roots, and in the sap of many trees. Photosynthesis effects the combination of carbon dioxide with

water to manufacture sugar (sucrose) and other starches and sugars. Our species cannot manufacture sucrose, only consume it. Ingestion of carbohydrates, together with inhalation of oxygen, allows glucose (blood sugar) to be transformed into energy, and is accompanied by the exhalation of carbon dioxide: "sugar consumption is thus the reverse of sugar formation" (Hugill 1978: 11).

2. Of the six known species of the genus *Saccharum*, four appear to be domesticated, and of these, *Saccharum officinarum* ("sugar of the apothecaries") is most widespread and important (Warner 1962). The immense number of cultivated cane varieties is the consequence of a vast amount of applied research on the major source of one of the world's leading commodities. Sugar has ranked among the top half-dozen food imports worldwide for several centuries.

3. Deerr 1949: I, 63.

4. R. J. Forbes 1966: 103.

5. S. G. Harrison 1950: n.p.; R. J. Forbes 1966: 100–1.

6. *Tabashir* (*tabasheer, tabaxir*), or *Sakkar Mambu*, was much prized as a medicinal. When hardened, this vegetable gum becomes transparent or white, concreted, and sweet in taste. It may have been used in the same way as sugar in medical preparations. The word *tabaxir* means "chalk" or "mortar" in Urdu, according to the Shorter Oxford English Dictionary; it occurs with the same meaning in the dialects of Maghribi Arabic. The word "sugar" is believed to be derived from Sanskrit *śarkarā*, meaning "gravel" or "grit." Just as sugar came to be called a kind of salt by the physicians of seventeenth-century western Europe, so was *tabashir* called Arabian salt (*Salz aus den glücklichen Arabien*), "the salt of Arabia Felix." Opportunities for confusion between these substances were considerable—even though they are not really similar—because both were very rare, and probably some authors were describing them only second- or third-hand. Parallel confusion marks discussions of Biblical references to sweetness that mention neither manna nor honey. There seems no likelihood that sugar was known in the Near East in Biblical times, but scholars are not unanimous. See, for instance, Shapiro 1957.

7. Barnes writes: "Sugar cane is propagated commercially by the vegetative method, which involves the planting of sections of the stem of immature cane, this material being known as seed, seed cane, seed pieces, and setts. The true seed of cane arising from natural or controlled pollination of the female flowers is entirely unsuitable for producing commercial crops.... The asexual or vegetative method produces new plants in all respects like the canes from which the seed pieces were taken, though in very rare cases a new individual cane is developed from a bud sport which differs for unknown reasons from others derived from the same variety. The new crop thus

grows from the buds of the planted stem cuttings of the variety selected for commercial use" (Barnes 1974: 257).

8. Hagelberg 1976: 5.
9. *Ibid.*
10. The words for molasses (e.g., French *mélasse*, Spanish *melaza*, Portuguese *melaço*, etc.) come from the Latin *mel*, honey. The English term "treacle" is from the Latin *theriaca* (from Greek *thérion*, wild animal), an electuary or compound used in the treatment of poisonous bites. Both Galen and Dioscorides developed "theriacs," which often contained the flesh of poisonous serpents. Such theriacs (or treacles) eventually became enshrined in European medicine and did not disappear from official pharmacopoeias until late in the nineteenth century. F. Crane, writing in *Notes and Queries* (February 22, 1762), observes that only in England did the term "treacle" come to mean molasses, presumably by broadening its usage from a particular kind of compound to a general substance. The important point, it seems to me, is that treacles had been made with honey; that molasses, probably because of its rapidly declining price, supplanted honey; and that the term for the compound then could be transferred to the medium. We find "treacle" first written to mean "molasses" in 1694; the Shorter Oxford English Dictionary cites Westmacot, *Script. Herb.*: "good store of molossus or common Treacle to sweeten it." The term continues to be used to describe medicines as well, but the word "molasses" never achieved popular usage in England, whereas the liquid still called "treacle" (or "golden syrup") remains popular. The term "golden syrup" requires a passing comment in turn. Refined molasses can be made both thinner and lighter in color, so as to resemble honey, but with a readily varied consistency.

It achieved some kind of climax in the "golden syrup" perfected toward the end of the nineteenth century by the Glasgow-based giant of British sugar, Tate and Lyle. As Aykroyd (1967: 7) has pointed out, this product, one of the most important prepared foods in modern history, has been advertised by the invocation of a Biblical story that neatly confounds it with honey. The container shows a dead lion, the lion Samson killed, surrounded by bees: they have nested in the lion and made honey. Samson's riddle—"Out of the eater came forth meat, and out of the strong came forth sweetness"—could not be solved by the Philistines; but Delilah worried it from him: "What is sweeter than honey? and what is stronger than a lion?" (Judges 14:18). Aykroyd adds: The designers of the emblem ignored the fact that the source of sweetness [in the Biblical tale] is honey rather than sugar." Indeed they did, epitomizing thus a process of replacement that took centuries to complete.

11. Just as we cannot adequately discuss the place of sugar or sugarlike substances in traditional Greek medicine, we must omit any serious consideration of sugar in Indian medical practice. In all probability hardened sugar, crystallized from the processed juice of the cane, was being used medically in India by 400 A.D., if not earlier. But such hardened sugar was, it seems certain, not known to Galen and his contemporaries. The only sugar product—sucrose, that is to say—that may have figured in Galenic medicine was probably the doughy, ropelike, noncrystalline *fanid*—Arabic *al-fānīd*, English *pennet, penide, penidium.* These words probably come from some Indic language. (The term *phanita* is a Sanskrit-derived modifier of the word for "sugar" [*śarkarā*] employed in the Bower Manuscript, dating to c. 375 A.D., where it refers to a wholly liquid product. [Cf. Deerr 1949: I, 47]) *Penidium* gives rise to Spanish *alfeñique* and English *alembick*, meaning a still. In its earlier forms in English, such as "fanid," it refers to a taffylike sugar confection (or medicine) similar to the barley sugar of later English usage. "*Fanid,*" writes Pittenger (1947: 5), "originally nothing but the solidified cane juice after it had been boiled down and skimmed, consisted of a brown to black syrupy dough, later described as being yellowish and even as being whitish. It was evidently non-crystalline because of statements to the effect that before cooling off completely, it could be stretched into threads or leaves and rolled out." Pomet, writing in 1748, gives an admirably specific description of barley sugar, which makes clear its affinity with the *fanid* (*pennet*, or *diapenidium*) of European pharmacopoeia at the time: "Barley-sugar is made either of white sugar or brown; the first sort is boil'd 'till the Sugar becomes brittle, and will easily break after it is cold. When it is boil'd to a Height, cast it upon a Marble, that is first lubricated with Oil of Sweet Almonds; and afterwards work it to a Paste, in any figure you fancy. The other Sort, improperly call'd Barley-Suger, is made of Cassonade, or coarse Powder Sugar, clarified and boil'd to a Toughness that will work with your Hands to any Shape, and is commonly made up in little twisted Sticks. This Kind of sugar is more difficult to make than the other, because of hitting the exact Proportion of boiling to fetch it to such a Height that they may work it as they please: This ought to be of a fine Amber-Colour, dry, new made, and such as does not stick to the Teeth: Some Confectioners, to make it of a fine Colour, stain it with Saffron" (Pomet 1748: 58).

It is not possible to do justice to this and other kinds of sugar in a work of the present sort. But it is worth noting that fanid or pennet could be made in combination with almond oil, and shaped afterward into different forms. This "sculptural" quality of some sugars was to play an important part in the later development of sugar uses.

12. Galloway (1977), building on Lippmann (1970 [1929]) and Deerr (1949, 1950), has advanced our knowledge of the spread and consolidation of the Mediterranean industry. A. M. Watson (1974) has documented the Arab contribution to Mediterranean agriculture. See also Phillips n.d.

13. Dorveaux 1911: 13.

14. A. M. Watson 1974.

15. Bolens 1972; A. M. Watson 1974.

16. Deerr 1949: I, 74.

17. Berthier 1966.

18. Popovic 1965.

19. See, for instance, Salmi-Bianchi 1969.

20. Deerr 1950: II, 536; Lippmann 1970 [1929].

21. Soares Pereira 1955; Castro 1980.

22. Baxa and Bruhns 1967: 9.

23. Benveniste 1970: 253–56.

24. Galloway 1977: 190 ff.

25. *Ibid.*

26. *Ibid.*

27. Greenfield 1979: 116.

28. Malowist 1969: 29.

29. Heyd 1959 [1879]: II, 680–93.

30. The first known exported sugar from the Canary Islands dates from 1506, but Fernández-Armesto (1982) believes that it began even earlier; indeed, he supposes that Canarian sugar production surpassed Madeira's during the first years of the sixteenth century.

31. Fernández-Armesto 1982: 85.

32. Wallerstein 1974: 333; Braudel 1973: 156.

33. Ratekin 1954.

34. *Ibid.*: 7. Here Ratekin follows Lippmann—wrongly, I believe—in attributing this mill type to Speciale. Mauro (1960: 209) reproduces a 1613 sketch of a mill said to have been introduced to Brazil from Peru by a priest, after a genuine innovation in milling there (1608–12). The new mill had three vertical rollers and a sweep bar, and allegedly replaced a two-roller horizontal mill then in use.

35. Ratekin 1954: 10.

36. *Ibid.* Ratekin quotes Peter Martyr's unsupportable claim that, by 1518, twenty-eight "mills" were operating, and Irene Wright's more reliable view of the growth of the industry in Santo Domingo (Wright 1916).

37. Ratekin 1954: 13; see also Sauer 1966.

38. Masefield (1967: 289–90) writes: "The first result of the extension of sugar cane production to Madeira and the Canaries in the fifteenth century was severe competition with existing European producers.

This was accentuated as the American colonies came into production. By 1580...the industry in Sicily was moribund....In Spain the industry languished....The small medieval sugar industries of southern Italy, Malta, the Morea, Rhodes, Crete and Cyprus all underwent a similar decline and eventually disappeared.

"In both Madeira and the Canaries sugar production involved the use of African slave labor....This use of slaves may have helped the islanders to undersell other European sugar producers, but Madeira and the Canaries in their turn succumbed respectively to Brazilian and West Indian competition."

39. K. G. Davies 1974: 144. Davies's mention of Javanese and Bengali sugar is slightly surprising. For England, at any rate, the bulk of sugars imported during the first half of the seventeenth century came from Brazil and the Atlantic islands.

40. Andrews 1978: 187.

41. Though the term "muscovado" (mascabado, moscabado, etc.) survives to describe some contemporary less refined brown sugars, "clayed" sugar is no more. When semicrystalline sugars were poured into inverted ceramic cones to permit the molasses and impurities to drain, it became the practice to cap them with wet white clay. The water in the clay, percolating downward, would carry with it much of the waste nonsucrose, the molasses and other materials, leaving the base of the inverted sugar "head" or "loaf" white in color. The apex of the cone would contain darker, less pure sucrose, which was of poorer quality. The whiter sugar was "clayed," the darker "muscovado." These were but two of the more important descriptive terms for sugar types, of which there were scores or hundreds. The British naturalist Sir Hans Sloane recounts the apocryphal story that sugar claying began when it was noticed that a hen, after foraging in wet clay, walked across wet sugar, and left it whiter in those places where she had walked. Once sugar making had passed the stage of removing molasses and impurities by drainage, claying disappeared.

42. Williamson 1931: 257–60.

43. Beer 1948 [1893]: 62–63.

44. *Ibid.*: 65.

45. Child 1694: 79.

46. Oldmixon 1708: I, xxiii.

47. Quoted in Oldmixon 1708: I, 17. The seventeenth-century political economist J. Pollexfen was prophetic: "Our Trade to our Plantations or *West-India* Collonies takes off great quantities of our Products and Manufactures, as well as Provisions and Handicraft Wares, and furnishes us with some Goods for a further Manufactury, and others in great abundance to be Exported to Foreign Nations, especially of

Sugar and *Tobacco*. And although some Objections may be made against the use and necessity of those Commodities, yet being so introduced amongst us as it may be impossible to prevent our having them from other Countries, and being a *Trade* which imployes vast numbers of Ships and Seamen, ought to be incouraged; for having lost so great a part of our *Fishing Trades*, these *Trades*, and that to *Newcastle*, are now become the chief support of our Navigation, and Nursery for Seamen. And if all back doors could be shut, that all the Products Exported from those Collonies might without diminution be brought to *England*, that what are not spent here, might be Re-exported from hence; and those Collonies, as the proprietors are *English*, made to have their whole dependance on *England*, the fruits of their labours to be as much for the advantage of *England*, as those that stay at Home, then all incouragement by easie Laws, Regulations and Protection, should be given to them, they having more opportunities, and being under a greater necessity of gaining more Laborious People, (from whence Riches must arise) to help to make great improvements than *England*, or any other of the Dominions belonging to it: And if it be considered what Forests and Deserts have been improved, and Riches acquired, in some of those Collonies, in so short a time, as the Age of a Man, it must be agreed what hath been asserted, *That the Original of moveable Riches is from Labour*, and that it may arise from the Labour of Blacks and Vagrants, if well managed" (Pollexfen 1697: 86).

48. Oldmixon 1708: I, 17.
49. Mill 1876 [1848]: 685–86.
50. Davis 1973: 251.
51. *Ibid.*
52. Gillespie 1920: 147.
53. Deerr 1949: I, 86.
54. Tryon 1700: 201–2.
55. Dunn 1972: 189–95.
56. Mathieson 1926: 63.
57. *Ibid.*
58. At the risk of digression, I mention that "free" labor and "slave" labor are not polar opposites, except abstractly; indeed, there are many intermediate forms of semicoerced labor, depending on locale, time, and specific circumstances. That capitalism is commonly (and, for analytical purposes, accurately) associated with the proletariat of course does not mean that capitalists were able to profit only from the use of free labor.
59. "In his letters describing the storming of Drogheda, Cromwell wrote that, 'When they submitted, these officers were knocked on the head, and every tenth man of the soldiers killed, and the rest shipped for

Barbados.' 'A terrible Protector this,' remarks Thomas Carlyle, '... he dislikes shedding blood, but is very apt to Barbados an unruly man: he has sent and sends us by hundreds to Barbadoes—so that we have made an active verb of it, 'barbadoes you'" (Harlow 1926: 295).

60. Curtin 1969.
61. Marx 1939 [1867]: I, 793, 738.
62. Gillespie 1920: 74.
63. Thomas and McCloskey 1981: 99.
64. A. Smith 1776: bk. IV, ch. VII, pt. III, quoted in Thomas and McCloskey 1981: 99.
65. Wallerstein 1980.
66. For a clear, elegant statement of this view, see Wolf 1982: 296 ff.
67. Banaji 1979.
68. Marx 1969: II, 239.
69. *Ibid.*: 303.
70. Marx 1965 [1858]: 112.
71. Genovese 1974: 69.
72. Genovese 1965: 23.
73. "Tremendous wealth was produced from an unstable economy based on a single crop, which combined the vices of feudalism and capitalism with the virtues of neither" (Williams 1942: 13).
74. Banaji 1979: 17.
75. Thomas 1968.
76. Quoted in Deerr 1950: II, 433–34.
77. Davis 1954: 151.
78. *Ibid.*: 152–53.
79. *Ibid.*
80. *Ibid.*: 163.
81. Marx 1939 [1867]: I, 776, 785.
82. Marx 1968 [1846]: 470.
83. Hobsbawm 1968: 51. Hobsbawm adds to his argument elsewhere (*ibid.*, pp. 144–45): "We ... expect to find, and do find, an increasingly large excess of imports over exports after 1860. But we also find—and this is rather odd—that at *no* time in the nineteenth century did Britain have an export surplus in goods, in spite of her industrial monopoly, her marked export-orientation, and her modest domestic consumer market.... The buyers of our exports reflect the limits of the markets to which Britain exported, which were essentially countries which either did not want to take much more British textiles or were too poor to have more than a very tiny per capita demand. But it also reflects the traditional 'underdeveloped' slant of the British economy, and also to some extent the luxury demand of the British upper and middle classes. As we have seen, between 1814

and 1845 about seventy per cent of our net imports (in value) were raw materials, about twenty-four per cent foodstuffs—overwhelmingly tropical or similar products (tea, sugar, coffee)—and alcohol. There is not much doubt that Britain consumed so much of these because we had a traditionally important re-export trade in them. Just as cotton production grew, as it were, as a by-product of a large international entrepot trade, so did the unusually large consumption of sugar, tea, and so on, which accounts for a large part of the deficit on current account."

I suspect this may be too neat an explanation. The consumption of tea and coffee diverged sharply in the eighteenth century, and these trends, once established, were never reversed. Even if the re-export trade in coffee maintained itself, tea won out over coffee in the British Isles, to some substantial extent because tea was an imperial production in a way that coffee neither was nor became. The same is even truer of sugar; its consumption solidified once British colonies produced it, and that has never changed.

84. Sheridan 1974: 19–21; italics added.
85. Coleman 1977: 118.
86. Deerr 1950: II, 532. Davis (1979: 43–44) summarizes eloquently: "Sugar was the largest British import for a century and a half, down to the 1820s when it was overtaken by cotton. Sugar was wholly imported from America, Asia or Africa; there was no British, and little European, production. Medieval Europe had lived without it, but once cheap and plentiful supplies appeared in the seventeenth century sugar rapidly became a conventional necessity, and it was one without a substitute. During the eighteenth century the slave-worked plantations of the British Caribbean colonies were virtually the only suppliers, but in the wars great amounts came in from British-occupied French West Indian islands and the Dutch East Indies; and Mauritius and India became important sources from the 1820s.

"Sugar was fairly homogeneous; that is, West Indian and Javan and Mauritius sugar were not basically very dissimilar, though they were imported at different stages of processing that gave them differing reputations. The colonial product was protected until 1844 by a discriminatory import duty that prevented foreign sugar import, but the duty on colonial sugar itself was very high, even after it was halved in 1845. Sugar prices were therefore not only influenced on the supply side by the opening of new sources to serve the British market, crop fluctuations and changing costs of transport, but also by changes in the general level of import duties and in colonial preferences. Britain's internal demand showed a strong long-run tendency to growth, because its rapidly rising population had firmly established habits of sugar consumption.

"Annual fluctuations in imports reflected crop variations and to some extent merchant intentions, but stock-holding was limited, and in any but the shortest run imports had to correspond with consumption. Year-to-year figures show a fair degree of price-elasticity, the British market responding to harvest variations by price changes as well as by adjustment of stocks. In the longer run, however, the picture is different. The slave revolution of 1791 in San Domingo (Haiti), which was Europe's largest supplier, caused some diversion of British supplies to Europe, and a sharp rise in prices which was continued by the first wartime increases in duties. Consumers seem to have been taken aback by this, but they soon returned to their old consumption habits despite continually rising prices. Throughout the war period the average consumer responded to the rising price of sugar by spending more money on it, and when prices fell after the wars he reduced his expenditure rather than greatly increasing his consumption. When the long post-war depression ended in the prosperity of mid-century, steeply rising incomes caused an even faster rise in sugar consumption.

"This pattern of buying, revealing a rather inelastic demand, might be expected for a non-substitutable article, on which few families spent more than a few pence a week, but which in some small quantity had become nearly a necessity, and which was attractive enough to invite a greater share of expenditure as more and more incomes rose well above the poverty line. Sugar retained its leading place among British imports over a very long period because it was much the most used of imported non-essential foodstuffs, and its relative importance sank only when the basic foodstuffs themselves began to figure on a great scale in British import trade."

87. Such calculations, at least for 1700, must be wildly imprecise, since both the amount of sugar consumed and England's population in 1700 must be guessed. It seems certain, however, that nearly 13,000 tons of sugar per year were reaching England by that time. If 10 percent of her citizens could consume as much sugar as they wished, leaving none for those poorer than themselves, each would have been using about 40 pounds per year, or 1.75 ounces per day. I think these guesses are not wild.

There were, to be sure, even earlier attempts to guess at per-capita consumption, and Joseph Massie's "incursions into political arithmetic" (Mathias 1979) include a sketch of differential sugar consumption by class, for the year 1759. Massie's purpose was to establish that the costs of the West India monopoly had been borne by the

English consumers, and he makes a good case. But I was not able to reconcile his enumeration of "ranks, degrees and classes" and his calculations of sugar consumed to arrive at any average figures.

88. The first modern writer to point to this issue may have been Eric Williams, in his *Capitalism and Slavery* (1944). But no reader of C. L. R. James's *The Black Jacobins* (1938) will have missed the thread of connection from Marx to James to Williams.

89. Mintz 1979: 215.

90. Mintz 1977.

91. Mintz 1959: 49.

92. Lewis 1978.

93. Orr 1937: 23. Leverett writes: "Dental caries was not prevalent in primitive societies apparently because their diets lacked easily fermentable carbohydrates. Although caries is clearly a disease with multiple causes, the principal mode of caries initiation is acid dissolution of tooth enamel. This acid is produced by several different microorganisms, most notably *Streptococcus mutans*, with fermentable carbohydrates, especially sucrose, as the nutrient source.... In England, for instance, there was a sharp increase in the prevalence of dental caries during the Roman occupation. There was a decline in dental caries after the departure of the Romans in the early 5th century A.D., and it did not significantly increase again until the second half of the 19th century, when sucrose became widely available to all levels of society" (1982: 26–27).

3. Consumption

1. A particularly moving representation is Nigerian author Chinua Achebe's (1973) story "Sugar Baby," in which a man's obsessive liking for sugar becomes the crux of his personal crisis during the Nigerian civil war.

2. McKendry 1973: 10.

3. Nonetheless there was some exportation of wheat and barley from England, even as early as the fourteenth century. Cf. Everitt 1967b, *passim*, especially pp. 450 ff.; and Bowden 1967: 593 ff.

4. Drummond and Wilbraham 1958: 41.

5. Appleby 1978: 5.

6. *Ibid.*

7. Drummond and Wilbraham 1958: 88.

8. Such general assertions are of course always risky and subject to exceptions. But J. E. T. Rogers called the fifteenth century "the golden age of the English labourer," and with reason; the depopulation

resulting from the Black Death had created a labor shortage resulting
in the doubling of wages in many regions (Bowden 1967: 594). "Not
until the nineteenth century," Postan writes, "was the wage-earner's
standard of living again so high" (Postan 1939: 161). In the seventeenth century, dearth fell especially hard upon the poor. The
evidence collected and assembled by Everitt and by Bowden in their
contributions to *The Agrarian History of England and Wales* makes
clear that "the third, fourth, and fifth decades of the seventeenth
century witnessed extreme hardship in England, and were probably
among the most terrible years through which the country has ever
passed" (Bowden 1967: 621). These were the years immediately
preceding the large-scale introduction of sugar and other commodities (such as tea) into England.

9. Drummond and Wilbraham 1958: 68–69.
10. *Ibid.*: 51.
11. *Ibid.*
12. Murphy 1973: 183.
13. *Ibid.* See also note 8.
14. Not all of these particular items—saffron, for instance—are pro-
    duced exclusively in tropical or subtropical regions. Nonetheless,
    most were imported to England; all were rare and costly; and knowl-
    edge of their nature was for long imperfect and even fantastic. Ac-
    cording to tradition, it was Phoenician merchants who originally
    introduced saffron to Cornwall and Ireland. Hunt (1963) claims that
    the Cornish buns and cakes flavored with "saffran" confirm that
    tradition, while the saffron-dyed shirts of Ireland, the *leine caroich*
    worn by chiefs, supposedly are the origin of the tartan. England
    became a saffron producer in later centuries.
15. Joinville 1957 [1309]: 182.
16. Mead 1967 [1931]: 77.
17. Quoted in Salzman 1931: 461.
18. *Our English Home* 1876: 86.
19. *Ibid.*: 85.
20. *Ibid.*: 86.
21. Salzman 1931: 417.
22. *Ibid.*
23. *Ibid.*
24. Labarge 1965: 96.
25. *Ibid.*: 97.
26. Crane 1975 and 1976: 473.
27. Labarge 1965: 96.
28. Salzman 1931: 231 n.
29. *Ibid.*: 202.

30. Hazlitt 1886: 183.
31. *Ibid.*
32. Mead 1967: 44.
33. *Ibid.*: 55.
34. *Ibid.*: 56.
35. *Ibid.*
36. Austin 1888: ix.
37. R. Warner 1791: Pt. I, 7.
38. *Ibid.*: 9.
39. Lippmann 1970 [1929]: 352 ff.
40. *Ibid.*: 224–25. In an informative paper, K. J. Watson (1978: 20–26) describes the casting of sugar statues duplicating existing bronzes, which became common festive decor for the grand-ducal weddings of the fifteenth to seventeenth centuries in major Italian and southern French cities. Watson was not able to identify any pre–fifteenth-century references for such sculptures, and concluded that sugar's price precluded this kind of display, even for the wealthy, in earlier centuries. But since sugar was being imported to Venice no later than about the eighth century, while refining was being improved there by the thirteenth, earlier experimentation probably did occur. Sugar sculpture in Islamic North Africa was common by the eleventh century. The Italian sugar sculptures, Watson writes, were often called *trionfi* (triumphs): "table decorations for banquets, most frequently wedding banquets ... usually ... ornaments to delight the eye rather than the stomach ... sometimes presented to guests at the end of the event" (1978: 20). The subjects were drawn from heraldic imagery, themes of triumph, architecture, gods and goddesses, narrative groups from Biblical stories or contemporary literature, and animals. This "court art," Watson believes, was partially eclipsed in the early eighteenth century by the beginnings of hard-paste porcelain manufacture. The techniques, as well as the ceremonial specifications, were vey likely diffused from North Africa to northern Europe by way of Italy and then France.
41. Le Grand d'Aussy 1815 [1781]: II, 317.
42. Drummond and Wilbraham 1958: 57.
43. *Our English Home* 1876: 70.
44. *Ibid.*
45. W. Harrison 1968 [1587]: 129. William Harrison's *The Description of England* is generally regarded as the fullest single account of British social life in Elizabethan times. It was written, we are told, "to provide the introductory books to Holinshed's Chronicles" (Edelen 1968: xv), and deals with the whole of English society, but provides especially rich accounts of daily life. Harrison refers to sugar only

twice in his book, the first time to bemoan the sharp rise in price of all spices (sugar included) because they were being reexported; and the second, when describing the fare of the rich and privileged.

46. Warton 1824: I, clix. George Cavendish, the biographer of Cardinal Wolsey (1475–1530), rhapsodizes about the subtleties that graced the table of the Cardinal's installation: "Anon came vppe the Second Course w^t so many disshes, subtilties, & curious devysis w^{che} ware above an Cth in nomber of so goodly proporcion and Costly/ that I suppose the ffrenchmen neuer sawe the lyke/ the wonder was no lesse than it was worth in deade/ there ware Castelles w^t Images in the same/ powlles Chirche & steple in proporcion for the quantitie as well counte^{r}feited as the paynter sholld haue paynted it vppon a clothe or wall/ There ware, beastes, byrdes, fowles of dyuers kyndes And personages most lyvely made & counterfeit in dysshes/ some fighting (as it ware) w^t swordes/ some w^t Gonnes and Crosebowes/ Some vaughtyng & leapyng/ Some dauncyng w^t ladyes/ Some in complett harnes Iustyng w^t speres/ And w^t many more devysis than I ame able w^t my wytt to discribbe/ Among all oon I noted/ there was a Chesse bord subtilly made of spiced plate/ w^t men to the same/ And for the good proporcyon bycause that frenche men be very expert in that play my lord gave the same to a gentilman of fraunce commaundyng that a Case should be made for the same/ in all hast to preserue it frome perysshyng in the conveyaunce therof in to hys Contrie" (Cavendish 1959 [1641]: 70–71). "Spiced plate" refers to the hardened sugar from which these various forms and figures were sculpted. See also Intronizatio Wilhelmi Warham, Archiepiscopi Cantuar. Dominica in Passione, Anno Henrici 7. vicessimo, & anno Domini 1504. Nono die Martii, in Warner 1791: 107–24.

47. Partridge 1584: cap. 9 [unpaged].
48. *Ibid.*, cap. 13 [unpaged].
49. Platt 1675: nos. 73–79.
50. McKendry 1973: 62–63.
51. Glasse 1747: 56.
52. Warner 1791: 136. Surely one of the most interesting passages ever written about the subtleties is to be found here: "Hence arose an extraordinary species of ornament, in use both among the English and French, for a considerable time; representations of the *membra virilia, pudendaque muliebria*, which were formed of *pastry*, or *sugar*, and placed before the guests at entertainments, doubtless for the purpose of causing jokes and conversations among them: as we at present use the little devices of paste, containing mottos within them, to the same end.... Nor were these obscene symbols confined to the ornaments of the person, or to the decorations of the table, but, in

the early ages, were even admitted into the most awful rites of religion. The *consecrated wafer*, which the pious communicant received from the hands of the priest, on Easter Sunday, was made up into a form highly indecent and improper...." Not until 1263, according to Warner, did the English Church halt the apparently common practice of baking the communion wafers in the shape of human testicles: "Prohibemus singulis sacerdotibus parochialibus, ne ipsi parochianis suis die paschatis *testes* seu hostias loco panis benedicti ministrent, ne ex ejus ministratione, seu receptione erubescentiam evitare videantur, sed panem benedictum faciant, sicut aliis diebus dominicis fieri consuevit" (Stat. Synod. Nicolae, Episc. Anegravensis An. 1263). Warner adds: "Du Fresne subjoins, 'Ubi pro *evitare* legendum puto *irritare*, forte enim intelliguntur paniculi, seu oblatae in *testiculorum* figuram formatae, quas in hoc testo Paschali loco panis benedicti dabant'" (Gloss. Tom. III, p. 1109). A revival of such odd practices, now of course entirely divested of any religious associations, is evidenced by occasional stories in the contemporary American press. A January 1982 article in the Baltimore *Evening Sun*, for example, recounts the success of "adult" gingerbread cookies and "erotic chocolates." "I have people coming in," marvels one confectioner, "and saying: 'I want to see the gynecologist special.' Some women actually take these candies to their doctors and give their doctors candy after an examination." I intend to deal anthropologically with these rather bizarre materials in a subsequent publication.

53. Wallerstein 1974.
54. Schneider 1977: 23.
55. Pellat 1954. See also Hunt 1963.
56. Levey 1973: 74. It is tempting to try to combine Galenic humoral concepts with the "taste tetrahedron" proposed by Henning (1916) to show the interrelationships among the taste qualities. Galen himself had enumerated more than four taste qualities. But humoral medicine appears to be grounded upon a quadripartite organization of physical reality, and the taste qualities that were most often enumerated were four in number. The four elements of the natural world were air, fire, water, and earth; earth was dry, water moist, fire hot, air cold. Any two elements combined to produce a complexion; there were four, each with its own humor:

Complexion	Qualities	Humor
Sanguine	Hot and moist	Blood
Phlegmatic	Cold and moist	Phlegm
Choleric	Hot and dry	Yellow or green bile
Melancholic	Cold and dry	Black bile

All foodstuffs were made up of the same elements; their suitability as food depended upon these elements, relative to the temperament of the consumer. So lamb, which was considered moist and phlegmatic, was unsuitable for old men, whose stomachs had too much phlegm already. Children, by temperament phlegmatic, were to eat moderately hot and moist meats; as they grew older, becoming either sanguine or choleric, they were to eat cold salads, and colder meats (this is not, of course, a reference to temperature), reverting to hot and moist meats in old age. Appetite was believed to be a function of heat and dryness; digestion, of heat and moisture; retention, of coldness and dryness; expulsion, of moisture and coldness. Since foods had their characteristic states, they could be prescribed in dietary fashion. Moreover, the system was made more elaborate by the notion of degrees (so that, for instance, lettuce was cold and moist, while cabbage was hot in the first degree and dry in the second).

The "hot" and "cold" distinctions (which have nothing to do with temperature, of course, and occur in much-modified form in the contemporary folk medicine of much of the world) figured in Galenic humoral medicine (Kremers and Urdang 1963: 16–17), and were maintained and elaborated by Islamic scholars after the seventh century. Especially important in this semiscientific elaboration (and in its subsequent perpetuation in western medicine for centuries thereafter) was Alkindus (Abū Yūsuf Ya'qūb ibn-Ishāq al-Kindī), physician to the caliphs al-Ma'mun and al-Mu'taṣim at Baghdad. Alkindus "prematurely attempted to establish an exact method of prescribing by applying the law of geometrical progression to the Galenic doctrine of qualities and degrees of complicated mixtures. His geometrical prescribing combined with musical harmony is well illustrated in the following:

Cardamom is	1' warm	½' cold	½' moist	1' dry
Sugar is	2' warm	1' cold	1' moist	2' dry
Indigo is	½' warm	1' cold	½' moist	1' dry
Emblica is	1' warm	2' cold	1' moist	2' dry
Sum	4½' warm	4½' cold	3' moist	6' dry

This, according to Alkindus, means that the compound is dry to the first degree" (D. Campbell 1926: 64).

Honey and sugar were humorally different, it appears. But the humoral characterization of sugar probably developed within the Islamic world itself, later to be diffused to Europe. Because of this, the two substances were not used with complete interchangeability, though their uses overlapped, and sugar replaced honey more and more. Sweet-tasting foods seem generally to have been considered hot, the other three "qualities" or tastes being cold:

> Hic fervore vigent tres, salsus, amarus, acutus,
> Alget acetosus, sic stipans, ponticus atque
> Unctus, et insipidus, dulcis, dant temperamentum.
>
> (Harington n.d. [1607]: 50)

But a fleeting glance at the relevant materials gives no indication that sweetness was treated for diagnostic purposes as a "quality" separate from the food that produced the sweet sensation. My attempt to find some simple imposition of four tastes upon four humors (upon four fluids, upon four body processes, upon four elements, etc., etc.) failed. But serious study of the incorporation of sugar into the humoral pathology of the European world would probably reveal much about the way it was viewed, particularly in contrast to honey.

57. Levey 1973.

58. *Ibid.*

59. The influence of Arab pharmacology upon western concepts of liquid medicines and beverages is suggested in a small way by contemporary lexicon. It was through that influence that terms such as sherbet, shrub, syrup, and julep entered English; and these contributions of Arabic (and Persian, via Arabic) to English seem to have been based largely on the diffusion of sugar uses.

60. Pittenger 1947. Note that nearly all the ingredients are white in color. The association between purity and whiteness is ancient in Europe. White sugar was commonly prescribed in medicines, and combinations of white foods (chicken, cream, rice flour, almonds, etc.) seem to have enjoyed a popularity at times out of all proportion to their therapeutic efficacy.

61. Lippmann 1970 [1929]: 368.

62. An argument of a kind could be made for sugar's innocence or purity on grounds of its color—not so silly an idea as it sounds. See note 60. "Pure white sugar" still has two quite different meanings, which its manufacturers are happy to treat as one.

63. Pittenger 1947: 8.

64. Lippmann 1970 [1929]: 395.

65. Pittenger (1947) enumerates the following: (1) preservative; (2) antioxidant; (3) solvent; (4) to give consistency or body; (5) stabilizer; (6) to mask bitter and unpleasant-tasting drugs; (7) in syrups; (8) as a demulcent; (9) as a food; (10) as a replacement for glycerin; (11) in elixirs; (12) as a binder for tablets; (13) as an excipient; (14) as a coating; (15) as a diluent and sweetening agent; (16) as a confection base; (17) as an oil sugar base; (18) as an aromatic sugar base; (19) as a homeopathic medicated globule base;

(20) as a homeopathic medicated cone base; (21) as a candy cough lozenge base; (22) as a test diet base; (23) in calcium saccharate; (24) medicinally. Of these, I believe that nos. 1, 3, 4, 5, 6, 7, 8, 9, 11, 13, 14, 15, 16, 18, 21, and 24 were known and employed in the pharmacopoeias transferred to Europe in Latin translation beginning no later than around 1140; that nos. 2, 12, 17, 19, and 20 were possibly practiced; and that only nos. 10, 22, and 23 are probably European and recent. Though I have not consulted specialists in the history of pharmacy concerning this list, I believe the main point—that most such practices were developed or invented in the Islamic world, between the seventh and twelfth centuries—is unassailable.

66. Lippmann 1970 [1929]: 456–66. Serveto's essay on syrups seems innocuous enough to one ignorant of the deeper philosophical implications—which have to do with much more basic conceptions of orthodox Christianity. Pittenger's (1947: 9) suggestion that Serveto may have lost his life because of his hostility to sugared medicines is insouciant, to say the least. *On Syrups* can hardly be called medical in character, no matter how broadly one uses that adjective.

67. Pittenger 1947: 10.

68. *Ibid.*

69. Lippmann 1970 [1929]: 478. The translation by Pittenger (1947: 10–11) is abridged.

70. Vaughan 1600: 24.

71. *Ibid.*: 28.

72. Vaughan 1633: 44.

73. Venner 1620: 103–6.

74. Hart 1633: 96–97.

75. Slare 1715. Thomas Willis was one of London's most successful physicians of the Restoration period. He provided unusually complete descriptions of many diseases, and is especially known for his detailed study of diabetes mellitus ("the pissing sickness") or saccharine diabetes, in which he reported on the intensely sweet character of the urine of diabetics and speculated on the possible particular significance of this aspect of the disease. He is generally regarded as the discoverer of diabetes m. (cf. Major 1945: 238–42). Willis was one of the first medical men of his time to raise serious questions about sugar and health, thus incurring the wrath of Frederick Slare.

76. *Ibid.*: E4.

77. *Ibid.*

78. *Ibid.*: 3.

79. *Ibid.*: 7.

80. *Ibid.*: 8.

81. *Ibid.*: 16.

82. Oldmixon 1708: II, 159.
83. Anderson 1952: 154; Rosengarten 1973: 75.
84. Moseley 1800: 34.
85. Chamberlayn 1685. "As the Chinese would deem us barbarians for putting milk and sugar into our tea," writes Dodd (1856: 411), "so do the coffee-drinkers of tropical countries consider it to be barbarism to introduce such additions to the fragant decoction of their favourite berry. Lieutenant Welsted gives an amusing illustration of this: 'A party of Bedouins were disputing respecting the sanity of Lady Hester Stanhope,—one party strenuously maintaining that it was impossible a lady so charitable, so munificent, could be otherwise than in full possession of her faculties. Their opponents alleged acts in proof to the contrary. An old man with a white beard called for silence—a call from the aged among the Arabs seldom made in vain. "She *is* mad," said he; and lowering his voice to a whisper, as if fearful such an outrage against established custom should spread beyond his circle, he added, "for she puts sugar in her coffee!" This was conclusive.'"
86. Strickland 1878, quoted in Ukers 1935: I, 43.
87. Ukers 1935: I, 38–39.
88. *Ibid.*: I, 41.
89. Drummond and Wilbraham 1958: 116.
90. Heeren 1846 [1809]: 172–73.
91. E.g., Drummond and Wilbraham 1958: 116.
92. Ukers 1935: I, 67. The John Company's records reveal that in 1664 2 pounds 2 ounces of "good thea" were purchased by the court of Directors for presentation to His Majesty so that he might "not find himself wholly neglected by the Company" (Ukers 1935: I, 72). In 1666, 22¾ pounds of tea were provided to the king (purchased at 50s. per pound!); not until 1668 does a commercial order for 100 pounds of China tea occur in the records. Only after the English were driven out of Java by the Dutch in 1684 were standing orders for tea placed by the company.
93. Drummond and Wilbraham 1958: 203.
94. Ukers 1935: I, 133–47.
95. D. Forbes 1744:7.
96. MacPherson 1812: 132.
97. D. Davies 1795: 37.
98. *Ibid.*: 39.
99. Eden 1797: III, 770.
100. Hanway 1767. In an anonymous tract (whose author is undoubtedly Hanway) inveighing against both tea and sugar, we are told: "If you please, then, join them all together, and compute the expence, the loss of time taken in breaking and washing the dishes, sweetening

the tea, spreading the bread and butter, the necessary pause which defamation and malicious tea-table chat afford, and they will largely account for half a day in winter, spent in doing that which is worse, very much worse than doing nothing." That the tea and sugar might serve to make it possible for people to do much more than otherwise does not seem to have occurred to such critics.

Dorothy George has commented insightfully (1925: 14) on the school of opinion Hanway represented. In the latter half of the eighteenth century, there was, she writes, "a general cry of national deterioration. This is based largely on two ideas, one, the terrible effects of increasing luxury, as seen for instance, in the nabob, or the lamplighter with silk stockings, or the labourer's family consuming tea and sugar. The other is the decline of what Defoe called the Great Law of Subordination, a theory of course much stimulated by the fears of Jacobinism roused by the French Revolution. Though connected with opposite schools of thought, the two ideas merged; the well-dressed lamplighter for instance might be regarded as a symbol of either of the two great causes of degeneration. Contemporary denunciations of luxury and insubordination deserve a rather critical attention. They imply a higher standard of living and some improvement in education. The fine clothes, good food and constant tea-drinking so much complained of after 1750 were incompatible with the wholesale consumption of gin of the earlier part of the century. There was something paradoxical in a complaint by Dr. Price in 1773 that 'the circumstances of the lower ranks of people are altered in every respect for the worse, while tea, wheaten bread and other delicacies are necessaries which were formerly unknown to them.'"

But we can see clearly in retrospect that those who feared the moral and political consequences of increased and widened consumption were bound to lose out as the Industrial Revolution approached, the empire expanded, and as the trading, planting, and manufacturing classes grew apace, though not yet locked in competition with each other.

101. Burnett 1966: 37–38.
102. Drummond and Wilbraham 1958: 329.
103. *Ibid.*: 209.
104. Trevelyan 1945: 410; George 1925: 26.
105. Fay 1948: 147.
106. Quoted in Botsford 1924: 27.
107. Drummond and Wilbraham 1958: 112.
108. Ayrton 1974: 429–30.
109. Pittenger 1947: 13.
110. Drummond and Wilbraham 1958: 58.

111. *Ibid.*: 54.
112. Salzman 1931: 413.
113. Mead 1967 [1931]: 155.
114. *Our English Home* 1876: 73.
115. Salzman 1931: 417; see also Lopez and Raymond 1955. Balducci Pegolotti's (1936: 434–35) accounts from the thirteenth century are rich with references to different sorts of sugars reaching Venice (and passing through that city as well), mainly from the eastern Mediterranean. Included here are the once-, twice-, and thrice-"cooked" (refined) sugars; the various loaves (*mucchera, caffettino, bambillonia, musciatto,* and *domaschino*), which differed in form and quality; powdered sugar (*polvere di zucchero* or simply *polvere*); the various imperfectly refined, molasses-heavy sugars (*zucchero rosato, zucchero violato*), etc. There is also some mention of molasses, though such references are unsatisfactory. Heyd 1959 [1879]: II, 690–93) notes that such liquids were perceived, at least to judge by their names, as similar to honey: *mel zucarae, zuccara mellita, miel di calamele, meil sucre,* etc. While a reconstruction of both the distinctions among these sugars and some specification of their different uses is possible—Lippmann (1970 [1929]: 339 ff.) actually attempts to classify them—it is a task for the future. By turning instead to developing uses and preferences in England itself, I am able to cover some of the same ground.
116. Pomet 1748: 58–59. Pomet provides more than four pages of descriptive text, as well as a full-page plate of a West Indian cane plantation, showing mill and boiling pans. Each type or kind of sugar—Cassonade, Royal and Demy-Royal, Brown, White and Red Candy, Barley-Sugar, Sugar-Plums, etc.—is described fully, and its medical uses detailed.
117. Torode 1966.
118. Drummond and Wilbraham 1958: 332.
119. Burnett 1966: 70.
120. R. H. Campbell 1966: 54.
121. *Ibid.*: 56.
122. Paton, Dunlop, and Inglis 1902: 79.
123. R. H. Campbell 1966: 58–59.
124. Burnett 1966: 62–63.
125. Torode 1966: 122–23.
126. Austin 1888.
127. Mead 1967 [1931]: 159.
128. *Ibid.*: 160.
129. This issue is discussed in Taylor 1975 and Burnett 1966.
130. The short, unhappy life of Prince Henry, the sickly son of Edward I (who reigned 1272–1307), was sweetened by the prescriptions of

the court physicians, at a time when the medicinal uses of sugar were gaining recognition—rose sugar, violet sugar, *penidia* (pennet), syrups, liquorice—but all to no avail. They helped no more than did "the candles made to his measure" set to burn at all the famous shrines, or the thirteen widows who prayed all night for his recovery. See Labarge 1965: 97.

131. Hentzner 1757 [1598]: 109.
132. Rye 1865: 190.
133. Nef 1950: 76.
134. Lippmann 1970 [1929]: 288.
135. Renner 1944: 117–18.
136. Crane 1975 and 1976: 475. Eva Crane's excellent study of honey points out how very little formal attention was given to it in Great Britain. The first book on honey in English, John Hill's *The Virtues of Honey*, was not published until 1759, and dealt with honey mainly as a medicine. Crane's work is particularly important because of her insistence that honey was a food, a medicine, and a basis for manufacturing alcohol—but *not* a sweetener. She argues persuasively that sweetening was simply not valued that highly by the English before perhaps the thirteenth century.
137. Hentzner 1757 [1598]: 110.
138. Rye 1865: 190. I discovered too late to include in my discussion the interesting paper by Sass (1981) which deals with aspects of the English sweet tooth in medieval times. Sass indicates eloquently how much more historical research is needed on the subject of sweet preference.
139. Drummond and Wilbraham 1958: 116.
140. *Ibid.*
141. Sheridan 1974: 347–48.
142. Mathias 1967.
143. The new beverages provoked a flood of literature, most of it bad. The author of this poem is not identified, but Allen Ramsay, Robert Fergusson, Hartley Coleridge, and Shelley, among others, rhapsodized poetically about tea. One of the earliest devotees was Nahum Tate, whose "Panacea: A Poem upon Tea" was his most famous work; written in 1700, it includes the lines:

> With silent wonder mutually they Trace
> Bright joys reflected on each other's Face.
> Then thus the Bard—fear no Circean Bowls—this is the
> Drink of Health, the drink of Souls!
> The virtues this, and this the Graces quaff,
> Like *Nectar* chearful, like *Nepenthe* safe.

Not such the Plant which Bacchus first did nurse,
Heaven's Blessing changed by Mortals to their Curse,
Ah, Syren-Pleasure to Destruction turn'd!
Ah, woeful Mirth to be for ever mourn'd!

Not only is there an embarrassing supply of such "literature," but its very production raises interesting questions of social history. Sugar cane apparently excited similar excesses. Of James Grainger's interminable poem about sugar ("The Sugar Cane. In Four Books."), Samuel Johnson scoffed that he might as well have written of a parsley garden or a cabbage patch. But the role of so-called didactic poetry in influencing attitudes about these commodities should not be slighted.

144. Burnett 1969: 275.
145. Sombart 1967 [1919]: 99.
146. Shand 1927: 39.
147. *Ibid.*
148. *Ibid.*
149. *Ibid.*: 43.
150. Dodd 1856: 429.
151. Simmonds 1854: 138.
152. Though Oddy, emphasizing the nonsocial character of proletarian eating habits, cites a Liverpool dock laborer's wife interviewed before World War I, who did not offer tea to her friends because "women wouldn't thank you for a cup of tea" (Oddy 1976: 218).
153. Drummond and Wilbraham 1958: 299.
154. Taylor 1975: xxix–xxxi.
155. Oddy 1976: 219.
156. *Ibid.*: 219–20.
157. Reeves 1913: 97.
158. Drummond and Wilbraham 1958: 299.
159. Reeves 1913: 103.
160. Oddy 1976: 216.
161. Rowntree 1922: 135.
162. Reeves 1913: 98.
163. Oddy 1976: 217.
164. *Ibid.*: 13.
165. "The consumption of sugar was 20 lbs. per head. Now it is 5 times as great. Better class industrial workers in Manchester in 1836 consumed about ½ oz. of tea per head per week and 7 ozs. of sugar. Workers of a corresponding type today consume 3 ozs. of tea and nearly 35 ozs. of sugar in all forms. This five-fold increase in sugar consumption is the most striking change of the nation's diet during the last 100 years. It has, of course, been rendered possible by the

great fall in price. A hundred years ago sugar cost about 6d a lb. It now costs less than half" (Orr 1937: 23).

166. A dessert not yet forgotten. Margaret Drabble's hero, Len, in *The Ice Age*, thinks back: "Custard, the poor man's cream. Len, like many of his generation, did not taste fresh cream until he was a man: for a year or more he had surreptitiously preferred condensed milk, before weaning himself onto the real thing" (Drabble 1977: 97).

167. Burnett 1969: 190.

168. Klein, Habicht, and Yarborough 1971.

4. Power

1. Ragatz 1928: 50.

2. Ellis 1905: 66–67.

3. *Ibid.*: 78.

4. Rogers 1963 [1866]: 463.

5. Pares 1960: 40.

6. K. G. Davies 1974: 89.

7. Davis 1973: 251–52.

8. Quoted in DeVries 1976: 177.

9. *Ibid.*

10. *Ibid.*: 179. "Quotations of this sort," writes Elizabeth Gilboy, "could be multiplied without end," citing Sir William Temple: "... the only way to make them [the laborers] tempered and industrious is to lay them under the necessity of labouring all the time they can spare from meals and sleep, in order to procure the necessaries of life" (Gilboy 1932: 630). The citation in DeVries is from an anonymous 1764 tract entitled *Considerations on Taxes*.

11. *Ibid.*

12. *Ibid.*

13. Hobsbawm 1968: 74.

14. That apostle of colonization Edward Gibbon Wakefield, whom Karl Marx criticized so roundly, has some sprightly remarks upon the beneficial effects of the extension of markets. Of particular interest is his implication that sugar (among other things) reduced the costs of agricultural production in the metropolis: "It is not because an English washerwoman cannot sit down to breakfast without tea and sugar, that the world has been circumnavigated; but it is because the world has been circumnavigated that an English washerwoman requires tea and sugar for breakfast. According to the power of exchanging are the desires of individuals and societies [so much for

symbolic anthropology]. But every increase of desires, or wants, has a tendency to supply the means of gratification.... The sole ground on which it is supposed that the blacks of the West Indies will work for wages as soon as they shall be set free, is their love of finery. They will produce sugar, it is said, in order to buy trinkets and fine clothes.... As with individuals, so with nations. In England, the greatest improvements have taken place continually, ever since colonization has continually produced new desires among the English, and new markets wherein to purchase the objects of desire. With the growth of sugar and tobacco in America, came the more skilful growth of corn in England. *Because, in England, sugar was drank and tobacco smoked, corn was raised with less labour, by fewer hands; and more Englishmen existed to eat bread, as well as to drink sugar and smoke tobacco"* (Wakefield 1968 [1833]: 509; emphasis added).

15. Williams 1944: 37.
16. Pares 1950.
17. Pares 1960: 39–40.
18. Williams 1944: 96.
19. *Ibid.*
20. Drummond and Wilbraham 1958: 111.
21. Young 1771: II, 180–81.
22. Porter 1851: 541.
23. *Ibid.*
24. *Ibid.*: 546. Apparently no one in England thought it odd that the twenty million pounds sterling in indemnities paid at Emancipation should have gone to the planters, who owned the slaves, and to their creditors, and not one half-penny to the slaves themselves, whose labor had been taken from them. Porter, in making explicit his fear of "overrewarding" the ex-slaves, gives us a passage with a startlingly contemporary ring.
25. Lloyd 1936: 114–15. George Orwell (1984 [1937]:85–86) observed this problem firsthand, and commented upon it with his usual acuity. Analyzing the debate over the minimum food needed for continued survival, he cites a miner's family budget in which eight pounds of sugar *weekly* are consumed, and writes: "The basis of their diet, therefore, is white bread and margarine, corned beef, sugared tea, and potatoes—an appalling diet. Would it not be better if they spent more money on wholesome things like oranges and wholemeal bread or if they even, like the writer of the letter to the *New Statesman*, saved on fuel and ate their carrots raw? Yes, it would, but the point is that no ordinary human being is ever going to do such a thing. The ordinary human being would sooner starve than live on brown bread and raw carrots. And the peculiar evil is this, that the less

money you have, the less inclined you feel to spend it on wholesome food. A millionaire may enjoy breakfasting off orange juice and Ryvita biscuits; an unemployed man doesn't....When you are unemployed, which is say when you are underfed, harassed, bored, and miserable, you don't *want* to eat dull wholesome food. You want something a little bit 'tasty.' There is always some cheaply pleasant thing to tempt you. Let's have three pennorth of chips! Run out and buy us a twopenny ice cream! Put the kettle on and we'll all have a nice cup of tea!...White bread-and-marg and sugared tea don't nourish you to any extent, but they are *nicer* (at least most people think so) than brown bread-and-dripping and cold water."

26. Anonymous 1752: 5.
27. Malinowski 1950 [1922], Firth 1937, Richards 1939.
28. Mintz 1979. I am not interested here in the intentions of the British ruling classes, other than their internally divided—that is, conflicting—intentions to profit from their investments. If they are free, the proletarian and propertyless owners of their own labor power sell it to the owners of capital; if they are enslaved, the slave and propertyless nonowners of their own labor power surrender it under duress. In the first instance, all such labor appears as paid labor, paid for by the owners of capital; in the second instance, all such labor appears as unpaid surplus labor yielded to the owners of the slaves. "The value of labour-power resolves itself into the value of a definite quantity of the means of subsistence. It therefore varies with the value of these means or with the quantity of labour requisite for their production" (Marx 1939 [1867]: 172). As British workers responded to the availability of products such as tobacco, tea, and sugar, and later, even more intensely to their declining prices, they consumed more and more of them. Overall, they exchanged smaller and smaller quantities of their earnings for larger and larger quantities of these and like commodities. I have tried to suggest that the dietary and physiological consequences of this were mixed; it is certainly an open question whether all of such consequences were in the workers' best interests. As an interesting sidelight to this process, the development of exact and interchangeable measures of both substances and human effort in the same caloric terms gave new meaning to Marx's concept of labor power: a unit of work could be expressed exactly as a unit of sugar (in caloric terms), and vice versa. It seems unlikely that this exact rendering of the "weight" or "mass" of labor power, developed as part of the science of nutrition at the turn of the century, was not fully understood at an earlier time by some of those same sugar enthusiasts whose words have been quoted here. The relationship between nutrition and disciplined effort may have been learned first on the Caribbean sugar planta-

tions, in fact (as was so much else about labor exaction), before its
refinement in the free labor markets of Europe itself.

Turner comments: "There is a *prima facie* case for believing that
a dietary 'calling' to discipline the body by reference to a religio-
medical regimen would have been compatible with a spirit of capitalism" (Turner 1982: 27). Turner hypothesizes some "elective
affinity" between diet and the rise of capitalism, but has in mind
something both more abstract and quite differently generated from
my line of argument here.

29. Forster 1767: 41.
30. E.g., Gilboy 1932; McKendrick, Brewer, and Plumb 1982.
31. Dowell 1884: 32–33.

5. Eating and Being

1. No mystery here. In the developed countries, sucrose contributes a
bigger share of calories to the total food intake of the poor than of
the rich. Statistical support for this assertion is weak; but no one
seems prepared to contradict it. Sucrose is commonly rationed in the
West in wartime, in part because it is usually imported (except for
beet sugar in some countries) and its flow may be interrupted, in
part because it is politically wise to ensure that everyone gets at least
some of what there is. But for those for whom it may compose up
to perhaps as much as 30 percent of total caloric intake (Stare 1975),
response to its virtual disappearance from the market parallels the
response to scarcities of alcohol, tobacco, and the stimulant beverages.
2. "I know not why we should blush to confess that molasses was an
essential ingredient in American independence," wrote John Adams
in 1775. "Many great events have proceeded from much smaller
causes." The thirteen colonies were voracious consumers of molasses
and of rum, manufactured from molasses. Only after the Revolution,
and gradually, did Americans give up their preference for molasses,
rum, and tea, to replace them in large measure with maple syrup or
corn syrup, whisky, and coffee. Sugar consumption rose very sharply
in the nineteenth century. On rum and molasses in the British imperial trade, see Sheridan 1974: 339–59.
3. Bannister 1890: 974.
4. Material for a dozen different books, perhaps—but not this one.
Robert F. Smith's *The United States and Cuba: Business and Diplomacy, 1917–1960*, is one of many serious studies of American power
that touch on the place of sugar in the development of our foreign

policy. But the book that does the same generally for sugar and the activities of the U.S. Congress is yet to be written.

5. Sheridan 1974: 24–25.

6. Shand 1927: 45. The passage can be found in translation in Brillat-Savarin 1970 [1825]: 101.

7. Of course many unanswerable questions arise from such a conjecture. But probably most sophisticated persons in the West would rank both French and Chinese cuisines highly, and both stand in contradistinction to, say, American or British or German cuisines in their use of sugar—whether in terms of gross quantities, sugar's position in the sequence of dishes, or its forms of use. To advance the conjecture even more unreliably: sweetness is more often *unexpected* in Chinese and French cooking than in the other cuisines, and there is altogether less of it. Readers should not be misled by the drama of sweet and pungent dishes in Chinese cooking, or by French pastries. Consumption figures are markedly lower in these two countries, though the gap is closing rapidly.

8. "For approximately 50 years or more, sugar has provided 15 to 20% of total calories in the average U.S. diet.... Studies of actual intake among individuals suggest that the percentage of calories taken as sugar is higher during the growing and adolescent years, when energy demands are high, and lower during adult and later years.... The usual range of sugar intake may therefore be *between 10 and 30%* of total calories, with the average at 15 to 20%. *There being no valid evidence to the contrary, this rate of sugar intake may be considered moderate, and can probably be exceeded somewhat without overstepping the bounds of moderation"* (Stare 1975: 240; emphasis added). Professor Emeritus Frederick J. Stare, M.D., is not to be confused with Dr. Frederick Slare, the eighteenth-century champion of sugar cited frequently in this book.

9. Hagelberg 1974: 10 ff.

10. *Ibid.*

11. Stare 1948. 1975. Comparisons of this sort are inevitably inexact, since crop-yield figures are highly variable and cannot be averaged without introducing serious distortions. Nonetheless, the high caloric yield of sugar under the best conditions, relative to any other crop, and its amazing return of energy to the environment, make it a spectacularly efficient food.

12. Hagelberg believes that world consumption of noncentrifugal sugars is not falling, though he concedes that consumption of "direct consumption white" sugar is rising, particularly in the world's urban areas. There is more to the argument than I can deal with adequately here.

13. Timoshenko and Swerling 1957: 235. The rise of the European beet-

sugar industry, they write, provides "the earliest example of the market for an important tropical product being seriously eroded by the application of modern scientific methods in relatively advanced countries" (quoted in Hagelberg 1976: 13). This has happened with other tropical products since.

14. Page and Friend 1974: 100–3.
15. International Sugar Council 1963: 22.
16. Wretlind 1974: 81; Hagelberg 1976: 26.
17. Stare 1975; see note 8.
18. Wretlind 1974: 84.
19. Cantor 1978: 122.
20. Cantor and Cantor 1977: 434.
21. Page and Friend 1974: 96–98.
22. Recall once again that these are disappearance figures; and that the average consumption says nothing about probable differences in individual intake, or differences among economic, social, regional, racial, and age groups. Reliable data on this problem, if we had them, could prove immensely important in future policy-making.
23. The sugar-fat relationship has many facets; I intend to return to it in a later publication. The pioneering paper by Cantor and Cantor (1977) raises many of the relevant issues.
24. Douglas 1972: 62.
25. A "full-time household manager who lives with her family in Minneapolis," Linda Delzell tells us in her article in Ms. (entitled "The Family That Eats Together ... Might Prefer Not To"), says that her family's members are each in charge of their own nutritional needs since she quit planning and preparing meals three years ago. "David, 13," she asserts, "survives on cereal, milk, peanut butter, raisins, frozen pizza, orange juice, and McDonald's hamburgers, fries and shakes. At times I am almost certain that he will turn into a pizza," she adds, "but he's five feet nine and a very sturdy athlete" (Ms., October 1980). Delzell says her family could have arranged to eat together "with long-range planning, sacrifice of individual interests, sophisticated schedule juggling, or if need be, force. But all that came of it when we tried was strong resentment on the kids' part, added pressure on my husband, and frustration for me. The change in our lifestyle has meant that we have more time to spend together—though not at meals—and are more relaxed."
26. To impute the apparent feeling of a chronic shortage of time that most persons have in modern society to the intention of anyone is not my purpose here. But it seems to me at least possible—likely, even—that those who run a society so bent on "discovering" new consumption needs will have little interest in finding time for their satisfaction.

27. The example is borrowed (with some vulgar amendments) from Linder 1970, whose book deserves much more attention than it has received.

28. Though this is a subject that may seem remote from the history of sugar, my contention is that time and sucrose are closely linked. The classic paper by Edward Thompson (1967) comes to mind in this connection, as does the late Harry Braverman's work (1974). But anyone seriously interested in these connections must inevitably return to Karl Marx's concepts of commodity fetishism and alienation.

29. Page and Friend 1974: 100–3.

30. Fischler 1980: 946.

31. Cantor *in lit.* 5/1/80. Cantor (1975) discusses some of these issues.

32. Pyler 1973.

33. Sugar Association n.d. (1979?): 9.

34. Reports of research on a calorieless "sugar" began appearing in the daily press around 1980. But the rapid increase in the use of high-fructose corn syrup and the commercial development of low-calorie "Nutra-Sweet" (phenylalinine) have attracted more attention in the sweetener field in recent years.

35. Cantor (1981) projects a significant increase in the proportion of the market held by corn sweeteners before the end of the century:

	1965	1967	1980	1990
Beet	25.5	22.9	20.5	
Cane	59.6	61.9	46.3	
Corn	13.3	14.0	32.1	(47.5)
Sucrose	85.2	84.8	66.8	(52.5)

36. "The interconversion of one material to another for taste, economic advantage, status or other specific reason dominates our development activities.... The food and associated industries to an astonishing degree are involved in a vast (food) culture transfer—another kind of conversion" (Cantor 1969). Cantor 1981 provides an updated presentation of the interconvertibility concept.

37. Cantor 1981: 302.

38. This argument can be linked to the sugar-fat combination noted earlier, and to the odd but apparently real link between sweetness and sexuality. Though I will return to this theme in later work, it may be worth suggesting here that I believe these advertising adjectives contrast along symbolic lines associated with culturally conventionalized male-female differences.

39. Cantor and Cantor 1977: 430, 441.

40. *Ibid.*: 442.

41. Barthes 1975: 58. Lindsy van Gelder, in the December 1982 issue of *Ms.*, bemoans the ubiquity of food, particularly for those in urban

environments who wish both to diet and to see their friends: "There aren't an awful lot of places in New York City where an adult and child can sit down together after 5 P.M. without a sugar bowl in between them and a waiter hovering nearby." Her article, entitled "Inventing Food-Free Rituals," contrasts nicely with Delzell's abdication as family cook (see note 25): Delzell can't cook for her family and feel free; Van Gelder can't figure out how to see her friends without eating.

42. Cantor and Cantor 1977: 442–43.
43. Tiger 1979: 606.
44. *Ibid*.
45. The proliferation of impersonal (machine-dispenser) food outlets encourages the use of sucrose, which can increase shelf life and reduce the frequency of servicing, for instance. On reading this material, a colleague at a large American university wrote: "To gain space and save money the administration removed a large bank of milk, juice and yoghurt machines from a snack bar in the library, converting the room into a study hall. When students complained, they added vending machines in adjacent buildings. But the new vending machines are all for candy, barbecue-flavored potato chips, cheese–peanut butter atrocities, etc. My sense of it is that the latter machines are stocked very infrequently, in contrast to the others, which required daily stocking and refrigeration. Presumably here sugar's preservative and processing virtues are particularly important. And the consequences are interesting—while milk and yoghurt might be used as complements to a sandwich brought from home (as was my custom), their replacements have no role in a meal at all."

Overseas, the penetration of the nonwestern world by cold stimulant beverages provides different interruptions of meals and schedules. In much of the former British colonial world, the replacement of tea by Coca-Cola has an interesting symbolic weight: most of that world had first been converted to hot tea, a century or two ago, and its "retransformation" bespeaks American power. In the Soviet Union and the People's Republic of China, the growing success of cold stimulant beverages carries a similar meaning. The number of beverage salesmen who have become makers of foreign and military policy or journalistic commentators upon such policy, such as Weinberger and Safire, makes one think. See, for instance, Louis and Yazijian 1980.

46. Ortiz 1947: 267–82.

Index